Reckoning

TRANSGRESSING BOUNDARIES

Studies in Black Politics and Black Communities
Cathy Cohen and Fredrick Harris, Series Editors

Reckoning

*Black Lives Matter and the Democratic
Necessity of Social Movements*

DEVA R. WOODLY

OXFORD
UNIVERSITY PRESS

OXFORD
UNIVERSITY PRESS

Oxford University Press is a department of the University of Oxford. It furthers the University's objective of excellence in research, scholarship, and education by publishing worldwide. Oxford is a registered trade mark of Oxford University Press in the UK and certain other countries.

Published in the United States of America by Oxford University Press 198 Madison Avenue, New York, NY 10016, United States of America.

CIP data is on file at the Library of Congress
ISBN 978-0-19-760395-6 (pbk.)
ISBN 978-0-19-760394-9 (hbk.)

DOI: 10.1093/oso/9780197603949.001.0001

1 3 5 7 9 8 6 4 2

Paperback printed by LSC Communications, United States of America
Hardback printed by Bridgeport National Bindery, Inc., United States of America

For my family, blood and chosen

Contents

Illustrations

Tables

Figures

Preface: Who Am I to Write This Movement?

The timeline of my engagement in this project mirrors the timeline of the movement itself. I am a scholar of political discourse, public meaning, and political change. When I was in graduate school in the early 2000s, Black liberation movements in the United States and most places in the world were in what the social movement literature calls abeyance—a state of temporary disuse or suspension. The Black civil rights movement, which reached its zenith in the 1960s, had been, for better and worse, fully incorporated into the regular flow of common discourse and institutionalized politics, so it was not my primary subject of study. Because I wanted to examine the ways that social movements change our understandings of politics and create new political possibilities in real time, I wrote about the then active and growing struggles around the living wage and marriage equality in my first book, *The Politics of Common Sense*. Later, as I was getting into research on what I planned to be my second book, an empirical examination of popular understandings of "the economy," what it means to different segments of the American population, and how it might be changing, videos of Black people being murdered by police started circulating online in a terrifying proliferation. Without making a conscious decision, my nascent mappings of American economic discourse slowed, and I began researching and writing about the political implications of the movement that was rising in defense of Black lives.

Of course, I had been primed to pay attention to the mass demonstrations in Ferguson, Missouri, and other American cities because in 2013, I, like most other Black Americans, had followed the trial of Trayvon Martin's murderer closely. I had engaged in online discussions about the details of the case. I had talked to my parents, my colleagues, my friends. I was outraged that the prosecution slandered the teenager—a boy who died with Skittles in his pocket—after he had been hunted in the neighborhood where his father lived. I had been upset at the way both the prosecution and some Black people lambasted the testimony of Rachel Jeantel, critiquing her demeanor, her speech, her clearly present anger and sadness, as though she were not a human being, but instead a failed vessel for respectability. Even with these foreshadowing pieces of evidence that the purpose of the trial was not to judge the murderer, but to prove that Trayvon's life didn't matter, I was still hopeful that the man who had stalked and murdered this teenage boy would be found guilty.

But he wasn't.

I am a Black woman, the wife of Black man, and the mother of Black children. I was already aware that police could, would, and did harm Black, brown, and poor people without cause and based on their own whims and fears, but I had not understood the stultifying regularity with which police and vigilantes who believed themselves aligned with the state executed Black people—men, women, and *children*—for minor alleged infractions or no reason at all. And, more pointedly, I had not understood how easily they would *get away* with these acts of racial terror even when they murdered people on video and in plain view of the public. I was shocked by the excuses that were made for wanton police violence in public discourse, the ways that the Black victims of aggression and assault were demonized, always already deemed terminally guilty of *something*, having once smoked marijuana or being possessed of the gall to fight for the lives that vigilantes, police, and the state clearly indicated did not matter. It was heartbreaking. I can hardly describe my furious grief.

Almost four years before that savage acquittal, I had stood in Chicago's Grant Park on the evening of November 4, 2008, surrounded by an ebullient multiracial crowd of classmates, friends, and strangers as we waited for the results of the presidential election. I will never forget the roar of the tens of thousands of voices when, around nine o'clock, much earlier than we expected to know the outcome, an Obama campaign aide walked to the microphone on a raised stage facing the throng, and said into the hushed anticipation, "Check, check. Mic check. Mic check for the president-elect of the United States of America." The night seemed to explode with joy. We were carried away. The first Black president. Such a stunning declamation to kick off the second decade of the twenty-first century. Reader, I was never under any impression that the election of Barack Obama would usher in a so-called post-racial society, but I did think, "We have come so far." I did hope that it would be the beginning of something good, the clearing of a path forward, the sign that the American polity might be ready to become what it had always claimed to be.

But the next eight years showed that this hoped-for future had not arrived after all.

When Trayvon's murderer was acquitted in Florida, I took to my Facebook page and wrote the following:

I have been struggling with what to say. I'm a political scientist. And a political junky. I ought to say something politically productive. But my pre-
dominant response to this verdict—the very need for the 45 days of protest
to even bring this vigilante to trial—is pain. And fear. I am the mother of
Black children. The wife of a Black man. They are not safe. They are not safe.
They are not safe. I cannot keep them safe from eyes that have no capacity to
consider their humanity and no notion that they might be ordinary people,
innocent of any crime but walking around in their skin. My loves, my whole
life, everything we have built together, may be snuffed out by any armed
coward who takes it upon themselves to exercise their prejudice at any time
in any place. And there may be no recourse. And there will certainly be no
justice. Because all my pictures here of my beautiful, brilliant boy. My ebullient, gifted girl. Of my talented and dedicated and hardworking husband.
They mean nothing to a stranger with a gun. I am overcome with sadness
that this is my America. And sadder still that this sentiment is not new.
This fear is a fear that has flooded the heart of every Black woman since the
nation's inception. And the pity of it is, this fear recedes in moments. Many
moments. It recedes among my multi-racial and multi-cultural friends and
colleagues and associates. My family lives in a liberal, racially, and economically mixed artistic town on a beautiful river in a charmed valley. And it
is no accident that we do. Because here, this fear, this hurt, recedes. But
always, something like this brings that fear, that rage at being always out of
place, never ordinary, never innocent, back. And so I mourn. I mourn for
the life I wanted for my children. The country I wanted for them. Because that
world, that country is not to be. Listen, I am not naive, I know about prob-
abilities, I understand how rare justice is, how fundamental struggles are,
for all intents and purposes, unending. But I am an American. So I dream.
And my American dream, cherished and mostly unspoken, has been that
despite what I know of history, what I know of structural-isms, what I know
of the stickiness of old paradigms in new days, despite all of that, perhaps,
in my children's time, they could be free. Free of this fear and this rage. Free
to be an individual. Free. I have held this kernel of hope in my heart that
their generation would be gifted with struggles that were at least a little different. I know, I know. Impossible! Of course. But I am an American. So
I dream. Because honestly, how could I be who I am without the dreamers

who came before? The dreamers who worked and died for things the world could barely fathom? It is my birthright to "dream a world," as Langston Hughes wrote. And yet, the reality of my American life, of my son's and my daughter's, swirls down and down around the same narrow drain of possibility that has sucked us—all of us, every single American—down from the very beginning. So I turned my profile picture into a black box in mourning. Soon I will think about politics. Soon I will think about remedies. Soon I will think about struggle. Soon. Because these things give me hope. And something productive to do in the face of this great sadness. But today I mourn. Because though I should have known, though I did know in every measurable way, even still, I am shocked and more hurt than I thought I would be, that this is my America. Still.

My America. Some of you will read that cynically. During the course of the writing and review of this book, many have asked me: Why not let go of this American idea? It has never been. This place has always been a shining city built upon the unmarked and unremarked-upon graves of Black and Indigenous people. And, if the slaughter were not bad enough, all of the institutions of the country, and almost everybody who got rich under their auspices, have traded in our bones.

My first impulse is to give an answer about ideas. That the audacity of the American idea is worth nurturing, worth bringing into being, even if the apparatus built to enact it was built to fail Black, brown, and Indigenous peoples. But that answer is a dodge. Logically, a thing that is built to fail most people ought to be scrapped. So let me be honest. My attachment to the American idea is much more personal. Like most Black Americans who are descendants of enslaved people, my family can't trace all the generations that have been born in this land, but as far as we can tell, my roots in this country go back at least seven generations on both sides. Those generations include the often forced but sometimes passionately defiant intermixture of Black, white, and Indigenous bloodlines that make up most of the African diaspora. Those generations toiled to build and serve this nation while being brutalized, stolen from, disrespected, and disavowed. They built triumphantly, tragically effervescent human lives in the face of systematic dehumanization. They are owed—for both their unpaid labor and their faith that this American idea could one day justly serve the entire polity.

What that means to me is that this nation is mine. Mine to claim. Mine to hold to account. Mine to participate in reshaping. So I tell an American story because it my story to tell. It is why I reflected, in 2015, shortly after the coalescence of what had become the Movement for Black Lives:

> Listen, the movement was born, as all beings are, in pain. But what made it possible, what lets it live, is ecstatic, defiant, world-beating, unconditional love. The love of a people for our own breath. Our own raised hands. Our own spoken names. Our own queerness. Our own magic.
>
> Mine is the only story I can tell. I speak it. Sing it. Tweet it. Me and the rest of we who figured out how to love us and turn up. And so there are a million true tales whipping across the screen in real time. Vivid as fiction, but instead a history. This is what it looks like not to despair.
>
> We remember what every political animal has ever known: speech-is-action-that-creates. And all these players slaying, giving life, unapologetically declaring their political love as power because survival is not enough. We want to live.
>
> Let me tell you, there is no "post-". There is the unmasking. The deconstruction of grins and lies. The deferred dream of other possible worlds that are not yet. The breach to which we return.
>
> Listen, my grandmother was born to sharecroppers on a farm in North Carolina in 1924. At two years old, she was run over by a horse and buggy. Somehow, she stood up, unbroken, crying, ready. When she was grown, she moved north so she could work, vote, live. But my mother, a dentist's daughter, spent her youth wiping the spittle of white children from her face and learning not to let the word *nigger* knock her down. Later, I was told, *Black girls are never beautiful unless they look like white girls.* Good thing I was smart, "like Oprah." Smart enough to walk the halls of one ivory tower after another, not minding—not too much, not enough to fall—the loud whispers wondering how such a Black girl could take up so much white space.
>
> And of course, along the way, there have been too many losses. Unspeakable losses. In money and blood. Yet to mention reparation is not polite. We are supposed to get up (pants pulled up, hoodie shed, respectable). Unbroken, crying, ready. They call us to forgive. But the movement reminds us that the choice in answering is ours. That's how I know the movement loves us—*is* us—getting free.
>
> Listen, this hearing will be no easier than any other trial. The outcome, as uncertain. All I can report is what movements have long showed: together, we are a reckoning.

This book is an account of this ongoing reckoning. But let me be clear: I am not an architect of this movement. That honor and labor belongs to others, many, though not nearly all, named within these pages. I am not pretending to offer a definitive history of the movement or an inside look at how things unfolded. I cannot tell you what it was like to be a person on the ground, making decisions about how to keep people safe during direct actions or choosing what campaigns would be pursued, what policies written, or how resources would be allocated. I was not in the rooms where these historical decisions were taken. I do not know all the ins and outs of the conflicts that resulted, the tensions that festered, the friendships that grew and broke, or the sacrifices made. In the coming years, I hope that we have a plethora of histories and analyses from those who were in the rooms where these things happened.

For now, the task of this work is to shine a light on the sophistication and significance of the political work organizers and activists in the Movement for Black Lives have done to create the incredible change in common sense, public opinion, and the policy environment of the twenty-first-century American polity. I have done my best to report what has happened from a variety of evidence—most importantly, the accounts of people who were willing to share their experiences and reflections with me. My goal in this book is to present the implications, public meaning, and impact of this radical, innovative, and successful movement for our understanding of politics. Additionally, I aim to articulate the political philosophy I have observed animating the movement in a way that makes clear its complexity, depth, and usefulness to political and social thought. Herein, I put movement philosophers in conversation with canonical thinkers in political theory not to authorize the movement, but to show how it should disrupt, challenge, and revolutionize canonical thinking. I hope I have made legible the intellectual gift that the movement has given us, in addition to the practical changes that their work has enabled.

In sum, I assess and share what I believe the movement has to teach us about democracy, radicalism, persuasion, power, and the pragmatic paths toward making other worlds politically possible. My work is to make sense of things—to relate experience to concept and evaluate concepts in light of experiences. And though I am neither architect nor visionary of this movement, I am a witness. The movement made me a witness. And this book is my testimony, an act of political care rendered by way of scholarship, because that is the language I know best and the service I can render most faithfully.

Acknowledgments

This book has been nearly five years in the making, and it is difficult to begin to thank all the people who have contributed to its possibility, writing, and completion. First, I must thank my husband, Anthony Davis, who is a true partner in every sense of the word. He has provided the encouragement, logistical, and co-parenting support that has been critical to my ability to bring this long-term project to fruition. You are my home, and I am yours. That is a great gift. I would also like to thank our children, V and L Davis, who teach me, by example, what it means to be a fully engaged, totally messy, ever learning, immanently loving human in the world. My gratitude, also, to my parents, Ann and Donnell Woodly, who always believed in me and taught me to believe in myself—an indispensable, soul-saving armor for a person born, as Lucille Clifton writes, "nonwhite and woman."

There are those with whom I share no blood but who are, nevertheless, my family. So, I must thank the Friendsgiving crew: Daniel Reid, my first reader and longtime editor, who never fails to honor and lift up my voice amid the stew of words I drop in his lap. I love you avidly. Aaron Carico, who has processed every emotion with me since we were eighteen-year-olds sitting on porches and back steps trying to make sense of growing up and growing into who we wanted to be. Sarah Landres, who first taught me and keeps teaching me the crucial, life-giving difference between wasting time and spending time.

I am also blessed with an irreplaceable community of mentors and interlocutors who have helped to shape my mind and hone my thinking. In this capacity, no one has been more dedicated to my intellectual thriving than Danielle Allen, who possesses a colossal intellect, a kind soul, and a heart for service that I strive to emulate. I am continuously astounded by her capacious, heterodox mastery of so many subjects, which is nevertheless combined with an unfailing generosity. Cathy Cohen, who has always cheered, pushed, and challenged me to say what I mean and mean what I say, and who, with the appearance of this book in the series she co-edits, has welcomed me back to my intellectual home. Iris Marion Young, who left all our lives too soon but gifted me with a deep understanding of what it means to value clear, rigorous, and righteous thought and language. Because of her, I know what it means to be a scholar, and much of my work is an homage to her oeuvre, which still teaches me. I had no idea of my delirious good fortune in attending the University of Chicago at a time when I could learn political theory, American government, and Black politics from these women while also learning statistics from Melissa Harris Perry, who somehow managed to make this girl who had always thought she was bad at math, into a multi-method whiz. My thanks, also, to Patchen Markell and Jacob Levy, who each carried on their advising duties long past the time when they ought to have expired and made me feel smart and seen. I am also thankful to Barbara Ransby, who trusted me to get her footnotes together on *Ella Baker and the Black Freedom Movement*, giving me an exciting and educational sneak peek at what Black feminist scholarship in-progress looks like. She also continually shows what scholar-activism is with inspiring grace and aplomb and never fails to offer a thoughtful word of encouragement.

I also wish to offer my thanks to Shanelle Matthews, a blindingly talented, keenly smart, and boldly visionary communications expert and educator in the movement (and beyond), who just happened to be my very first interviewee. Without her, this book likely would not have happened. She trusted me and believed in this project enough to vouch for me in movement spaces when people were overwhelmingly busy with urgent and sometimes dangerous work and suspicions of outsiders were high. I will be forever grateful that she took a chance on me.

All books are challenging to produce, but this one was deeply personal to me in a way my first book was not; therefore, it took shape slowly and I was privileged to participate in several workshops and symposia that were essential to its development. I want to acknowledge them all and thank my fellow participants for their camaraderie and engagement. In chronological order these are: Political Theory In/As Political Science (May 2018) organized by Jacob Levy at McGill University; The Democracy and Freedom Conference (April 2019) organized by Neil Roberts at Williams College, including fellow participants George Shulman, Lawrie Balfour, Angelica Bernal, Nick Bromell, John Drabinski, Marisa Fuentes, Victor Muniz-Fraticelli, Emily Nacol, Keisha-Khan Perry, and Michael Hanchard. The Seeing Beyond the Veil Symposium (November 2018) organized by Melvin Rogers and Juliet Hooker at Brown University, with fellow participants Baron Hesse, Michael Hanchard, Michael Dawson, Ainsley Lesure, Alexander Livingston, Erin

Pineda, Jasmine Syedullah, Neil Roberts, Candice Delmas, Charles Mills, David McIvor, Shatema Threadcraft, and Stephen Marshall.

I would also like to acknowledge the Edmond J. Safra Center for Ethics at Harvard University, which extended me a fellowship in 2019–2020 that was crucial for the completion of this manuscript. My thanks to my fellow members of the 2019–2020 Safra Center class: Anna Lewis, who generously extended an invitation to me to room with her during my time in Cambridge, Roni Hirsh, Attila Mraz, Naomi Scheinerman, Allison Stanger, Adom Getachew, Eric Beerbohm, Jacob Fay, John Basl, Greg Keating, Meira Levinson, Rebecca Henderson, Josh Simmons, Leah Downey, and essential staff members Emily Bromley and Vickie Aldin.

I also want to thank the Center for hosting my manuscript workshop, allowing me to bring together Shanelle Matthews, Quincy Mills, Jenn Jackson, Jasmine Syedullah, Shatema Threadcraft, Melvin Rogers, Neil Roberts, and Danielle Allen for crucial and helpful commentary on the first complete draft of the book.

In addition to these venues where I was gifted with more formal commentary and critique of this project, I am also privileged to have a fantastic group of scholar friends who push me and inspire me through their own work and through regular engagement with mine. Let me extend my eternal thanks to Jasmine Syedullah, my writing partner and soothsayer, who is full of bold, poetic ideas, rare knowledge, and trenchant critiques. Melvin Rogers, whose intellect is patient and profound. He always makes time to chat with me and lend a word of advice, despite his busy schedule and full life. Shatema Threadcraft, whose keen mind and good humor keeps me sharp, informed, laughing, and connected to all the good stuff the academy has to offer. Neil Roberts who has been sharing his intelligence and intellectual generosity with me since graduate school. Andrew Dilts, who pushes and challenges me with his unique combination of cranky determination and fierce love. Sina Kramer, whose serene manner and loyal friendship is underpinned by a ferocious and careful mind. Chris Harris, who is a passionate advocate for and articulator of the Black radical tradition and whom I had the pleasure to learn from and teach during his graduate studies at the New School. Thanks also to Will McKeithen, who sat through the longest run-through of the talk based on this book and helped make it better. And, last but far from least, buckets of gratitude to my research assistant Liam Bouquet, who provided invaluable support.

I would also like to shout out my thanks to the Geek crew, who buoyed my spirits and provided invaluable community, especially during the plague year 2020: Chris Lebron, Chris Robichaud, Utz McKnight, Daniel Silvermint, Elizabeth Barnes, Ross Cameron, Marisa Parham, Zachary Callen, Nolan Bennett, and Tilda Cvrkel.

My heartfelt and humble thanks to organizer and artist Kei Williams for agreeing to design the beautiful cover of this work. I am in awe of your many talents and so grateful you agreed to share them with me and the world.

To anyone I have omitted, please accept my apologies. It is a failure of my brain and not my heart. I am full of gratitude for every person who has touched my life during this process because I know, as Octavia Butler writes, that "all that you touch, you change and all that you change, changes you." My cup overflows. Selah.

PART ONE
DEMOCRATIC PRECIPICE

The whole history of the progress of human liberty shows that all concessions yet made to her august claims, have been born of earnest struggle . . . If there is no struggle, there is no progress. . . . Power concedes nothing without demand. It never did and it never will.
— Frederick Douglass, 1857

The cause of freedom is not the cause of a race or a sect, a party or a class—it is the cause of humankind, the very birthright of humanity.
— Anna Julia Cooper, 1892

We who believe in freedom cannot rest.
— Ella Baker, 1964

It is our duty to fight for our freedom.
It is our duty to win.
We must love each other and support each other.
We have nothing to lose but our chains.
— Assata Shakur, 1987

There is no end to what a living world will demand of you.
— Octavia Butler, 1993

Introduction

The Democratic Necessity of Social Movements

In 2016, three years after the emergence of the Movement for Black Lives, President Barack Obama chided the movement by saying that it had been "really effective at bringing attention to problems," but claiming that "once you've highlighted an issue and brought it to people's attention . . . , and elected officials or people who are in a position to start bringing about change are ready to sit down with you, then you can't just keep on yelling at them." As reported in the *New York Times*, he went on to say that "the value of social movements and activism is to get you at the table, get you in the room, and then to start trying to figure out how is the problem to be solved" (Shear and Stack 2016).

Obama's view is a common one, but it is also incorrect. The value of movements is something much more profound. They are necessary, not only to address the concerns of those engaging in public interest, nor only for the ethical purpose of achieving more just conditions for all, but also for the health and survival of democracy, as such. Movements are what keep democracy from falling irrevocably into the pitfalls of oligarchy and the bureaucratic iron cage described by Max Weber, chiefly dehumanization, expropriation, and stagnation. Democracy demands a broad political orientation toward participation and citizenship from "the people" who are to govern. A democracy where people have come to believe that voting is the only kind of participation that matters, that their vote, in any case, doesn't count, that the system is fundamentally "rigged," and that those who govern are not "like them" and, worse, are unresponsive is a polity that will struggle (and perhaps fail) to bear the burden and responsibility of self-governance. If citizens, from whose authorization the legitimacy of democratic government arises, come to believe that their capacity to act as authors of their collective fate is a fiction, then what follows is what I call a *politics of despair*.

In this book, I argue that the force that counteracts the Weberian pitfalls of bureaucratization and oligarchy and that can counteract the politics of despair by "re-politiciz[ing] public life" (I. Young [1990] 2011, 81) is social movements. Social movements infuse the essential elements of pragmatic imagination, social intelligence, and democratic experimentation into public spheres that are ailing and have become nonresponsive, stagnant, and/or closed. However, this book is not only a theoretical exploration of the place of social movements in democracy. If social movements help to repoliticize public life, we should see some observable changes in the polity. Therefore, I undertake an examination of the ideas and impacts of one of the most influential movements of our moment: the Movement for Black Lives (M4BL).

To be clear, I do not intend to claim that M4BL is the only movement making a political difference in the second decade of the twenty-first century. In fact, I would assert that since 2009, the United States and, arguably, the world have been in what social movements scholar Sydney Tarrow (1998) calls a "cycle of contention," which is a "phase of heightened conflict across the social system." Contentious cycles are characterized by the rapid diffusion of collective action and mobilization; innovation in the forms of contention; the creation or major change in collective action frames, discourses, and frames of meaning; coexistence of organized and unorganized activists; and increased interaction between challengers and authorities. In the United States, the 2009 emergence of the Tea Party movement, followed by Occupy in 2011, #BlackLivesMatter in 2014, #Me Too in 2017, and March for Our Lives in 2018 evinces all the above.

In the following chapters I explore the Movement for Black Lives as a case study, not only because it has had a measurable and dramatic political impact on American (and, indeed, global) politics, but because as it persists over time, it has the promise for effecting transformative, historically unique change. This is because the movement has a peculiar political philosophy that I call radical Black feminist pragmatism (RBFP). This philosophy is new—no historical corollary combines all of these elements—and it has struck an unusually resonant political chord, resulting in the transformation of our understanding of racial justice and of the entire political environment in 2020.

I undertake this study not only to outline the sophistication and significance of the Movement for Black Lives, but also to explicate what social movements *do* for democracy in general. The importance of social movements goes beyond the political claims they make on behalf of marginalized groups and cuts right to heart of what makes democracy, as such, sustainable. Herein, I explain how movements can reinvigorate the public sphere and what such remembrance and recommitment to politics, if it occurs, means for the polity as a whole.

The Political Context

The graphic and bewildering 2016 electoral contest, and its surprising outcome, seemed to make the world anew overnight, especially for the 73.68 million voters who had cast their ballots for someone other than President Trump (figures from Federal Election Commission). However, the political tumult that gave rise to the contentious and surprising election cycle began much earlier. Already the twenty-first century had put the lie to the 1990s notion that America and the world had reached "the end of history," in which the liberal international order and increasing development would lead to ever-growing tolerance and prosperity. The first year of the new millennium saw the birth of a new form of international conflict and the first decade ushered in the largest financial collapse the world had seen since the 1930s. During what was dubbed the Great Recession, one-quarter of American families lost at least 75 percent of their wealth, and more than half lost at least 25 percent (Pfeffer, Danziger, and Schoeni 2013). As with almost every indicator of American well-being, for African Americans, the news was even worse: the median net worth of black families fell 53 percent (NAREB 2013). The national unemployment rate had climbed to above 10 percent; for Blacks, the rate topped 17 percent (US Congress Joint Economic Committee 2010). When the wave of job loss began to recede in 2013, it left in its wake occupations that did not provide as much stability or income as the ones that had been swept away.

But the economic devastation of the Great Recession and the precarity that it laid bare were not the only upheavals testing the temerity of American dreamers by 2016. Already, a Black teenager named Trayvon had been hunted and gunned down by a vigilante as he walked home in a small town in Florida. Already, Rekia Boyd had been shot dead by an off-duty cop on a burger run, while standing in her neighborhood park. Eric Garner, a Black man selling loose cigarettes on a New York City street corner, and pleading "I can't breathe," had already been choked to death on video by a police patrolman. Twelve-year-old Tamir Rice, mistaken for a twenty-year-old man, had been slaughtered by law enforcement while playing behind a community center. Already, Sandra Bland had been disappeared into the cell where she would die for behaving as though she were free during a traffic stop. And Michael Brown's cooling body had already lain uncovered on the hot concrete for four hours after being shot dead by a police officer who claimed the unarmed teen looked like a "demon." In each case, the killings were deemed justified. The perpetrators left free.

The justice system's shrug of acceptance in the face of the violent, unnecessary deaths of Black people at the hands of vigilantes and the state mirrored the unconcern that seemed to suffuse all the institutions of power as they witnessed the post-recession suffering of ordinary people of all colors, and seemed to do little or nothing in response. Indeed, in the second decade of the twenty-first century, the world had already witnessed a series of uprisings demanding democratic accountability and economic fairness. This context suffused organizer Alicia Garza's hastily typed cry that "black lives should matter" with grief and gravitas. Garza's friend and fellow organizer Patrisse Khan-Cullors put the exhortation behind a hashtag that yet another organizer and collaborator, Opal Tometi, pushed onto what were in 2012 the lesser-used social media platforms of Twitter and Tumblr. #BlackLivesMatter quickly diffused across social media and became a part of national discourse, and later a rallying cry for mass mobilizations in the streets. But what characteristics created a "political opportunity" for the commotion that has characterized America's early twenty-first century?

The Politics of Despair

In the early twentieth century, social movements were regarded as purely emotional mobs reacting to some stimulus of deprivation. After the Black civil rights movement of mid-century, along with the rise of the New Left, social movement scholars tended to downplay the emotions stirred by social movements in order to emphasize their strategic and political impacts. Contemporary scholars, particularly those who have studied the role that emotions played in the militant politics of ACT UP in the 1980s and 1990s, eschew the division between emotions and effective political strategy, instead investigating how emotions inform and shape the collective commitments, agenda-setting, and political strategies of social movements. Veterans of the gay rights movement, most notably the sociologist Deborah Gould, began insisting that studying movement organizations without taking note of the emotions that motivated, animated, and complicated them overlooks major dynamics of the emergence, maintenance, and demobilization of movements.

In 2012, Gould introduced the concept of "political despair," which she described as a "feeling of inefficacy and hopelessness, the sense that nothing will ever change no matter what some imagined collective 'we' does to try to bring change" (Gould 2012, 95). Gould describes political despair as a part of the "affective landscape of the early twenty-first century" (95). But political despair is more than a public mood, it is also a *politics*, "the activity through which relatively large and permanent groups of people determine what they will collectively do, settle how they will live together, and decide their future" (Pitkin 1981, 343). Politics "concerns all aspects of institutional organization, public action, social practices and habits, and cultural meanings insofar as they are potentially subject to collective evaluation and decision-making" (I. Young [1990] 2011, 9). For citizens, a politics of despair is characterized by a lack of institutional investment and public trust, suspicion of the social practices and habits of others in the polity, cultural meanings that are illegible across difference, and deep cynicism about the possibility of political efficacy. For governors, a politics of despair is characterized by a Weberian retreat to bureaucratized oligarchy particularly marked by either indifference or inability to respond to the concerns of constituents.

Evidence that the United States can be described as in the grips of a politics of despair can be found in several trends that have been intensifying for decades: (1) rising inequality, (2) declining political trust, (3) declining interpersonal trust, (4) declining civic knowledge, (5) declining and stratified political participation, and (6) declining political efficacy. The data demonstrating each of these trends is voluminous and robust. Social and economic inequality has been rising since the mid-twentieth century, with income inequality currently more stark than it has been since the Gilded Age imploded in 1928. The top 1 percent of income earners saw their share of total income rise from 8.9 percent in 1973 to 21.2 percent in 2014, where it has remained (DeSilver 2015; Schaeffer 2020). This startling proportion does not capture the fact that income growth during that time has accrued almost exclusively to the top 1 percent of income earners, or that for all but top earners, incomes have been stagnant since 2000. Moreover, the proportion of Americans who are middle income has been decreasing, falling from 61 percent in 1971 to 51 percent in 2019 (Schaeffer 2020).

The data on the increasing wealth gap is even more severe, with America's upper-income families possessing 75 times the wealth of lower-income families and 7.4 times the wealth of middle-income families, the largest gap recorded by the Federal Reserve in the thirty years it has been collecting data (Kochhar and Fry 2014; Kochhar and Cilluffo 2017). When these numbers are parsed by race and ethnicity, the already wide divide reveals itself to be a chasm, with the median wealth of white households increasing by 2.4, from $138,600 to $141,900, between 2010 and 2013, while Hispanics' median wealth *decreased* by 14.3 percent, from $16,000 to $13,700, and Black households' fell 33.7 percent, from $16,600 to $11,000 (Kochhar and Fry 2014). As of 2016, the picture had barely improved for Black and Hispanic Americans, while white Americans had, on average, recovered the wealth they lost the previous decade (Kochhar and Cilluffo 2017). These gaps in income and wealth are not unique among indicators of well-being. Egregious and persistent gaps by class, race, and gender are evident in everything from education to physical safety, health, maternal and infant mortality, and contact with disciplining institutions, including carceral and welfare agencies (Pew Research Center 2016a; Atkinson 2015; Piketty 2015; Bonilla-Silva 2013).

Additionally, trust in government is at a historic low (Smith and Son 2013). According to the Pew Research Center (2019), only 17 percent of respondents trust the government in Washington to do what is right "just about always" or "most of the time." By comparison, 73 percent of Americans answered this question affirmatively in 1958, and 49 percent did so in 2001. Questions about individual institutions reveal similar skepticism. According to Gallup's Historical Trends data, the only institutions that a majority of Americans trust are the military (73 percent) and police (53 percent). Only 38 percent trust the president and the Supreme Court, 29 percent trust organized labor, 24 percent trust the criminal justice system, 23 percent trust newspapers, and 11 percent trust Congress (Gallup 2016).

Alongside this lack of trust in institutions, Americans have become much more likely to sort themselves by party sympathies now than they were two decades ago (Lupia 2015). This partisan sorting is not limited to issue positions, with more Democrats and Republicans espousing policy preferences that align with their chosen party, but also includes social sorting. Democrats and Republicans are now less likely to participate in the same entertainment, live in the same neighborhoods, or consume the same goods (Pew Research Center 2014; Bingham 2012; E-Poll Market Research 2016). In addition, 80 percent of Democrats believe the Republican Party has been taken over by racists, and 82 percent of Republicans believe the

Democratic Party is now run by socialists (PRRI 2019). Perhaps because of this sorting, there has also been a stunning increase in personal antipathy between Democrats and Republicans, with 86 percent of Democrats reporting that they have an "unfavorable" view of Republicans and 55 percent "very unfavorable." Likewise, 91 percent of Republicans report that they view Democrats unfavorably and 58 percent very unfavorably (Pew Research Center 2016c).

The personal antipathy between partisans hints at an even more troubling phenomenon: Americans' declining trust in each other generally. In 1974, 46 percent of Americans reported that they trusted most people; by 2012, only 33 percent said the same, with millennials reporting less trust in others than any other generation (Twenge, Campbell, and Carter 2014). To make matters worse, Americans know less than ever before about how their government is structured and how it is supposed to function, with only one-quarter of Americans able to name the three branches of government, and one-third unable to name any of them (Annenburg Public Policy Center 2016; Lupia 2015).

These changes in fortunes, trust, and knowledge have taken a toll on the belief that democratic government can be responsive to most citizens, producing dramatic and widespread disillusionment with the idea that political participation by ordinary citizens can create positive change. This bleak view of the effects of traditional political participation is not merely the result of a cynical outlook. Americans have good reason to doubt their ability to effect national politics. Political scientists have shown that government responsiveness is stratified by socioeconomic status (Gilens and Page 2014; Hetheington and Rudolph 2015). Is it any wonder, then, that political participation is stratified in the same way, with the wealthy and educated much more likely to contribute their "money, skills, and time" in the political arena than those who have fewer resources, but need more responsiveness? (Schlozman, Brady, and Verba 2012; Verba, Schlozman, and Brady 1995). For Black Americans, the reality of stratified representation is even more severe. Though the civil rights movements of the 1950s and 1960s opened pathways for more African Americans to participate in the political process and elect some members of the group as political representatives, the price of the ticket has been electoral capture by one increasingly unresponsive party, and the decline of a politics dedicated to confronting racial inequality head on (Frymer 2010; Harris 2012). Given these realities, the breadth of the crisis we now face is profound.

Analysts of democracy spanning diverse political times and traditions—from Thomas Jefferson to Frederick Douglass, Max Weber to John Dewey, and Rosa Luxemburg to Angela Davis—have warned that though democracy is based on the idea that the people will govern, checking governors' and institutions' tendency toward consolidating power and ruling in the interest of the few is work that requires muscular and often rebellious engagement from the people.

The American pragmatist John Dewey reasoned that since "progress is not steady and continuous [and] retrogression is as periodic as advance" (Dewey [1927] 2016), citizens will often find themselves in a situation in which they must "build power external to the state" in order to "create, through protest or violence, a new space where inquiry may once again thrive in the service of collective problem-solving" (as explained in M. Rogers 2010, 84). Because democratic institutions derive their legitimacy from the people and exist to serve them, the bureaucratic disconnect is particularly toxic in democratic systems. Indeed, that disconnect's resulting lack of responsiveness, lopsided responsiveness, and malign neglect creates conditions ripe for a politics of despair.

A series of pointed and urgent questions arise from these facts: What helps members of the polity recover from the cynicism wrought by insufficiently responsive governance? What reminds us of the power of the public sphere? What causes governing officials to be responsive to new or neglected constituencies and attentive to their causes? What helps us to feel that our opinions and political actions matter—that "we the people" have power? What makes a citizenry both believe and act on behalf of the belief that "another world is possible?"

The answer is social movements.

Theorizing Social Movements as Democratic Institutions

When people think of the structure of democratic societies, they often think of the institutions formalized in the US Constitution: the legislature, the executive, the judiciary, and the press (as acknowledged and protected in the First Amendment). I argue that a complete theory of democratic politics ought to include social movements as another essential institutional element, a Fifth Estate that is an indispensable check on institutional tendencies toward bureaucracy and oligarchy. Although social movement scholars generally do not spend much time contemplating the function of social movements in democracy, the sociologist Hank Johnston writes in *States and Social Movements* that it is crucial to understand the role that social movements have played in the formation of the modern state:

> Let us be clear: for most of history, when a ruler's attention turned to the common folk, it was usually not from compassion or concern for their well-being or a desire to protect their interests, but for practical considerations of maintaining power and squelching the threat of rebellion. The long-term effects of popular mobilizations and protests have been to force the ruling classes . . . to consider the popular will in state politics. . . . Although this is not usually the intended consequence of social movements, to this day they continue to bring new challenging groups, new ideas, new coalitions, and new interests into today's system, such that the strong undemocratic tendencies are often mitigated to the extent that social movements mobilize. (Johnston 2011, 3)

Democratic theorists sometimes point out the essential functions that movements play, but often without realizing that movements are not an intervention from outside a routinized democracy, but are, in practice, an essential part of democracy. Sheldon Wolin, for example, famously declared that democracy cannot be had as a form of governance or through a set of procedures, and that, indeed, the form of government usually devolves into "democracy without the demos as actor" (Wolin 1994, 13). Wolin goes so far as to dismiss contemporary instantiations of representative democracy as "various representations of democracy" bolstered by "the political burlesque hustled by the pundits" (14). Democracy worthy of the name, by this account, only erupts spontaneously and temporarily, via revolutions that "activate the demos and destroy boundaries that bar access to political experience" (18). This activated populous, though, creates a tumult, "one that comes to appear as surplus democracy once revolutions are ended and the permanent institutionalization of politics is begun" (19). Wolin contends that this is because the democratic notions of "citizen-as-actor" and "politics-as-episodic" are incompatible with the modern choice of "the State as the fixed center of political life," and consequently that "[d]emocracy in the late modern world cannot be a complete political system, and given the awesome potentialities of modern forms of power . . . it ought not be hoped or striven for" (23). Instead, he asserts, we ought to make our peace with the idea that democracy "is doomed to succeed only temporarily, but is a recurrent possibility as long as the memory of the political survives" (23). Wolin concludes that "the possibility of renewal draws on a simple fact: that ordinary individuals are capable of creating new cultural patterns of commonality at any moment . . . renewing the political by contesting the forms of unequal power" that characterize society (24).

I agree with Wolin's account of the way that democracy is, in practice, periodically recalled to itself because of the political action of resistant and organized members of the polity. However, what if these periodic democratic renewals are not outside the bounds of regular democratic politics? What if they are not paradoxical or contradictory? What if they are not evidence, as Wolin colorfully puts it, of "democracy . . . betraying its own values" (24). Perhaps these seeming disruptions are actually part and parcel of the democratic package and should be theorized as such. More pointedly, what if periodic insurgency is democracy's way of keeping itself alive?

We might look to the physical sciences for an analogy. Take the concept of "swailing," a word used in forestry and farming, which means "controlled burn." Swailing is the practice of setting small parts of the forest on fire to reduce hazards that accumulate during the colder seasons and prevent hotter, more destructive fires from erupting in the spring. This process also stimulates the germination of some desirable forest trees, and reveals soil mineral layers that increase seedling vitality, thus renewing the forest. Without seasonally appropriate swailing, forests become moribund. I contend that the democratic environment, one filled with the hazards of structural inequalities and manifold cross-cutting difference, is one that requires the political swailing that social movements provide.

The Failures of Interest Group Pluralism

Contrary to the theoretical balm of balanced pluralism offered by American democratic theorists in the mid-twentieth century (e.g., Dahl 2006), social scientists have consistently demonstrated that, empirically, the "heavenly chorus"—that is, the collection of voices raised to speak their interests and policy preferences in democracies—sings with a decidedly upper-class accent (Schattschneider 1960). To wit, nothing explains differences in political participation better than socioeconomic stratification (Schlozman, Brady, and Verba 2012). Likewise, elected representatives are most likely to listen to upper-class constituents and make policy in accordance with their wishes (Gilens and Page 2014). Suppositions by mid-twentieth-century political scientists that stratified participation in electoral politics was voluntary, and therefore a benign expression of disinterest rather than a reflection of structural disadvantage, have been proved false (Verba, Schlozman, and Brady 1995; Bartels 2008; Schlozman, Brady, and Verba 2012). Equally optimistic notions that perhaps the policy preferences of the upper and lower classes were not very divergent have also shown themselves to be incorrect (Page, Bartels, and Seawright 2013; Flavin 2012; Kelly 2009). Additionally, though socioeconomic status is the most predictive indicator of political participation and influence, race and gender matter most in terms of the way members of the polity understand the political world as well as how they develop and express political attitudes and policy preferences (Hochschild 1996; Kinder and Sanders 1996; Dawson 1994; Sears, Sidanius, and Bobo 2000; López 2004; Lien 2001; Dittmar 2015; Caroll and Fox 2013; Pew Research Center 2016a; Fingerhut 2016).

These stratifications do not balance out at any point in the electoral process, national or local, during campaigns, or once representatives are situated in office. Instead, our regular electoral process routinely leaves some—usually white, upper-class men and associative conglomerations thereof—on top and others arrayed in an intersectional hierarchy that cascades below. The well-documented stratification evinced in the electoral system means that the United States is (in fact, not hyperbole) governed by and for the benefit of the few, rather than the expansive swath one might imagine with the echo of the words "we the people" ringing in the *doxa* of our imagined community (B. Anderson [1983] 2006).

This idealized form of this arrangement, which Iris Young calls "interest group pluralism," is predicated on the idea that coalitions of interests will be voluntary, based on associative rather than structural or immutable categories, and able to combine in a variety of ways. The acknowledgement of difference is an underpinning of the idea of democratic pluralism, but the understanding of difference—and its implications for justice and the possibility of a well-functioning democracy—is so flawed as to be counterproductive for the ideal. The kind of contestation that proponents readily acknowledge as endemic to the political includes competing interests, competing values, competing ethics, competing norms, competing discursive lexicons, and so on. Traditional proponents of pluralism like Robert Dahl argue that such conflict can and should be salved through the normal process of institutional politics, because satisfying the demands made in these contests is simply a question of organization on the part of citizens and responsiveness to that organization on the part of elected officials. Those with competing views must organize with others who share their perspective, and the most organized interest will win out, with no win ever being permanent and power shifting over time. However, the problem, as we know, is that pluralism is characterized not only by conflict between equals who have differing perspectives, but also by inequality, structural disadvantage, and, if not immutable, then demonstrably enduring exclusion based on ascriptive characteristics.

The issue of inequality is of great concern because it is not simply a matter of inequality among different social groups in the current generation, but inequality that compounds over time, giving rise to a cumulative effect or legacy that, while it does not always arise from the actions of the current members of the polity, nevertheless conditions the material opportunities granted in their lives, shaping the political meaning of their social understandings and the effect of their political actions. In short, interest-group pluralism might, in ideal theory, be able to solve the problem of difference, but it is only because the concept of difference is so thoroughly misconceived as to leave out consideration of the reality of inequality and its political and economic consequences.

But inequality is not the only concern. Interest-group pluralism also "depoliticizes public life." Because we carry out democratic politics in a way that restricts legitimate political concerns to personal interests, we have developed the habit of making "no distinction between the assertion of selfish interests and normative claims to justice or right" (I. Young [1990] 2011, 72). Indeed, the most common political insults leveled in contemporary politics, "snowflake" and "social justice warrior," treat genuine emotional investment in political topics and commitment to the ideal of justice, respectively, as infantile, undesirable attributes.

Politics is supposed to be made of sterner stuff, namely a naked "competition among claims," where the only worthy consideration is winning and "one does not win by persuading a public that one's claim is just," but instead by "making trades and alliances with others, and making effective strategic calculations about how and to whom to make your claims." This process "collapses normative claims to justice into selfish claims of desire" (I. Young [1990] 2011, 72). This way of conducting democratic politics is not damaging merely because it presents ethical problems, but also because it "fosters political cynicism" and convinces people that democratic politics is less about participation, representation, and problem-solving, and more a great game where the powerful compete and the rest of us clamber through our lives trying to stay out of the dangerous messes they make.

A further concern is that when the goal is only to win and not to deliberate and persuade your fellows regarding what is right, the range of arguments that circulate in public discourse is narrower and the content more superficial. Young contends that this leads to "a fragmented public life" in which people only give an audience to the arguments of their group. Today, the media environment, which features cable news subdivided by political attitudes, websites, and blogs precision-tuned for ideological preferences, and social media feeds personally and algorithmically curated to perfect comportment with our preexisting ideas, this tendency has only grown worse. Our discursive environment now provides structural support for public fractionalization. This means that "there is no forum within the public sphere of discussion and conflict where people can examine the overall patterns of justice or fairness produced by these processes." Additionally, because the political habit is to evaluate politics based on who's winning and who's losing (Bartels 1988; Capella and Jamieson 1997; T. Patterson 2005), rather than what is just or good and for whom, it is exceedingly difficult to bring "the basic structures, assumptions, constraints, and decision-making procedures" that coalesce to produce political outcomes into public discussion, "because, for the most part, these [structures] are not effectively public" (I. Young [1990] 2011, 73). The consequence is that political proposals are not directed at "persons as such, but at persons constituted piecemeal as taxpayers, health service consumers, parents, workers, residents of cities, and so on" (73). This kind of fragmentary public sphere's most negative impact is not polarization, but incoherence. Not only is there a dearth of public forums for discussion of issues outside the rubric of our selfish interest, but even if there were such settings, our political culture has not taught us what we ought to do in them. This kind of depoliticization, more than conflict or polarization, is the death of democracy because it means that the nation has become a mere territory, rather than a polity, because people have forgotten how to be citizens.

I have listed the empirical and conceptual deficiencies of interest-group pluralism, but it is also important to remember that any way of arranging power that starts from the world as it exists will require long-term and ongoing commitment to adapting to the realities of structural inequality and social difference in order to approach just political and social relations. Likewise, there are no ideologies, procedures, or policy agendas that can permanently or entirely undo the material and political consequences of the historically compounded legacies of domination and oppression. Of course, that is not to say we cannot and should not strive to do better.

An Antidote to the Politics of Despair

What is required is a political project that can meet the world where it is and take it someplace new. Such a politics requires an ethic for deciding what political remedy looks like and a political culture that facilitates revising structures, laws, and routines so that they can be in comportment with what the polity conceives as being as just as possible in a given time and place. Fundamentally, this iterative balancing act is what democracy is built to do. However, since democracy, like all governing systems, develops strong oligarchic tendencies over time, it is necessary to push through periods of political stagnation, and social movements provide the way.

It is for this reason that social movements are a potential antidote to the politics of despair. They allow us to enact citizenship, not only through performing duties, but also by authoring new understandings, priorities, and even governing institutions. Unlike other forms of participation, which can also teach valuable civic skills, social movements show us how to make change. Even if we do not immediately change policy or restructure institutions, we change our ideas, we change our minds, we change our associations, we change public understandings, and we change the scope of political possibility.

It is important to note that I do not assume that all social movements will be progressive. Nor do I think that political swailing is only delivered from the left. Democracy is difficult and risky—it is so because it entrusts people who have divergent understandings of the world and deviating interests in it to govern themselves collectively, with no power above them that can right the ship of state should they decide, through recklessness, blundering, or honest error, to dash it against the shores of history. A democratic society is ever in danger of doing itself in, but democratic polities are also incredibly resilient when they maintain public belief in and commitment to engaged citizenship that relies on debate, persuasion, and participation rather than resentment, cynicism, and violence. That is to say, when the democratic polity remains properly political.

At the point when belief in the efficacy of politics becomes tenuous in the majority, when people begin to despair—not about the consequences of decisions they have made in collective contestation, but instead about the very possibility of governing themselves—then the only hope for repair is a repoliticization of public life, an exercise of the political that reminds people that they are citizens. When antidemocratic movements arise and do this work, it is the responsibility of the citizenry to evaluate and answer. Sometimes, as we learned from the rise of the Third Reich in Europe at the beginning of the twentieth century, the polity will make catastrophic choices. But at others, it will author principles and construct institutions that bring future generations closer to the ideal of justice. For these reasons, it is important to take social movements seriously as a pragmatic political solution to a real democratic problem.

The Repoliticization of the Public Life

Social movements' greatest good derives from repoliticizing the public sphere—that is, reminding "the people" that they are the root of all legitimate democratic authority. When movements arise, they disrupt the formation of the bureaucratic "iron cage" that Max Weber warned of, in which elites organized into efficient establishments forget that their purpose is to serve the polity and instead spend their energy and resources defending the perpetuation of power and knowledge as it most benefits the organization (Weber [1922] 2013; Weber 2004). As such, "movements arise within welfare capitalist society, on the fringes of bureaucratic institutions or carving out new social spaces not dreamt of in their rules" to "exploit and expand the sphere of civil society" and challenge the forms of oppression and domination that structure contemporary social and political relations (I. Young [1990] 2011, 82).

Movements are a pragmatic politics in process; they are the performance of the political. They remind members of the polity that there is a public sphere where politics can and must take place if democracy is to be both authorized by and responsive to the people. In this way, social movements are not only instrumental, but institutionally important in themselves. They teach us how to reclaim citizenship in times when public life has become anemic or repressive, and many have forgotten that their political action is both necessary and beneficial.

In 2013, #BlackLivesMatter arose as the current iteration of the Black liberation movement. My book explores how it has inspired new political activism, developed a unique political philosophy, imagined new horizons for institutional change, invented new tactics for contestation, and transformed the public sphere. In original interviews, participants report how they developed a belief in their ability to be authors of the social and political arrangements that will characterize the new century. I explore their theory of politics, which I call radical Black feminist pragmatism, and examine their organizations and tactics, evaluate their influence and impact, and envisage the possibilities that their action has revealed to the American polity.

Plan of the Book

In the chapters that follow, I analyze the emergence of the Movement for Black Lives, its organizational structure and culture, and its strategies and tactics, while also laying out and contextualizing its political philosophy and measurable political effects in terms of changing public meanings, public opinion, and policy. Throughout the text, I interweave theoretical and empirical observations, rendering both an illustration of this particular movement and an analysis of the work social movements do in democracy.

In chapter 1, I relate the story of the emergence of the movement, beginning with the shocking though, for some, not surprising acquittal of Trayvon Martin's murderer. I discuss the way the activist hashtag #BlackLivesMatter coalesced into an offline movement during the uprising responding to the police murder of Michael Brown in Ferguson, Missouri, and soon after matured into the Movement for Black Lives, which is the name of a coordinating organization that helps to harmonize the autonomous efforts of individuals, groups, and organizations who take their mission to be defending Black lives from systematic oppression, domination, and premature death. In the second chapter, I outline the components of the political philosophy I have observed in the Movement for Black Lives. I argue that radical Black feminist pragmatism (RBFP) is a new approach to politics, one that takes lessons from many twentieth-century ideologies and forges them into a political ethic for our times. In the third chapter, I build out an analysis of one of the key elements of RBFP, the politics of care, which holds that the activity of governance in a society that hopes to be just must be oriented toward the responsibility to exercise and provide care for those most impacted by oppression and domination. The fourth chapter is an exploration both of the concept of organizing as distinct from mobilization, as an understudied yet critically important part of creating political change, and of the unique semi-federated organizational structure of the Movement for Black Lives. Chapter 5 reports the political impacts of the movement thus far, including the way it has reshaped public discourse and political meanings, transformed public opinion, and influenced public policy. The concluding chapter returns us to the consideration of what it means to repoliticize public life and how a public politicized by racial justice, and specifically a political philosophy oriented toward the radical imagination of pragmatic futures, promises to revolutionize the terms on which the twenty-first century will be lived.

1

Emergence

A Contemporary History

If the soil of the United States could speak, before saying a word, it would cough up our blood.

—BYP100

We believe it is our right and responsibility to write ourselves into the future.

—Walidah Imarisha and adrienne maree brown

A Movement Born in the Caul

Trayvon Martin was not the first Black American boy killed for being out of his proper place. Because homicide statistics are poorly kept, and vary wildly between reporting agencies, we do not know how common it is for Black people to be hunted in neighborhoods where they are deemed suspicious.[1] We do know that America has a long history of attacking and killing Black people deemed to be in the wrong place at the wrong time. From "sundown towns"[2] to "stop-and-frisk" policing,[3] to be Black in America is to be suspiciously out of place, perceived, as W. E. B. Du Bois wrote, as "a problem," and therefore to be ever in danger of violent, preemptive retaliation.

---

[1] "The FBI's Uniform Crime Reporting Program tabulates death at the hands of police officers. So does the National Center for Health Statistics. So does the Bureau of Justice Statistics. But the totals can vary wildly" (Wines 2014).

[2] Sundown towns are municipalities or neighborhoods that enforced segregation by excluding people of non-white races via some combination of discriminatory local laws, intimidation, and violence. The term came from signs that were posted in such places stating that "colored people" had to leave the town by sundown. Most famously, "Nigger, don't let the sun set on YOU in Hawthorne," which was posted in Hawthorne, California, during the 1930s. These towns have been located all over the United states, not only in the old Confederacy. See Loewen 2006.

[3] "Stop-and-frisk" policing, or the "Terry stop," is a practice of temporarily detaining, questioning, and at times searching civilians on the street on suspicion of the possession of weapons and other contraband. The overwhelming majority of people detained are Black or Latino. Between 80 and

Alicia Garza recalls that on July 13, 2013, when the jury finished its deliberations on the fate of George Zimmerman, she was in a bar with her husband and two friends awaiting the verdict. When it was announced, "Everything went quiet, everything and everyone. And then people started to leave *en masse*. The one thing I remember from that evening, other than crying myself to sleep that night, was the way in which as a black person, I felt incredibly vulnerable, incredibly exposed and incredibly enraged. Seeing these black people leaving the bar, and it was like we couldn't look at each other. We were carrying this burden around with us every day: of racism and white supremacy. It was a verdict that said: black people are not safe in America" (quoted in Day 2015).

Alicia Garza wrote a Facebook status that soon went viral. She called the status "a love letter to black people":

> The sad part is, there's a section of America who is cheering and celebrating right now. and that makes me sick to my stomach. We GOTTA get it together y'all. Stop saying we are not surprised. That's a damn shame in itself. I continue to be surprised at how little Black lives matter. And I will continue that. Stop giving up on black life. Black people. I love you. I love us. Our lives matter. (quoted in Lowery 2017)

Though young Trayvon's murder was the occasion for Alicia Garza to write her "love letter," which her friend and fellow organizer Patrisse Khan-Cullors hashtagged #BlackLivesMatter, in the years to follow the mobilizations of the movement were most often aimed at what Vesla Weaver calls the "carceral state" (Lerman and Weaver 2014). This is because it wasn't Zimmerman's murderous actions that were most shocking, but the fact that the system charged with "justice" legitimized them.

It was difficult to believe that though Trayvon's killer was known, he wasn't arrested until after Black people protested for forty-five days. And more astonishing still, District Attorney Angela Corey, who was reluctant to bring charges against Zimmerman on the basis of a presumed "stand your ground" defense, two months later quickly charged Marissa Alexander, a Black woman who fired a warning shot in the direction of her abusive husband,

---

90 percent of the time, those stopped have no weapons or contraband. Additionally, stop-and-frisk policies are ineffective, having no correlation with crime reduction. In 2013, a federal judge ruled that the practice was discriminatory and unconstitutional. See Bump 2016.

with aggravated assault with a lethal weapon, a charge that carried a mandatory minimum sentence of twenty years. In one case, a known neighborhood bully claimed self-defense as he gunned down a boy walking home with Skittles in his pocket. In the other, a Black woman could not claim self-defense though she was a documented survivor of domestic violence and no one was harmed. The common denominator in the two cases seemed depressingly clear: Black people are not allowed to defend themselves. And they are never, ever innocent.

This heart-rending supposition was given even more credence as the boy whose life was cut short was posthumously presented at trial as guilty for his own murder. The evidence of his culpability was that the high school junior had trace amounts of marijuana in his system and once played hooky from school. On the strength of these marks against Trayvon's character, the jury acquitted Zimmerman after sixteen hours of deliberation, with one juror opining afterward that she was convinced that "George Zimmerman had his heart in the right place" (quoted in Ford 2013). Meanwhile, the domestic violence survivor, Marissa, was convicted and condemned to twenty years in prison by the jury who heard her case, after only thirteen minutes of deliberation. None of the jurors at her trial publicly speculated about the disposition of her heart. Most white people's collective and habitual disregard for the humanity of Black people is also evidenced by the fact that although most Americans avidly followed the news of the Zimmerman trial, nearly eight out of ten Black people felt the case raised important issues about race and that the verdict was unsatisfactory, while only about three of ten white people agreed (Pew Research Center 2013).

None of these phenomena—from the lethal vigilante violence to the indifference of the legal system in the face of Black suffering and death—are new, but the Zimmerman trial focused America's attention on the fact that despite the attractive African American family living in the White House, Black people continued to be unsafe. Ta-Nehisi Coates writes:

> It is hard to face, but all our phrasing—race relations, racial chasm, racial justice, racial profiling, white privilege, even white supremacy—serves to obscure that racism is a visceral experience, that it dislodges brains, blocks airways, rips muscle, extracts organs, cracks bones, breaks teeth. You must never look away from this. You must always remember that the sociology, the history, the economics, the graphs, the charts, the regressions all land, with great violence, upon the body. (Coates 2015, 10)

Patrisse Khan-Cullors, a longtime anti-incarceration organizer and one of the three founding women of the Black Lives Matter Global Network Foundation, was visiting a young mentee, an inmate at a prison in Susanville, California, when she learned the verdict. "The first thing I did was literally drop my jaw. And then I felt intense amounts of heat in my chest" (quoted in King 2015). She started crying, but beyond the heartbreak, she reports, "I was clear that the acquittal couldn't be the only thing that people remembered from that day. There must also be this movement" (Khan-Cullors interview, 2017).

In this chapter, I provide an account of the emergence of the Movement for Black Lives (M4BL). The movement was born twice, first as #BlackLivesMatter, a primarily online reaction to the shock of the Zimmerman acquittal, and second as the street mobilization in Ferguson that would inspire the invention of the Movement for Black Lives, an umbrella organization Jessica Byrd has called "a political home of political homes," which was created "as a space for Black organizations across the country to debate and discuss the current political conditions, develop shared assessments of what political interventions were necessary in order to achieve key policy, cultural and political wins, and to co-create a shared movement-wide strategy under the fundamental idea that we can achieve more together than we can separately" (from an organizing email of June 22, 2020, to the group's listserve).

Ferguson: Genesis of the Movement

The killing of Trayvon Martin and the trial and acquittal of George Zimmerman were a political shock. Wesley Lowery, an African American reporter who covered the uprisings in Ferguson, Baltimore, and other cities around the country, wrote about the movement for the *Guardian*:

> That year was a major awakening point not just for me but also for other young black men and women across the country. Each story of a police shooting solidified the undeniable feeling in our hearts that their deaths and those of other young black men were not isolated. Peaceful black America was awakened by the Zimmerman verdict, which reminded them anew that their lives and their bodies could be abused and destroyed without consequence. Trayvon's death epitomized the truth that the system black Americans had been told to trust was never structured to deliver justice to

them. The "not guilty" verdict prompted the creation of a round of boisterous and determined protest groups, initially Florida-based, although they would eventually expand nationally. (Lowery 2017)

Social media platforms allowed that shock to generate what social movements scholars call a "political opportunity," a "consistent dimension of the political environment that provides incentives for people to undertake collective action by affecting their expectations of success or failure" (Tarrow 1998, 19–20). But political opportunities can be fleeting. The moment of political awakening many experienced at the acquittal of Martin's killer could have subsided without blossoming from grievance into movement if not for the August killing of Michael Brown in Ferguson. Of the Ferguson firmament, activist Matt Nelson writes, "This became the epicenter of a major political earthquake, shifting the ground underneath us, shaking the core of how America sees police and policing, and jolting us into a new, more-politicized normal" (M. Nelson 2015, xv).

What was it about Michael Brown that acted as such a catalyst for the movement?

There are four characteristics that made Ferguson the conflagration that forged the movement into a formidable political entity: (1) Michael Brown's killing represented a recursive trauma; (2) the city of Ferguson was at the center of a particularly vivid confluence of not only racial but also economic injustice, in the form of anti-Black extortionist schemes perpetrated by county government; (3) St. Louis County has a wealth of what Doug McAdam calls "indigenous organizations"—established, local, Black-led social justice nonprofits and churches; and (4) Black activists with extensive professional experience in a variety of sectors mobilized from all over the country to provide advice, support, and long-term planning services for the budding insurgency.

Recursive Trauma

The murder of Michael Brown hit Black America, and especially African American political activists, as a recursive trauma. People watching felt they had seen the story before. With the murder of Martin, there was some hope that the system would work—that Zimmerman would be arrested, charged, indicted, and convicted. When he was not, it shocked Black people. It made people understand that not as much had changed since the mid-twentieth century as our national narrative suggests. It made people believe that justice would not come, because the ideology of white supremacy and the institutions that serve it could justify killing Black people with impunity and blithely blame the dead for their mortality, regardless of circumstances. After Trayvon, seventeen-year-old Jordan Davis had been killed while sitting in a parking lot with a car full of friends, because an armed white passerby was annoyed by the volume of the music they enjoyed. Twenty-two-year-old Rekia Boyd had been shot by an off-duty police officer while standing in the park eating takeout with her friends. John Crawford had been shot by police for holding a toy gun he had picked up off the shelves while browsing at Walmart. Eric Garner had been choked to death by a cop for selling loose cigarettes without a license, while he begged for his life, saying that he couldn't breathe. These were only the cases that had been most widely publicized. Garner's murder had been videotaped by a bystander with a cell phone. The cop who killed the father of six was never charged with a crime.

By 12:00 noon on August 9, 2014, when Michael Brown was gunned down on Canfield Drive, a street in his neighborhood, the disbelief of the Zimmerman verdict had long since turned to a simmering, bitter anger. Brown's friends, neighbors, and parents gathered at the edges of the hastily strewn yellow police tape, frantic for answers and mourning the death of their college-bound boy, in the face of indifferent white police officers who stood impassively just outside the coagulating spread of Mike Brown's blood. The immediate aftermath of Brown's execution was documented by bystanders in pictures and video. At 12:03 p.m. Twitter user @TheePharoah tweeted a picture of Brown prone on the ground, uniformed police standing over him, with the caption "I JUST SAW SOMEONE DIE OMFG" (quoted in Lurie 2014). Thus began the real-time documentation of events in Ferguson by people who happened to be in proximity to the event. In the days and weeks to follow, professional journalists would come to Ferguson to report on the story, but in the first hours, bystanders took to social media to share what they witnessed, unmediated by police accounts or news editors, related in still images, 30-second clips, and 140-character observations that were raw, emotional, bewildered, and, as the hours ticked by, enraged.

This outrage was undeniably fueled by the "gruesome, dehumanizing spectacle" of Brown's body lying in the street for four and half hours after Darren Wilson pumped eight bullets into his body. Michael Brown's remains were not transported from the scene or logged into the county medical examiner until 4:37 p.m. (Lurie 2014). Wesley Lowery reflects:

> For some, first in Ferguson and later around the nation, the spectacle of Brown's body cooling on the asphalt conjured images of the historic horrors of lynchings—the black body of a man robbed of his right to due process and placed on display as a warning to other black residents. (Lowery 2016, 25)

One person who came into the streets in that first afternoon commented, "It's like we're not even human to them" (quoted in Lowery 2016).

At first, those gathering in the street were there to mourn. They set up a memorial of flowers and teddy bears, around which people stood and sought information and prayed. But as afternoon turned to evening, Ferguson police began to mass around the crowd. Several had police dogs on leashes. One officer allowed his canine to urinate on the makeshift memorial. In late afternoon, Louis Head, Brown's stepfather, was photographed holding a handwritten cardboard sign that read "Ferguson police just executed my unarmed son!!!" The image quickly went viral (Lurie 2014).

By 6:30 p.m., police from several jurisdictions had arrived and formed a line to separate the growing crowd from the yellow-tape-cordoned scene. In addition, they prohibited all vehicles from passing through Canfield Drive except their own. Around 7:00 p.m., Leslie McSpadden, Brown's mother, spelled out Michael's name in tea-light candles and rose petals over the bloodstains that remained all over the street after his body was finally removed. At 7:18, a group of people broke off from the mourners to march toward the Ferguson police station to demand answers, some kind of explanation for why eighteen-year-old Mike had been gunned down. Around 8:00, someone set fire to a dumpster on Canfield Drive. When the fire department responded, two police officers climbed atop the fire truck, surveying the area. People in the crowd began to taunt them. The officers called for backup and the police "swarmed the area," according to a tweet by St. Louis alderman Antonio French. At 9:02 p.m., French reported that "police cars trampled rose petals and candles at the memorial for #MikeBrown." Missouri state representative Sharon Pace, who was also with her constituents that evening, told *Mother Jones*, "[t]hat made people in the crowd mad, . . . and it made me mad. Some residents began walking in front of police vehicles at the end of the block to prevent them from driving in" (Follman 2014). Witnesses tweeted out photos of the mangled memorial and the growing volume of heavily armed police. More people came into the streets to lend support to the family, to bear witness, and to express growing anger. By 10:00 p.m. that night, most of the crowd in the neighborhood had dispersed, but a growing number would return to the streets of Ferguson to demonstrate their outrage and demand accountability every day for the next four months (McFadden 2014).

The more than one hundred days that activists spent in Ferguson were not spent only in outrage. During those months, people began to strategize about how they could turn the moment of what Emile Durkheim called "collective effervescence," into a movement. Maurice "Moe" Mitchell, cofounder of the movement-facing, capacity-building consultancy Blackbird, said,

> It's hard to explain . . . that experience, the first weeks, basically from when Mike Brown died to his funeral, you had to be there in order to understand what that was. To this day I've never experienced anything like it. . . . From August 9th to the funeral, was the uprising—a completely organic black uprising. . . . When you hit Florissant [Ave.] there were Black people as far as the eye could see. Of every age group. Every part of our community. It wasn't just the activist class or "woke" people. It was everyone. And it wasn't organized—there was no center of gravity, there was no Sharpton, there was no St. Louis version of Sharpton. It was everyone. There were people from gangs/street organizations out there, there were church people out there, there were very, very young people who were holding their own rallies and making their own signs. It was a legitimate, grassroots, organic, homegrown, working class Black people who had been super politicized. It was amazing . . . [it] was what I had always dreamed of as an organizer. . . . Everybody chipping in, the sense of community and love. It was beautiful. (Mitchell interview, 2017)

In their accounts of the genesis of the movement, activists describe their reaction to the police killing of Mike Brown in remarkably similar ways. While the Zimmerman affair had come as a shock, Brown's murder and the response of the state was, by then, familiar. But that familiarity was far from a comfort; instead, it was a triggering trauma, one that many activists, both lay and trained, had prepared themselves for by vowing not to miss the opportunity to respond in a way that was more active than commiseration and despair.

Moe Mitchell describes what brought him to Ferguson this way:

> I remember when Trayvon was killed. It just hit me. It's hard to understand why certain cases, certain stories hit you in certain ways, but you know the Trayvon story—and I felt like, as an organizer—I been organizing since I was 16 years old and I'm 37, will be 38 in July—I remember, I helped organize a mobilization in New York. . . . And afterwards, I saw the way that case was handled, I saw the Sharpton-led mobilizations and other stuff. And I felt really hollow, just hollow. And then when—I'm not even gonna mention his name—when dude got off, it just really hurt. And I was like damn, I'm an organizer, I need to be doing something. I didn't know what I needed to be doing, but I needed to do something. And <u>Black death needs to mean more.</u> I mean, our lives need to mean more. If they take our lives, they need to feel the repercussions of every one of our lives. Every one of our lives, they need to feel it. They don't. That's why they do this. Because they can, essentially. And so, I thought, if there's ever a situation like this, I'm gonna lean into it. I'm going to do everything I can do. I'm going to use all of my resources, all of my relationships, all of my organizing skills and I'm going to lean into that moment. So, when Mike Brown was killed, I felt something. I was so inspired by how people responded on the ground in St. Louis. I was like, I've never seen anything like this. (Mitchell interview, 2017)

Many young organizers made personal vows like Moe Mitchell's, and when the time came, they headed to St. Louis, determined to use all their resources, relationships, and organizing skills to do everything they could do.

Confluence of Injustice

The City of Ferguson was not only unique in the ferocity and duration of the uprising that took place there in August 2015, it also presents an extreme, local example of the horrors of what Cedric Robinson calls "racial capitalism" (C. Robinson [1983] 2000). A Department of Justice investigation found that Ferguson is a community that had been subject to the routine and systematic exploitation of its Black residents by police for the purpose of collecting revenue for the city (US Department of Justice 2015). Municipalities all over Missouri profit from Black poverty by targeting Black people and levying large, accumulating fines against them for minor and imagined violations of the law (Balko 2014a). Racial capitalism consists of the common material practices that result from white supremacy as a structuring—not interpersonal—condition in Western social and political life. Specifically, the City of Ferguson uses its monopoly of force, enacted by the police department, and institutional authority, enacted by municipal courts, to gobble up the lives of the Black and brown people within its borders, both metaphorically through tickets, fees, and arrests that impede or end employment, and literally via summary execution on neighborhood streets. The threat of these state terrorisms of both an economic and physical nature put Black and brown citizens who are marked for sacrifice in an untenable position. It creates situations in which even an idealized "personally responsible" working individual's entire life, and that of their family, can be decimated by a traffic ticket. Barbara Ransby writes in her contemporaneous history of the movement, *Making All Black Lives Matter*, "It was evident that, while Brown's killing was the catalyst, the Black working class of Ferguson was angry about much more, and their anger resonated around the country and beyond" (Ransby 2018, 6).

In a wonderful example of in-depth reporting from the *Washington Post*, Radley Balko describes in detail confirming the Department of Justice's 2015 findings of racially motivated municipal exploitation of Black residents in Ferguson, and how St. Louis municipalities profit off the poor Black residents within their borders. Balko tells the story of Nicole Bolden, who had a fender bender with another town resident. When the police arrived, Bolden was filled with dread because she knew that she had unpaid parking tickets. True to her fear, she was arrested on site in front of her children and taken to jail.

Some of the towns in St. Louis County can derive 40 percent or more of their annual revenue from the petty fines and fees collected by their municipal courts. A majority of these fines are for traffic offenses, but they can also include fines for fare-hopping on MetroLink (St. Louis's light rail system), loud music and other noise ordinance violations, zoning violations for uncut grass or unkempt property, violations of occupancy permit restrictions, trespassing, wearing "saggy pants," business license violations, and vague infractions such as "disturbing the peace" or "affray" that give police officers a great deal of discretion to look for other violations.

"These aren't violent criminals," says Thomas Harvey . . . of Arch City Defenders. "These are people who make the same mistakes you or I do— speeding, not wearing a seatbelt, forgetting to get your car inspected on time. The difference is that they don't have the money to pay the fines. Or they have kids, or jobs that don't allow them to take time off for two or three court appearances. When you can't pay the fines, you get fined for that, too. And when you can't get to court, you get an arrest warrant." Arrest warrants are also public information. They can be accessed by potential landlords or employers. So they can prevent someone from getting a job, housing, job training, loans or financial aid. "So they just get sucked into this vortex of debt and despair," Harvey says. (Balko 2014a)

Some will say that the only answer to these crippling, systematic impediments to self-development and self-determination is "personal responsibility." This is often the refrain in American policy and rhetoric—and it was the explicit reason cited by the police and city officials questioned by the Justice Department about the bald disparities in Ferguson. That being the case, how can one resist political despair? The answer that occurred to the people of Ferguson and hundreds of African American activists watching the events unfold was to follow some advice embedded in Black vernacular English: "show up," "show out," and "shut it down."

Local Organizations and Professional Help

The longing to do something positive that had been percolating among Black activists around the country might not have come to fruition if not for the "indigenous organizations" that existed in St. Louis County. Indigenous organizations, according to Doug McAdam, are local institutions that enable and support those who have developed an "insurgent consciousness" or shared sense of injustice as they mobilize in response to "political opportunity" or observed vulnerabilities and interruptions in the regular arrangement of power and privilege that govern social institutions, habits, or mores (McAdam 1982). St. Louis County has several long-established community organizations that have worked tirelessly to combat the local effects of discrimination, domination, and oppression. One of those establishments, Organization for Black Struggle (OBS), played a pivotal role in supporting people who gathered in the street to mourn Mike Brown when protests erupted on August 9, the day of his funeral.

OBS was founded by veterans of the Black Power wing of the civil rights movement in 1980. By their own account, they are "one of the oldest

Black-led, mass organizations with radical politics in the state of Missouri";
they work to address issues in the areas of "prison industrial complex (including police violence and court corruption), workers' rights, women and
youth"; and their political focus is the "fight for political power, economic
justice and cultural dignity for African Americans, especially the Black
working class," according to the group's website (Organization for Black
Struggle, n.d.).

For Black organizers who wanted to come to Ferguson in the days after
Brown was gunned down, OBS was often the first point of contact. Moe
Mitchell relates the way OBS and outside organizers came together:

> I finally reached somebody from the Organization for Black Struggle, and
> I was like, "Hey Sis, I don't know you that well but from afar this is my read
> of the situation. And it seems like y'all could use more capacity, y'all could
> use more hands. And, I know there's probably a lot of people coming at you
> with all different types of politics, all different types of tensions, but I know
> really, really dope and really, really honorable Black organizers who would,
> if they could, support you." (Mitchell interview, 2017)

Another organization that provided support to local protestors and a point
of contact for outside organizers was Saint John's United Church of Christ,
known locally as The Beloved Community church. The church's stated mission, according to their website, is to "nurture the closeness, care, fellowship
and faith of the congregation; to be a catalyst for neighborhood wholeness
and growth; and to work toward the elimination of violence" (St. John's
Church, n.d.). The pastor, the Reverend Starsky Wilson, endorses "political
docetism," which emphasizes the political nature of Jesus's life and ministry
(Hendricks 2007). The church served as one of the major bases of operations
and respite during the uprising. Organizers and activist met in the pews to
connect with each other, rest, and strategize. Direct action trainings and
wellness workshops were held, and the pastor preached sermons to fuel and
fill the spirit of those participating in and/or supporting the rebellion. At a
sermon during the uprising, Wilson preached:

> [Jesus] lived under Roman occupation and there were militarized forces in
> his neighborhood. Jesus lived under an elite priestly system that turned the
> temples over to Rome to exact taxes on people that kept them oppressed.
> These priests were in bed with the Roman establishment to keep people

poor. . . . We don't call it taxes today. We call it profiling and being ticketed for driving while black. Somebody got here today and didn't know that there were three arrest warrants for every household in Ferguson. . . . It was noted that there were people who were so poor, that they decided to act out against the system by looting people who came down the pathways in Galilee. Crucifixion was an execution reserved for insurrectionists and rebels. Jesus was not killed between two thieves, but between two looters or "social bandits." . . .

There are those who have attempted to forget . . . the political nature of [Jesus'] ministry. They suggest that Jesus was more concerned with individual morality than he was with social justice—that he was more concerned with inward evil than systemic evil and oppression. Jesus' political climate is our political climate, and therefore we must not forget the revolutionary reality of our religious roots. (quoted in Vaughn 2014)

These community institutions provided an entry point and anchor for a network of educated, mostly young, Black people trained as organizers, who had honed their skills in social justice-focused nonprofits. Black organizers from all over the country abandoned their work at large nonprofits and redirected their efforts, in part or wholly, toward the movement. Although it is tough to pinpoint the total number of activists who traveled to Ferguson from elsewhere, we do know that hundreds of people, mostly self-funded and on a volunteer basis, flocked to Ferguson.

People like Maurice Mitchell, who at the time was serving as the coordinator for the New York State Civic Engagement Table, a project of the New York Foundation. In his capacity as coordinator, he served as a liaison and communications hub for more than sixty social justice nonprofits, helping them share information and technology, and assisting them with messaging for public campaigns. His friend and fellow organizer Thenjiwe McHarris was at the time working for the US Human Rights Network, heading up the Human Rights at Home Campaign, which sought to hold the United States accountable for human rights violations the organization had documented when it came up for UN review in 2014. Mitchell gave this report:

I got down on the ground, Thenjiwe was coming back from Geneva, she did a lot of work with the UN and with other international [human rights groups]. So, she hit me up on Facebook and was like, "Yo, I hear you're out in St. Louis," and I was like, "Yeah, you should come." And so, I got in that night, the next morning, she was there. I picked her up. And then, that was history. . . . I came for five days and stayed for five months. (Mitchell interview, 2017)

During those months, Ferguson frothed with protest and the eyes of the nation turned to the small city, debating what caused the uprising, what it meant, and when and where it would end. But for the activists in the city, the goal was that it never would. In those early days, the daily demonstrations felt like a revelation, a communal purgation, an example of what Emile Durkheim (1995) calls "collective effervescence," a moment when a group comes together to communicate the same thought and participate in the same action, a ritual that unifies the group. Interviews with people who participated in the protests convey a feeling of organic rupture, a welling-up of sentiment and the ebullient sense of people coming to recognize their own power. In the midst of mass uprisings, this feeling that everything is happening spontaneously and without having been planned is common. Writing of the sit-ins that swept the South in the 1960, Francesca Polletta (2006, 32) reports that students described their motivations for participating "unplanned, impulsive, and, over and over again, spontaneous. 'It was like a fever . . . everyone wanted to go.'" While the energy of mass protest does effervesce unpredictably, creating its own velocity, it is almost never the case that no one has organized a framework for protest to become sustained. As Polletta points out, "student activists called up 'spontaneity' in the same breath as they pointed toward (and stood within) the local spaces in which they organized, deliberated, gathered, planned, and theorized" (148). Likewise, in Ferguson there existed an "ecosystem of local organizations" (Ransby 2018, 7), including those planning actions and campaigns as well as movement-facing support organizations that provided communications and logistical support, trainings in direct action, health and healing support, legal aid, and more. In the midst of this cathartic, "organic" organizing tumult, many new organizations had their founding. For example, Mitchell, McHarris, and their friend Mervyn Marcano founded Blackbird, a movement-facing, capacity-building, and public relations nonprofit that exists to provide "communications, organizing, [and] policy/advocacy support to a growing field committed to ending racism in the United States" (according to McHarris's LinkedIn page). While the combined efforts of local organizers and outsiders who came to support the Ferguson uprising were crucial to its duration and success, there were tensions that resulted from the combination of forces. Ransby reports that Brittany Ferrell, one of Ferguson's most prominent local organizers, said "she sought advice from those with more experience" and said "I would never downplay the knowledge that Merv [Marcano from Blackbird], Patrisse [Khan-Cullors], and Alicia [Garza] brought to the situation," but notes that there were a lot of local people whose names never made it into the paper: "Tony Rice, Ebony Williams, Derek Robinson, Diamond Latchison, and Low-Key from Lost Voices" (Ransby 2018, 52). There were also the steady efforts of Kayla Reed, founder of St. Louis Action Council, and Jamala Rogers ("MamaJamala") of the Organization for Black Struggle, who was "often the first person people called when they arrived in town to help, or when they encountered a problem or dilemma locally" (55). Rogers framed the main message of the Ferguson uprising this way: "We are moving from an era of police impunity and the perception that police killings are rare and isolated occurrences into an era of heightened awareness, consciousness, organizing, and mobilization." Put more bluntly, "[t]he Ferguson Rebellion is a statement that it will not be business as usual in this country. It's time to choose your side" (J. Rogers 2015, xxi, 130).

The combined knowledge and effort of organizations that had long been fighting racism in the St. Louis area with the skills-based expertise of organizers who offered to support their efforts made the uprising in Ferguson uniquely sustainable. Patrisse Khan-Cullors writes,

> We understood Ferguson was not an aberration but, in fact, a clear point of reference for what was happening to Black communities everywhere.... When it was time for us to leave, inspired by our friends in Ferguson, organizers from 18 different cities went back home and developed Black Lives Matter (BLM) chapters in their communities and towns.... People were hungry to galvanize their communities to end state-sanctioned violence against Black people, the way Ferguson organizers and allies were doing. Soon after, Opal, Alicia, Darnell and I helped create the BLM network infrastructure. (Khan-Cullors 2016)

From BLM to the M4BL

The atmosphere of the summer was tense because Brown's killing came after a season filled with the viral images of Black people being detained and killed by police. Khan-Cullors and her friend Darnell Moore, a queer activist and reporter, decided that they should develop a way for Black people outside St. Louis to actively learn from and contribute to the uprising that was taking place. Khan-Cullors and Moore quickly put together what would become the Black Lives Matter Rides.

Brittney Cooper, an academic and activist based in New Jersey, relates the story of her recruitment to the rides this way:

> Like most Black folks, I was sitting in front of my TV in August of 2014 horrified every night at the tanks and the tear gas and the way our folks were being treated. And I get this text from Darnell one night and he says, "Do you want to ride to Ferguson this weekend?" and I was like, "Yup, let's do it." And as he kept talking to people, it became, "Well, let's take a bus of folks." Really, I knew something was going on when I got on the bus to Ferguson. It was a terrible bus. It had no outlets, no Wi-Fi, we had all been promised that these things were going to be on the bus. So, that meant we were going to have to talk to each other for 20 hours. A couple things happened on the bus, some of it, I don't even have the language for it. There was this feeling that folks were engaged and that we all knew that something—we were using all this moral language and so you had all these young folks who were disconnected from religious institutions—yet, there was still this sense that something uniquely evil had happened. And that it required us to show up. (Cooper interview, 2017)

Although Moore and Khan-Cullors had planned the rides in only two weeks, by utilizing their personal contacts and social media networks and putting out a call for participants on YouTube, as well as setting up GoFundMe accounts to raise money for busses and basic accommodations, the action drew hundreds of people. Modeled after the Freedom Rides of the 1960s, the BLM riders were five hundred strong and hailed from Boston, Philadelphia, Chicago, Detroit, Houston, Los Angeles, Portland, and Tucson, among other cities. The stated goal of the rides was to "support the people of Ferguson and help turn a local moment into a national movement" (Solomon 2015).

In Ferguson, the riders from around the country were greeted by St. Louis-based organizers who had been sustaining the protests in Ferguson since Brown was gunned down, including Organization for Black Struggle, Hands Up United, and Missourians Organizing for Reform and Empowerment. The riders, who included students, scholars, journalists, lawyers, nurses, organizers, pastors, and tech mavens, among others, converged on Saint John's United Church of Christ, which served as a home base for the four days of the riders' sojourn.

Accounts of the Black Lives Matter riders' experiences in Ferguson emerged on personal blogs as well as on popular news sites all over the Internet. Three riders—Tamura Lomax, Stephanie Troutman, and Heather Laine Talley—wrote up their experience for *The Feminist Wire*:

> We were asked one question over and over again, "Are you committed to transforming this moment into a movement?" Our final conversations in Ferguson reveal that the answer to that question is quite simply, "Yes." We emphatically believe that Black Lives Matter—all Black Lives Matter. And changing the narrative and ultimately socio-political praxis from Black insignificance, which enables all kinds of structural and interpersonal violence and dehumanization to innate Black importance and value will require the concerted and strategic works of all of us. (Lomax, Troutman, and Talley 2015)

In a September 2014 editorial for the *Guardian*, Darnell Moore and Patrisse Khan-Cullors underscored this point:

> But the real work begins now: Nearly a month after Brown's brutal killing, after the camera crews have left and in a moment when justice has yet to be realized, many more of us have decided that we could not allow Ferguson to be portrayed as an aberration in America: it must remain understood as a microcosm of the effects of anti-black racism.

Underscoring the political conviction was an emotional, even spiritual, experience. Participants reported that they were moved by the experience of standing in the place where Brown's body had lain. That they were made more determined than they had been because they witnessed the pain and fear of the people who lived in the town. That they were impressed by the commitment of all those who gathered—a commitment that was made concrete by the promise activists made to each other to take what they had learned and discussed during the rides back with them as they planned actions tailor-made in and for the cities from which they hailed. A BLM rider and writer for *Colorlines* magazine, Akiba Solomon, related the aftermath of the rides this way:

On Facebook I friend everyone I recognize from the trip. . . . Throughout the week, tag-filled testimonies begin to appear. Several people (including me) say they can't find the right words to describe our journey. One rider describes a change within: "I felt something shift in me and more importantly, I bore witness to an emergent Black political consciousness and a movement led by our youth." (Solomon 2015)

Activists working for different organizations, on different coasts, and in locales in between, used the Black Lives Matter Rides to forge the popular injustice frame "#BlackLivesMatter" into a movement with a collective identity. This is a rare accomplishment for a collectivity that is neither single-issue, nor located in any one organization, nor coalesced behind the charismatic presence of any one person. Instead, the movement for Black lives repurposed the "freedom ride," a successful tactic of the twentieth century's racial justice movement, and made it their own. In this way, activists were able to build relationships upon face-to-face encounters that gave participants the selective emotional incentives that Fancesca Polletta and James Jasper (2001) note are necessary to the formation of collective identities that are meant to endure during sustained political challenges. These relationships were later able to be maintained and deepened online. This style of organizing, rooted in real life but bolstered by a vibrant and variegated virtual civic space housed on Facebook, Twitter, Instagram, Vine, WhatsApp, GroupMe, and other platforms, adopted as needed by participants, gave the collective action frame and slogan of the movement additional meaning for the leaders and residents who converged in Ferguson that fall. Not only did Black lives matter in the abstract, as an aspirational political goal, but their politicized and mobilized Black selves, very clearly and concretely, mattered to each other.

The Convening in Cleveland

As winter came, the protests in the streets of Ferguson waned. However, organizers and activists who had worked together in those streets, and many others who had supported those efforts from afar, continued to come together. Barbara Ransby recounted that in December 2014, activists gathered in New York to reflect on their experiences and to try to strategize about how to continue the political work that had begun. It was there, she says, that "the Movement for Black Lives was born." After the meeting in New York, there were additional regional meetings in Los Angeles and Selma, Alabama. It was decided that the newly formed Movement for Black Lives would have its first convening in the Midwest. Blackbird helped organize M4BL's first convening in Cleveland, Ohio, in July 2015. It brought together over two thousand Black organizers. There, seven "tables" were organized: "strategy, action, communication, policy, organizing, electoral strategy, and resources" (Ransby 2018, 153).

In Cleveland, people representing dozens of organizations based in cities around the nation came together again, including Ferguson Action, BYP100, Million Hoodies, Project South, Dream Defenders, and many others. The gathering was called the Movement for Black Lives Convening. It was organized as a series of sessions on broad topics covering the activity, strategies, tactics, vision, and trajectory of the growing movement. One of the planners, Los Angeles–based organizer Tanya Lucia Bernard, reported in *The Root* that "when we started planning the Movement for Black Lives Convening, we had our love for our community at the center of the planning. From the outset, the team wanted to come together not only to process and heal from the trauma we'd suffered over the past couple of years, but also to love one another and build lasting relationships" (Bernard 2015). Brooklyn-based organizer Mark Winston Griffith described the gathering as "less about creating a definitive agenda or a centralized leadership and coordination structure than it was about framing the moment in a legacy of resistance and grounding it in black-on-black love" (Griffith 2015). He goes on to describe the horizontal organization of the gathering, noting that the session agenda was set by participants and that there were no keynote speakers:

The planning and organizing team, which included the three co-founders of #BlackLivesMatter, barely introduced themselves to the attendees, and there were no pictures or bios of them to be found in the program or on the official website. This horizontal form of leadership and relinquishing of ego has emerged as one of several generational markers in this movement. There were plenty of elders, old-school black nationalists, and middle-aged nonprofit professionals in effect, but the weekend and its dominant sensibility belonged to radicalized, under-35-year-old social-justice organizers. The Cleveland gathering was not only conspicuously devoid of white people but, unlike more traditional political and cultural events, there were neither headliners nor lionized personalities.

The workshops were conceived and provided by the participants themselves. Several hundred were proposed, and the final line up was decided by online voting. Sessions on political prisoners, the legacy of the Black Panther Party, queer and transgender leadership, reparations, and the intersection between nationalism, gender, and sexuality, stood side by side with sessions on healing and self-care, organizing for resilience, urban farming, and intra-community conflict resolution. (Griffith 2015)

At the convening, organizers attempted to create a democratic experience utilizing a politics of care in line with their values. Organizers spent time making sure that people could be housed and assisted with costs of travel, and that groups that tend to be marginalized, like trans activists and sex workers, would have a significant voice in setting the agenda. However, conflict still arose. Mary Hooks, an organizer homed at Southerners on New Ground (SONG), remembers:

I was one of the folks on the planning team. . . . What I was clocking at the time was some of the magic of it, which was palpable, . . . and some of our contradictions and tensions. . . . What were the plagues we were seeing inside the movement and what was the medicine? It showed up in that people didn't always know how to struggle in a principled way. We saw the tactics that we were using in the street to shut down political candidates, taking over mics, and you know, folks were using that inside of a movement space. . . . What I saw were people elbowing out space when an invitation had already been made. And so, some tensions showed up. [The convening] was at a college and the city had already passed an emergency ordinance to limit protesting and to say that anyone caught protesting without a permit would be held in jail for a minimum of forty-eight hours, because they knew that we were coming. They put in a curfew. The city was really responding [to our presence]. (M. Hooks interview, 2018)

In the midst of all of the tension created by the hostile external conditions, there was also trouble brewing internally. She goes on:

We were setting up the space, making the bathrooms gender neutral by putting up signs. But the school was mandating the mostly Black janitors to take down any signs. So then, we would put them back up. Finally, the Black janitors were like, "We see what you all are trying to do, but if you keep doing this, our jobs are at stake." And we knew that our fight wasn't with them. But, then, when we opened the doors for the M4BL meeting, people were immediately triggered because the bathrooms were not accommodating. And they were like, "Y'all are transphobic." And we didn't say this, but we should have said it: "Y'all, we were expecting 800 people, because that's how many registered, but then 600 of you have called to say you're coming since registration. And the 20 people organizing this have been hustling to make sure all of y'all have a place to sleep." Real talk, people were pulling out their own personal credit cards, booking flights for families who had lost someone and felt they had to be there. And we were like, "Of course!" Trying to get as many families as possible who had been impacted. And I was like, "Really, y'all mad because of the signs? Because also, y'all know us. Some of y'all we have relationships with. Look at our body of work!" But there were still those tensions, and people were turning up on each other. And we were all really grappling with how to be principled in this struggle. (M. Hooks interview, 2018)

Hooks reports that these kinds of disagreements about what it meant to live the principles of the movement in their own organizing space did not go away, but that there was also a unique energy.

There were so many traditions of Black organizing in that space. There were the nationalist folks, people who were doing political prisoner work, queer organizers, people coming out of the church, it was all different manifestations of Black struggle. It was all of us. And the magic of that. What happens when all of us get together and share space? There's a recognition and a rhythm. Somebody would get on a drum and people would begin singing. Even in moments of tension, you could feel the power rise as people came and stayed, you could feel the power rise. It was cool. It was new. You could feel the possibility, that's what we felt. (M. Hooks interview, 2018)

Nevertheless, there were also tensions around what kinds of direct action would be planned. It was June 2015, and thirteen-year-old Tamir Rice had just been murdered by police in Cleveland while playing with a toy gun in the back yard of a community center. People argued about what level of confrontation was appropriate. Some having traveled very far to make clear and uncertain statements that "turning up on the State" was not a tactic confined to the streets of Ferguson. Some had come expecting to shut down highways and sit in at municipal buildings and were disappointed that others were more interested in more limited actions like guerilla theater or legal processions on sidewalks as opposed to marching in the streets, which had been made temporarily illegal by the city. People couldn't agree, so no action was planned. This was a source of extreme frustration for many, and as the convening ended, it was unclear what next steps for collaboration among this diverse group would or could be. However, as people were leaving, the Cleveland police presented a stark reminder of the injustice that the fledgling movement was fighting. Hooks goes on:

I was walking from my room and saw a comrade just sitting on a bench reading a book and looking across the street. I looked over and saw a police officer yelling at a young boy in handcuffs. I went over to sis and said, "Sis, you been watching this?" She said "Mmhmm. They've been there about seven minutes, the officer said this, this, and this." I mean, she was like staying ready. And then she pointed out that there was a bottle of beer or something right there next to the boy and the police were trying to say he was drinking. At that point, I saw some of the comrades from BYP coming up from the other side of the street. And we went over there and said, "Hey, young man? Have they called your mama? Have they called your people? How old are you?" The boy said he was fifteen although the officer had told us he was older than that. And the officer also claimed when talking to us that the boy's own mother was the one who called the police on him. But the boy gave us his mother's number and we called her [and told her the situation]. She said, "Why would I *ever* call the police on my son?" I said, "They haven't arrested him yet, with your permission, can he come with us?" And she said, "Yes! I'm going to get there as soon as I can." So it started escalating because the police were by then taking him to try to put him in the paddy wagon [away from us]. And all the people coming out of the convening were like "not today!" People kept gathering—folks got off their buses, folks missed their flights—there had been about 1,200 people at the convening and I would say at least four to six hundred of us massed in the streets to protect this kid. We surrounded the police car. Shit got tense. The police [sprayed] Mace at everybody. But, guess where people were? All the queer and trans folks who had been upset were on the front lines fighting to keep this boy from being taken. And all the churchwomen who had been upset because they thought they didn't have a space in movement anymore. And the healers, who had been concerned about what kinds of direct actions would be traumatizing for our people [and problematized many ideas] were on the grass putting milk in people's eyes so they could see and be ready to fight. I mean, people got *in formation*. And it became clear. We sit in these rooms so that we can support, love, and protect each other outside, where none of us is in control of what the police decide to do. We all put our bodies on the line, and we understood what was at stake. And if people went to jail, we would still think with our principles. Who will be the most harmed? When we get the bail fund together, we know, get the transwoman out first, the folks who are on medication, the disabled, get them out first, but we all put our bodies on the line. (M. Hooks interview, 2018)

Finally, the boy's mother came. The boy was transferred from the paddy wagon to an ambulance that had been called. They tested his blood alcohol and it turned out, just as the boy had been insisting, that he had not ingested anything illegal. The boy was released into the custody of his mother and, as she walked him from the ambulance to her car, Hooks describes the jubilance of the crowd:

My God. People formed like—almost like a soul train line so it was like a corridor for them to walk—and they were shouting "We love you, we love you!" And I promise to God, there were two or three butterflies that followed after that boy and his Mama. And I was like, y'all, if we could leverage this alchemy. This is what we should do every time the police roll up on someone. We refuse to get in the car. We demand that they give us back our people. It was so much. So much. (M. Hooks interview, 2018)

Brittney Cooper, who was also present in Cleveland adds:

We unarrested that kid and gave him back to his Mama. We forced the cops to give him back to his Mama! It was incredible. And there's video of this—when the boy and his mom drive off, the crowd—hundreds of Black people—just goes into a rendition of Kendrick Lamar's "We Gon Be Alright." And, you know, that is on an album called *To Pimp a Butterfly* and as we are doing this, I shit you not, a butterfly, a Black butterfly fluttered through the crowd where the boy had been. And it was like, Oh My God! So that was a moment. I mean, there are these moments where it felt like a spiritual experience, for real. Because it came out of nowhere! And everyone sees this and you have this moment where you just feel *this is the work we're supposed to be doing.* (Cooper interview, 2017)

The fact that this highly effective action took place spontaneously, after participants in the convening failed to agree about how to conduct a planned action, served up a key lesson: Everyone didn't have to agree about everything. In the midst of tactical divergences, concerns about health and safety, tense conversations about harm, conflicts over differential resource levels, and even petty jealousies about credit claiming, one thing was clear—none of it could or would outshine the movement's reaffirmed purpose: fighting for, protecting, and defending Black life.

The convening thus served as the moment when the coalition, dubbed the Movement for Black Lives, began to acquire an offline structure. One year after the convening, in the summer of 2016, The M4BL released the Movement for Black Lives Platform. The platform is a six-plank policy document (published in English, French, Spanish, Arabic, and Chinese) outlining the areas of concentration and policy goals of the movement, including details about the organization's working in each policy area, the campaigns underway to promote policy goals, and the successes and challenges advocates have faced in each case. The document was produced in stages, first through a large convening of people with expertise in public policy, law, and communication to gather ideas and prioritize issues called the Black Lives Matter Policy Table. The policy table was assembled after the convening and worked for a year soliciting "feedback from hundreds of people through surveys, national calls, organizational membership, [and] engaged dozens of other organizations, researchers, and other individuals for their insights and expertise to begin developing a framework for shared policy priorities" (Justice Roundtable 2020).

Anyone who reads the platform, organization or individual, can "endorse" it by signing their name and giving their contact information on an online form linked to the M4BL platform website. Those who endorse the platform are added to a list of people who can opt to receive texts and emails about movement actions, including street protests, bail fund actions, giving circles, and policy education webinars.

A final point about the M4BL organization: though the movement is decentralized in its structure, there are leaders in what historian and activist Barbara Ransby calls the Ella Baker style. She writes,

Baker represented a different leadership tradition altogether. She combined the generic concept of leadership—"A process of social influence in which a person can enlist the aid and support of others in the accomplishment of a common task"—and a confidence in the wisdom of ordinary people to define their problems and imagine solution. Baker helped everyday people channel and congeal their collective power to resist oppression and fight for sustainable, transformative change. Her method is not often recognized, celebrated or even seen except by many who are steeped in the muck of movement-building work. (Ransby 2015)

It is in acknowledgement of this model that M4BL founders describe their organization not as leaderless, but as "leaderful." This leaderful model corresponds to the ethic that demands that the movement seeks political justice from margin to center, but it also has strategic advantages that movement participants recognize. Cooper observes:

This is the model that the movement strives for, it wants to have multiple leaders and the brilliance of that is that we know the disarray of the civil rights movement after King gets assassinated. So, I think the thing that they have figured out and that I've heard said is, you can kill some of us, but you can't kill all of us. And at the point that the leadership is diffuse, then you can't kill the movement by targeting key actors. This is the strategy, that you want people to feel like they can just step into the movement at any given place and do work because you don't ever want . . . folks to feel like they have figured out who the movement people are, they know where its gonna come from and then they can, sort of, target and shut it down. (Cooper interview, 2017)

Though this lack of centralization provides many advantages, there are disadvantages as well. According to some of the participants I have interviewed, the process for those who sympathize with the movement to become involved beyond getting text notifications about where to show up to protest or where to send money is less clear. A drawback to eschewing a national coordinating body beyond task-based committees, given the autonomy and diversity of organizations affiliated with the movement, is that there is no clear pathway for people to become involved between mobilizations. Instead, those interested in supporting the movement must find their own way in, whether through local organizations that chose to affiliate with the movement or by developing and cultivating relationships with people who are already involved through online engagement with social media or the thriving Black news, opinion, and commentary sphere that has come into being and has been sustained, in part, as a result of the significant cultural impact of the movement's emergence in 2011. These include websites like The Root (2008), Very Smart Brothers (2008), Black Youth Project Blog/Opinion (2011), RacebaitR (2014), and HuffPost Black Voices (2011) (Silva 2017).

Conclusion: A Movement, Not a Moment

In this brief overview of the emergence of the Movement for Black Lives, I have related the story of its genesis, using the words of activists to illuminate the motivation for the reinvigoration of this iteration of the Black liberation movement. I have argued that there were four characteristics that made Ferguson, Missouri, the catalyst for the movement's consolidation following the murder of Michael Brown. The first is that Brown's killing represented a recursive trauma for Black Americans in general, and for young Black activists in particular. Second, the city of Ferguson was at the center of a particularly vivid confluence of not only racial but also economic injustice, and that combination created a seethe of grievances that outside observers rightly took to be representative of a larger set of unjust structural conditions. Third, St. Louis County had several established organizing institutions, or "indigenous organizations," that provided the resources needed to extend the initial gathering of mourners into a set of demonstrations that lasted several months. Fourth, Black activists with extensive experience in social justice nonprofits mobilized from all over the country to provide advice, support, and long-term planning services to the people who had massed on the ground. And as all these actors worked together during the Ferguson uprising, they authored new ways of articulating Black striving and founded new organizations to support their emerging vision.

In the following chapter, I outline the major tenets of the movement's political philosophy: radical Black feminist pragmatism (RBFP). I emphasize that the philosophy of the movement cannot be easily collapsed into the Black visions that we are familiar with from the 20th century (Dawson 2003). Instead M4BL takes a point of view that is characterized by a belief that appeals for justice must begin with concrete lived experiences rather than abstract universalisms, and that the diagnostic and evaluative imperative of justice must be one that centers capabilities rather than rights. Further, for radical Black feminist pragmatists, the experiences of the most marginalized are the ones that speak the truth of political problems and which must be the beginning of political solutions.

PART TWO
DEMOCRATIC NECESSITY

My parents' generation taught us that we can be somebody, our generation knows that we can make something.
—Black student activist, Amherst College[1]

There is no such thing as a single-issue struggle because we do not live single-issue lives.
—Audre Lorde

Freedom is a constant struggle.
—Angela Davis

[1] As reported by Professor John Drabinski at the exploratory conference "Race and the Imagination in African American Political Thought," held at UCLA, April 28–29, 2017.

2

Political Philosophy

Radical Black Feminist Pragmatism

The Movement for Black Lives (M4BL) is often misperceived as merely a reaction against police brutality. On the contrary, M4BL is based on a rich and dynamic political philosophy that is unique in that it is distinct from twentieth-century ideologies and, perhaps more profoundly, because it embraces an inductive approach to theory building. The immediate subject of the philosophy, which I call radical Black feminist pragmatism (RBFP), provides a lens through which one can view all of the forces that inhibit Black people's ability to live and thrive. However, in this chapter, I will also show the deep contribution RBFP makes to political thought in general, gifting us with the first political philosophy born and bred in the twenty-first century. This political philosophy should be thought of as akin to Imani Perry's notion of "liberation feminism," a set of practices for understanding and working against domination and oppression rather than a doctrine (Perry 2018, 6). This is because, from the perspective of the movement, doctrinal dictates cannot rise to the task of undoing oppression, a state that Prentis Hemphill, a leading practitioner of somatics and healing justice in the movement, defines as "the requirement that you hold another's center at the cost of your own" (Instagram post, July 1, 2020). This focus on addressing politics from lived experience, simultaneous with the belief in a duty to imagine transformative solutions to the systemic plagues that make Black life precarious, is the key to radical Black feminist pragmatism.

That the political philosophy is new does not mean that it has been invented out of whole cloth. RBFP contains within it elements of political thought that have come before but have been reconstituted and supplemented to create a natal expression of political thought. In other words, I argue that the political philosophy of the Movement for Black Lives cannot be collapsed into what Michael Dawson has called the "Black visions" of the twentieth century, and that it instead offers something new.

Each word that identifies the political philosophy of the movement is important in its explanation: *radical* is a mode of questioning, *Black feminism* is an ethical system, and *pragmatism* is a mode of judgment that guides action. Substantively, RBFP has nine elements, four constitutive and five substantive (summarized in Table 1). The constitutive elements of the theory—those ideas that function as the framework or scaffolding for the substantive principles—are recognizably in the tradition of American pragmatism (West

Table 1. The Elements of Radical Black Feminist Pragmatism

PRINCIPLE	DEFINITION
Constitutive	
Pragmatic Imagination	Imagination toward action; speculative, not make-believe; the world it conjures may be fantastic, but it is practicable. The pragmatic imagination is concerned with "not yet here" rather than "nowhere."
Social Intelligence	The ability to connect old habits, customs, institutions, beliefs, and new conditions. The movement seeks to press foundational American ideals into service to salve and correct the structural conditions that enable domination and oppression in present day.
Democratic Experimentation	Characterized by the importance of meaning, evidence, accountability, fallibility, and revision while enacting practical ideas.
Liberatory Aim	Marronage and the practice of freedom—rejecting the binary free/unfree, instead preferring a congregational flight toward liberation, a "constant struggle."
Substantive	
Political Claim	Socio-ontological claim—Black being matters *as such*, but phenomenological understanding of Blackness as not a what or a who, but a *how so*.
Radical Mandate	To aim at the root of systemic injustice, that is, social and political structures (ideologies, institutions, politics) that organize the consequences of racial categorization.
Intersectional Lens	Oppressions are not additive, but intersect given the material, social, and psychological consequences of politically relevant categories of disadvantage.
Margin-to-Center Ethic	Reasoning about justice from the evidence of the lived experience of those at the margins or exterior rather than from an abstract ideal.
Politics of Care	Oriented toward intentional community rather than natural rights/laws; acknowledges trauma; upholds political action/change as integral to healing.

1989). These include a belief in the Deweyan concept of social intelligence, a fundamental investment in pragmatic imagination, a commitment to democratic experimentation, and an aim toward liberatory ends. The substantive elements of the theory—those ideas that give the philosophy content and meaning—combine new thinking with ideas that have surfaced in a variety of traditions, most significantly Black feminism. They include the political claim that Black Lives Matter, the radical mandate, an intersectional lens, a margin-to-center ethic, and a politics of care. The substantive elements are ideas about the meaning and ends of politics, and the constitutive elements relate those ideas to a theory of political process.

Radical Black feminist pragmatism is specific and experience-based; it calls out anti-Blackness directly and forcefully because without that direct address, our political tendency is to look away toward abstract universalism. However, the fact that this philosophy is built from the specific lived experience of Black peoples should not obscure what the vision has to offer everybody: the idea that we deserve to thrive because life is valuable and the only way to build a society, polity, and world where this is possible is to devise ways to change the *lived experience* of the most marginalized in the direction of what we all deserve.

This chapter proceeds in two parts. In the first, I explore the constitutive elements of RBFP, both the pragmatist roots and the creative ways that movement actors demonstrate their adherence to this framework in action. In the second, I explicate the substantive elements of the new political philosophy, putting the explanations of movement actors in the forefront while pointing to some of the places where RBFP touches more familiar theoretical accounts.

The Four Constitutive Elements
Pragmatic Imagination

The movement's philosophical commitments come from inductive observation of the problem of injustice, building the theory by examining the structural, institutional, and political forces and practices that allow Black lives to be "systematically and intentionally targeted for demise" (Garza 2016, 23). This basis in experience makes RBFP divergent from the abstract humanisms that have characterized modernity. Instead of asking, "What constitutes justice?," this philosophy asks, "What does it mean to experience justice?" The form of that question is what makes the philosophy pragmatist. Charles Sanders Peirce wrote that the aim of pragmatist inquiry is to think about what the truth of statements means in terms of action—that is, to think of not only the concept, but also of what it means for the concept to be enacted in reality. Now, importantly, pragmatism is not identical with consequentialism (or utilitarianism). This is because pragmatism does not require using consequences as the basis of moral judgment—pragmatism is a mode of judgment that guides action, but it may have any kind of organizing ethical system (in this case, Black feminism), and the pragmatists' decision-rule for what is better and what is worse is not prescribed.

In addition to the pragmatic foundation, there is an insistence on the centrality of radical imagination. We often think of imagination as flights of fancy. Not so. Imagination is the faculty or action of forming new ideas, or images or concepts of external objects not present to the senses. Imagination is the creative divergence from the well-trod habitual and lexical paths that are set in the common sense of a given time and place. Political imaginaries are very important and have all kinds of uses. We imagine communities. We imagine the good life. We imagine our futures. Pragmatic imagination also understands that the circumstances that currently condition our lives were also once imagined. In this way, imagination is a normal political faculty, its opening is useful for political change and its closure is useful for the maintenance of status quo relations of power and privilege.

In her book *Emergent Strategy*, adrienne marie brown points out that "[i]magination has people thinking they can go from being poor to being a millionaire as part of a shared American dream. Imagination turns Brown bombers into terrorists and white bombers into mentally ill victims. Imagination gives us borders, gives us superiority, gives us race as an indicator of capability. I often feel I am trapped inside someone else's imagination, and I must engage my own imagination in order to break free" (brown 2017, 18).

In this way, the imagination of social movements is political, and it is political because when movements like the Movement for Black Lives insist that another world is possible, they do so with a philosophically pragmatist, not utopian, conviction. Utopia, a term the novelist Thomas More coined in 1519 from the Greek οὐ (*ou,* no or not) plus τόπος (*topos,* place) is no place, it's make-believe. A utopian world is not in the midst of becoming, it simply doesn't exist, it's pretend.[2] You can describe a utopian world in detail, but it's an exercise of pure fantasy, there is no philosophy of action that attends it (M. Rogers 2007). Those whose political thought is utopian exhibit a refusal to capitulate to the present and to engage in building a bridge from the world as it is to the world that might be. Instead, they wait for a metamorphosis, for new political subjects who are not forged in the trenches of ordinary political struggle, but instead appear after a collective revelation. Further, utopians are not fond of uncertainty. In politics, utopians cannot fail. From their point of view, it is the world that fails to become what it ought to be. As such, utopians make political judgments based on counterfactual (perfect) situations rather than whether their actions can create conditions that enable the world they must actually build.

Unlike utopian imaginaries, the pragmatic imagination is rooted in inquiry about current conditions and oriented toward actions given those conditions. This kind of imagination does not rely on any single ideology to show the path from the world as it is to the desired one that might be. Instead, it demands that those who desire the change make the way. This includes not only imagining what could be, but also, crucially, plotting a course and designing the process and means that those involved will use to make strides toward their goals.

When asked why she is involved with the Movement for Black Lives, Patrisse Khan-Cullors, one of the founding women of the Black Lives Matter Global Network Foundation, answers, "I'm involved in Black Lives Matter because it pushes me to think creatively . . . about what actions, what kind of strategy, what tactics can come from a call like Black Lives Matter" (quoted in Caspar 2014). Likewise, Charlene Carruthers, former director of BYP 100, argues, "[i]t is within the spaces of imagination, the dream spaces, that liberatory practices are born and grow, leading to the [ability] to act and to transform" (Carruthers 2018, 25). Paris Hatcher, an organizer in the movement and executive director of Black Feminist Future, argued in a 2018 online reading circle discussion that "what our current system does is kill the Black radical imagination. It kills our ability to dream. We start to accept some things as inevitable—like capitalism, like prisons—when they actually are not inevitable, and we have the ability to build something new. The

[2] Utopia is also not necessarily good, the root εὖ (eu) would need to be used to indicate a specifically positive utopia, but in English these sounds are homophones, so we make no distinction in modern usage.

autonomy to create alternatives." Notice here the seriousness with which these women talk about building, rather than arriving, in a new world. This is an artifact of joy as a political resource. It is what Erving Goffman calls *jouissance*, the bliss of discovering oneself as the author of experience; the ecstasy that allows people to explode traditional ways of understanding themselves in the world, including our beliefs about whether and how we change it. What is radical about the Movement for Black Lives is not merely their policy recommendations, but the fact that they claim the authority to author new possibilities for the arrangements of decision-making power, sociality, and governance.

adrienne maree brown opines, "At this point, we have all the information we need to create change; it isn't a matter of facts. It's a matter of longing, having the will to imagine and implement something else." She goes on to paraphrase the novelist Toni Cade Bambara, describing the task of movement as making "just and liberated futures irresistible." In her view, people in movement "are all the protagonists of what might be called the great turning, the change, the new economy, the new world. And I think it is healing behavior, to look at [the world as it is] something so broken and see the possibility of wholeness in it" (brown 2017, 19, 21).

Social Intelligence and Democratic Experimentation

Pragmatic imagination gives rise to unusual approaches to leadership, organization, and political situations. Political science often envisions leadership through the lens of "great men" or "charismatic authority." In the study of American politics, this vision is largely based on the presidential or executive style of leadership, where we ponder and analyze the strengths and weaknesses of particular individuals as they inhabit and reshape their office. The literature on social movements, which originates mostly in sociology, takes a different tack, having no single idea of leadership, but instead focusing on producing typologies of the kinds of leader-structures found in social movement organizations. This literature notes that the dominant style of charismatic leader(s) heading up centralized, hierarchal organizations went out of fashion at the end of the twentieth century, giving way to nonhierarchal, decentralized, loosely organized new social movements, which preferred lifestyle- and culture-shifting ethos to top-down political battle plans. Though there is no single notion of leadership in the study of social movements, there is the underlying theory that <u>leadership is a yoke borne by individuals or groups (who usually inhabit formal organizations) that either happen to be or place themselves at the nexus of favorable structural forces, allowing them to leverage environmental and social forces toward their own ends.</u>

The Movement for Black Lives does not approach leadership in this way. People in movement understa[nd] ... [that is] less useful than it seems, and a my... [a] movement goals than is generally acknow[ledged] ... ds writes,

> Sustained engagement with ... [pe]rspectives,
> movements, stories, and pla... [a] history
> of black American moveme... [a]l progress
> requires both historicizing ... [so]cial trans-
> formation is impossible in t[he] ... leadership.
> Charisma is a political fiction ... [ab]out authority
> and identity that works to structure how political mobilization is conceived
> and enacted. This fiction is staged in real time and in media playback: its
> narrative thread is woven into the fabric of what might be called the charis-
> matic scenario. (Edwards 2012, 3)

[Handwritten note on attached sticky note:] On pg 44, Woodly describes the drawbacks of non-central leadership. If this makes it difficult to organize, why include democratic experimentation as a/principle? Does Woodly underestimate the dr[awbacks]... essential

This charismatic scenario was particularly reified in the late nineteenth and early twentieth centuries, but there have always been competing models of leadership. One of those competing styles is a "leaderful" approach and was famously championed by Ella Baker, one of the most influential and effective organizers in the Southern Christian Leadership Conference (SCLC). In an opinion piece in the *New York Times*, the historian Barbara Ransby explains:

> The idea behind that model is that when people on the ground make
> decisions, articulate problems and come up with answers, the results are
> more likely to meet real needs. And that's more sustainable in the long
> run: People are better prepared to carry out solutions they themselves cre-
> ated, instead of ones handed down by national leaders unfamiliar with real-
> ities in local communities. Such local work allows people to take ownership
> of the political struggles that affect their lives. (Ransby 2017)

The dominant myth of the heroes shaping the times they inhabit through particularly savvy use of their innate ability to amass, leverage, and wield power

is widespread, but it is antithetical to the political philosophy of the movement, which values decentralized leadership for practical reasons: assessing and addressing the conditions that shape people's lives is most effective when one begins at the local level. At the same time, building movement demands from the diversity of data provided by "on-the-ground" lived experiences helps the movement develop political demands aimed at the national (even transnational) level that are both resonant for the values that they call to mind and concrete in terms of local impact. Ransby further elaborates:

> The Movement for Black Lives is distinctive because it defers to the local wisdom of its members and affiliates, rather than trying to dictate from above. In fact, the local organizers have insisted upon it. This democratic inflection will pay off if they persevere. Brick by brick, relationship by relationship, decision by decision, the edifices of resistance are being built. The national organizations are the mortar between the bricks. That fortified space will be a necessary training ground and refuge for the political battles that lay ahead. (Ransby 2017)

The view of leadership prevalent in the movement refuses the dichotomy between charismatic leaders and structural serendipity and/or strategy. Instead, drawing heavily from both the tradition of American pragmatism and Black feminist thought—especially that of Ella Baker as currently expanded and annotated by organizers in the Movement for Black Lives—people in movement assert that leadership is the process by which individuals and the groups they are situated in intentionally and successfully shape political and social change. I take as given, as William James writes, that "the fermentative influence of geniuses must be admitted . . . [but] not every 'man' fits every 'hour.' A given genius may come either too early or too late. . . . John Mill in the tenth century would have lived and died unknown . . . [and] an Ajax gets no fame in the day of telescopic-sighted rifles" (James 1880).

Rather, leadership comes from the interaction between genius and the social and political environment—what John Dewey calls "social intelligence." Dewey argues that "[t]he office of intelligence in every problem that either a person or a community meets is to effect a working connection between old habits, customs, institutions, beliefs and new conditions" (Dewey [1935] 1991, 56)." Intelligence does not arise from the "mere abstraction of a native endowment unaffected by social relationships, but [is instead built] upon the fact that native capacity is sufficient to enable the average individual to

respond to and use the knowledge and the skill that are embodied in the social conditions in which he lives, moves and has his being" (58). Intelligence
is not book learning or a high IQ. It is at once a fact of human capacity and a
method of human engagement. According to Dewey, "intelligence develops
within the sphere of action for the sake of possibilities not yet given," and is
exemplified by the "remaking of the old through the union with the new. . . .
It is the conversion of past experience into knowledge and projection of that
knowledge in ideas and purposes that anticipate what may come to be in the
future and that indicate how to realize what is desired" (56). Even more interestingly, Dewey contends that intelligence is not only the result of the creative and practical process of understanding the relationship between old
or extant circumstances and new possibilities, but that this process is also
"constitutive of the agent" (Rogers 2007, 93). Therefore, while the vision for
the movement arises from imagination, its end goal is neither fixed nor utopian, but is instead guided by an ethic of care and a habit of inquiry that is
embedded in an intelligent and iterative political process aimed at both changing the subject and ushering in new worldly possibilities. Dewey writes that
intelligence is the "remaking of the old through the union with the new. . . .
It is the conversion of past experience into knowledge and projection of that
knowledge in ideas and purposes that anticipate what may come to be in the
future and that indicate how to realize what is desired" (Dewey [1935] 1991,
56). Further, "[i]ntelligence develops within the sphere of action for the sake
of possibilities not yet given" (Rogers 2012, 64).

   This intelligence is not just a matter of the acuity of thought. Instead, it is a
union of three elements that comprise the skills one needs to connect existing
belief to new purposes. First, it is a critical orientation that questions and
interrupts old habits of thinking and acting. Second, it includes what Melvin
Rogers calls a "theory of action," or a sense of how new ideas about governance and justice can become real in the world through changes in beliefs,
habits, custom, institutions, law, and policy. Third, and finally, it involves a
group commitment to and demonstration of those experimental actions in
the world, or, as Dewey puts it, "organization." In this way, social intelligence
involves the ability to see existing political opportunities where they may
not be obvious. It involves a foresight that includes yet exceeds the recognition of political opportunity and instead verges on prophecy—the ability
to see through what is not yet but might be—it is a faculty of what people in
movement call "radical imagination," and a product of what Amna Akbar (in
a tweet) calls "visionary labor." These radical imaginings are taken up with

practical ends in mind, and the labor in envisioning the world that might be is one of translation into language and action that is broadly accessible.

The Movement for Black Lives believes in the efficacy of radical imagination; that is, the imagination of conditions and outcomes that cannot be achieved in the world as it is and would require the transformation of common beliefs, practices, laws, and institutions. But that radicalism is also grounded in the philosophically pragmatic orientation toward the world. Radical imaginings of systems of care that enable the well-being of the most marginalized are never wholly untethered from observations and analysis of the world as it is and are always meant to return to the critical questions: What do we have to do to get from here to there? What kinds of logics do we have to articulate to the polity? What kinds of institutions do we have to build? What kinds of constituencies do we have to engage? What majorities must we build? Which kinds of policy do we have to author? Which elections must we win? How do we make the world we have imagined not only possible, but also irresistible? I therefore talk about the essential imaginative component of the M4BL as pragmatic imagination, because it is rooted in inquiry, focused on producing practical wisdom, and ultimately focused on problem-solving. This pragmatic orientation toward transformation means that movement organizers are keenly aware, as Dewey was, that their knowledge is contingent and that experience may cause them to change their minds, revise their vision, or alter their tactics.

It is in this context that leadership takes on its significance. Ella Baker defines leadership as "a process of social influence in which a person can enlist the aid and support of others in the accomplishment of a common task" (quoted in Ransby 2015). In order for this process of social influence to be successful, the task must truly be held in common. That means that the charismatic leader is always a red herring: the messianic authority is only ever as strong as the belief in the principles embraced, and the social relationships—made through interpersonal connection, mass communication, and social and political organizing—that they foster and maintain.[3] In other words, Black feminist thought illuminates and expands the pragmatist argument that leadership inheres in the fortuitous and purposeful interaction of genius and environment with the insight that this interaction, in its most effective form, does not and should not inhere in only one compelling individual.

---

[3] Here, "organizing" is defined as meeting and discussing the causes and solutions of mutually defined and acknowledged problems with the intention to act to solve them as a part of some self-acknowledged and mutually claimed collectivity.

Instead, leadership is group work. Borrowing from the physics definition of "work," this means the group process of amassing a force that can move a sociopolitical object in the desired direction. This is something that cannot and should not be done alone.

Organizers in the Movement for Black Lives call this Black feminist vision of leadership "leaderful." The movement has often been chided for not elevating a charismatic figure to take charge of message and tactics; however, I submit that such a demand misunderstands the nature, purpose, and potential of leadership's efficacy in general, and of social movements, in particular. I make this assertion for two main reasons. First, as Aristotle observed over two thousand years ago, if one wishes to convince a broad and diverse crowd, it is not the messenger who is most important, but the message. This may be truer today than ever before, given the advent of social media, in which a 280-word tweet can go viral and become an instant common frame for understanding current events regardless of the identity of the author.[4] The movement has taken this fact to heart by building itself not around a single leader or dominant organization, but instead around a common set of messages that are discussed, debated, and deployed by a tightly networked yet decentralized organizational structure. As adrienne maree brown explains, a leader's main priority is not to "build bases" so they can "scale up"; it is instead their task to learn how to "create more and more possibilities. Not one perfect path forward, but an abundance of futures, of ways to manage resources together, to be brilliant together" (brown 2017, 22–23).

Second, the movement is committed to democratic experimentation, and implements this experimentation both within the organizations that function under the umbrella of the Movement for Black Lives and with the campaigns those organizations author. The Movement for Black Lives itself, described by Jessica Byrd as a "home of political homes" utilizes a unique organizing structure—a networked, decentralized grouping of institutions and individuals that make it less easily co-opted or incorporated into traditional electoral and institutional politics. Let me pause here to say that such co-optation is not a danger to movements because it dilutes their purity,

---

[4] One of the potential problems with the force of leadership inhering in the message instead of the authoritative messenger is that when the original speaker is irrelevant, it may be more difficult to assess truth claims, because one cannot quickly ascertain whether the commenter is reliable or knowledgeable. However, the identity/source of a claim has only ever been a heuristic for evaluating the truth of a statement. In order to ascertain the relevance or validity of a claim, the one who is receiving it must have tools for evaluation independent of the identity of the source, otherwise we are left only with the opinions of demagogues and tyrants.

but because it limits their power. The Movement for Black Lives does not wish to be what Paul Frymer has termed a "captured constituency," but instead a countervailing political force. The structure of the movement allows it to utilize a full range of tactics, both confrontational and conciliatory, to shape political change. It allows the movement to essentially say, "We're not endorsing a candidate, but by all means, you who are involved as individuals or affiliated organizations, feel free to work for a candidate, or register voters, or draft policy. Or protest outside conventions and campaign rallies, if that's how you think the movement is best served."

This approach creates a situation in which decision-makers must adopt the frames and address the concerns present in movement messaging because they are unable to silence the claims or change the subject by wooing individuals with prizes and perks. It also means that no entity in traditional politics can claim to absorb the movement by supporting or employing any particular individual. The Movement for Black Lives is aware of arguments like those of Frances Fox Piven and James Cloward, who warn that organizations and their incorporation are often the end of movement influence rather than its beginning (see Piven 1977). And yet they have not thrown away the advantages that come with having professional organizers and skilled, full-time leadership at the heart of movement activities. The Black feminist pragmatism that underlies M4BL gives rise to a rhizomic, leaderful style that best enables the group work of liberatory politics.

In terms of novel approaches to political situations, the example of the Louisville, Kentucky, chapter of the Black Lives Matter Global Network Foundation stands out. Louisville, like many cities, is geographically segregated. Most of the Black population lives in the West End, where poverty rates are high and housing insecurity is common. Since BLM chapters are not directed by a central office, they are able to tailor campaigns to the circumstances that obtain in their specific localities. Given the deep need for housing assistance in West Louisville, the chapter, guided by cofounding director Chanelle Helm, decided that their primary work would be reclaiming vacant land and restoring crumbling properties in the West End. This endeavor would include not only salvaging space for the BLM chapter, but also emergency housing for Black people facing eviction, and, most ambitiously, permanent homes for Black single mothers that the BLM chapter would purchase, fix up, and gift to them, deed and all (M. Jones 2018; Warfield 2019).

The goal of the project is unique—gifting homes to vulnerable people who are usually the target of blame and shame—but even more interesting is the way that Helm and the chapter framed their work. It was not an act of charity that they sought to do, but an organized practice of reparation. They sought out donations from wealthy white people and businesses in the area, but did not appeal to their altruism, but instead to reparative justice. Through practices like redlining, the federal government had colluded with state and local authorities to deprive Black people of ownership of their own neighborhoods while subsidizing the stability and prosperity of white neighborhoods. Black people, Helms argued, were not to blame for the blighted West End; instead, they were *owed*.

In August 2017 as the chapter began raising money, a khaki-clad army of white supremacists infested Charlottesville, Virginia, to protest the removal of a statue of Confederate general Robert E. Lee. During their multiday rally, one of the members killed the young, white, anti-racist activist Heather Heyer, and shocked the country with the return of publicly avowed and open racist hatred. The day after the events in Charlottesville, Louisville's mayor, Greg Fischer, announced that he was forming a commission to evaluate and remove any public art erected to honor "bigotry, racism, and slavery" (Fischer 2017).

Helm, seeing what social movement scholars call a "political opportunity," wrote her own response to the events in Charlottesville, where she argued that removing monuments to racism was not enough to address the harms of structural racism. She called her contribution to the discussion "10 requests from a Black Lives Matter Leader." Among, them she urged "white people, if you don't have descendants, will your property to a Black or brown family. Preferably one from generational poverty. . . . If you are a developer or realty owner of multi-family housing, build a sustainable complex in a Black or brown blighted neighborhood and let Black and brown people live in it for free. . . . White people, re-budget your monthly [income] so you can donate to Black funds for land purchasing" (Helm 2017). These radical, practical suggestions exemplify the kind of thinking that is motivated by M4BL's political philosophy.

Liberatory Aim

The inductive and pragmatic question "What does it mean to experience justice?" also yields a distinctive notion of freedom, close to the concept that Neil Roberts articulates in his 2015 book *Freedom as Marronage*. Conceptualizing freedom as marronage means rejecting freedom as a binary (one is either free or not) and holds that a linear, developmental view of progress toward a definitive freedom will always yield a distorted picture that cannot account for empirical conditions of oppression and domination. Instead, freedom in this sense affirms that we are always in the process of flight toward freedom as liberation, which is the ongoing undoing of common understandings, systems, and practices that (re)produce oppressive conditions. Put differently, RBFP points to the wisdom that the task of those who care about justice is always and ever will be a striving to continue to *get free*.

The Movement for Black Lives has at its root a philosophy that holds that freedom and justice will always be woefully lacking if we expect it to trickle down from the most powerful and advantaged to the least. Instead, if we expect freedom and equity to be lived realities, then we must look at untangling the structures of disadvantage that constrain those who are most impacted by systematic domination and oppression.

Liberation, then, calls for political, social, and interpersonal strategies that take aim at identifying and mitigating the complicated structural and institutional causes and effects of domination and oppression. This is not an easy task. In fact, identifying and undoing these structures can only ever be an iterative process, one that just societies have a political habit of returning to. In a liberatory framework, the future is wholly possible. That does not mean it is unconstrained by material and other worldly realities, but instead that our futures are natal and unpredictable. Therefore, liberation is a collective and imaginative ongoing process of perception, analysis, experimentation, and implementation.

Domination must be understood as structural, rather than as the imposition of the directed will of a malevolent individual or class of individuals, because "the constraints that people experience are usually the . . . unintended product of the actions of many people" operating according to the laws and habits of institutions that predated their existence or intentionality (I. Young [1990] 2011, 32). Individuals have choices, but those choices are constrained by the world as it currently exists, by the laws, customs, and common ways of understanding that characterize the way people live their lives in a particular time and place. These constraints can and do produce outcomes that are both patterned (e.g., systematic) and unintended by individuals that are both acting independently and imbricated in rules and mores beyond their control. This reality of situated individuality is true both for those who have positions that afford them relatively more power and those whose positions restrict them to having relatively less. Take, for example, the dominative institution of law enforcement.

This story, told to me by a police officer attempting to navigate his job in light of the questions that the Movement for Black Lives has made salient, perfectly illustrates how individuals can enact domination without intending to do so:

> I have exercised authority as an officer that I considered abusive and created some serious moral dilemmas for me at times. As a relevant example, I was recently called to an apartment because a maintenance worker went inside and found three children left alone, ages two, five, and eight. We tracked down mom, who was working a shift at Walmart. Mom was cooperative and honest, and it appeared she typically left her children alone during six- to eight-hour shifts at night (4 to 10 or 4 to midnight). My sergeant and I did not want to arrest her. She was violating the law by leaving an eight-year-old to care for her five- and two-year-old siblings which was not safe, but she was in a really tough spot. My [sergeant] and I came to the conclusion that not taking charges could create liability for us if she continued to leave her children alone at night to work and they were harmed in the future while she was away. I made sure to pursue the least severe charge, in both severity and number of counts, but my ability to address the situation is limited by my professional function. I also involved CPS of course, with the aim of getting some sort of social service in place for the mom, but I have limited influence over how a social worker handles their case. (Police Officer interview, 2017)

This police officer knows the circumstances that caused this mother to break the law are well beyond her own control and intentionality. And he further knows that enforcing the law in this case will cause more harm and damage than the situation ostensibly being addressed. The time and expense of adjudicating those charges will have a measurably negative and potentially devastating impact on the lives of this mother and her children. This mother will likely lose her job because she's been charged with a crime, and if she is convicted of a felony, she will have trouble finding employment in the future. She is also in danger of losing custody of her children. The children are in danger of being separated from both their mother and one another. Or, if they are able to remain with their mother, who will now be more financially strapped and less employable, they are in danger of sinking into a poverty that grabs hold of generations.

The institutional conditions that precipitate this dominative situation—
one that prevents the self-determination of *both* the mother and the police
officer—is a symptom of oppressive conditions. M4BL seeks to take aim at
domination and oppression by actively trying to imagine and enact a world
in which Black people, and all people, might be free. Indeed, it is hard to
overstate the place of "freedom" in the conception of movement activists.
When asked about the ultimate goal of the movement, to a person, each activist described a world in which Black people could be free of domination
and oppression. Shanelle Matthews, the former communications director
of the Black Lives Matter Global Network Foundation, put it this way: "The
work is about changing people's behavior so that Black people can live free,
full lives in this democracy. And we don't have to be afraid. We can parent
our children into adulthood and have access to the rights, the resources,
and the recognition that we all need to live our best lives" (Matthews interview, 2017). Brittney Cooper, an activist and professor of Africana Studies at
Rutgers, remarks,

> [B]eing in movement spaces over the last three years [what I learned] is that,
> these are some really big dreamers. And I really think that these are folks
> who are thinking broadly about transformation. They're not reformers.
> They don't think—it's not like, we can just tweak the system and these
> things will happen. But a real sort of sense that, what does it look like—I
> think the sort of core goal is—what do Black people need to live and thrive?
> And so, how can we put structures in place so that Black thriving is actually
> a political priority. Not just Black survival. (Cooper interview, 2017)

It is important to note that freedom, in the political philosophy of the movement, bears little resemblance to the most popular liberal formulations of that
term. The conceptions of freedom that are most common in American public
discourse emphasize rights and choice. It is also a static conception—you are
either free or you are not, as determined by the rights you are accorded and
the choices you are allowed to make. The movement, by contrast, emphasizes
that freedom is a process, one that must be measured by the capabilities that
people are able to exercise in their lived experience and the health and efficacy of the communities they live in.

In this conception, freedom is fundamentally relational and dynamic instead of fixed and absolute. This is because *marronage*, a term that originates
in part of the Caribbean colonized by the French, means "flight." It is the

description of a "multidimensional, constant act of flight" that involves trying to improve one's lot in terms of "distance, movement, property, and purpose" (N. Roberts 2015, 9). "Distance," Roberts elaborates, "denotes a special quality separating an individual or individuals in a current location or condition from a future location or condition." Movement "refers to the ability of agents to have control over motion and the intended directions of their actions." Property is the "designation of a physical, legal, [or] material object that is under possession and ownership of an individual, institution, or state." Purpose, in his conception, "denotes the rationale, reasons for, and goal of an act begun by an individual or a social collective" (9–10). Notice how these "pillars," as Roberts calls them, serve as modes of response to the problems of domination and oppression that Young details. If you are facing a social and political situation in which you and your social group are systematically deprived of self-determination (domination) and self-development (oppression), then it makes sense to measure your freedom by the distance the group has (in the past) and can (in the future) put between present conditions and future desired conditions. Likewise, thinking about one's control over one's own "movement" as a measure of freedom, and specifically of "flight" as the motion that conveys departure from oppressive conditions, provides another method of assessing degrees of oppression or freedom. Property and purpose are pillars that allow one to assess degrees, or relative levels, of domination— these degrees of freedom exist not only between people(s) but also within time. That is, one's freedom is relative, not only to how free others in your political time and place are positioned, but also to how free one is compared to a future desired state. The Movement for Black Lives is fundamentally concerned with futurity. Patrisse Khan-Cullors puts it this way:

> I am hopeful for Black futures. And I say that because we live in a society that is so obsessed with Black death. We have images of our death on our TV screen, on our Twitter timeline, on our Facebook timelines. But what if, instead, we imagined Black life—we imagined Black people living and thriving? That inspires me. (Khan-Cullors interview, 2017)

Importantly, these ways of understanding freedom as relational and dynamic are more useful and important for understanding what one is actually capable of doing, given the structural constraints of the "actually existing" world (Fraser 1990), than are rights and choices that one may formally be accorded but that are, in practice, difficult or impossible to exercise. In this way, marronage describes a "capabilities approach" (A. Sen 1992) to freedom, one that attends to the relational basis and dynamic nature of the concept, and that is simply and potently expressed in the movement slogan #getfree.

The Five Substantive Elements
The Political Claim

The most fundamental, animating principle of the movement is its name, a name that springs from a socio-ontological claim: Black lives—all Black lives, as such—matter. This claim has a phenomenological expression, which is to say that Blackness (indeed, any raced-ness) by this reckoning is not a *what* or a *who*, but a *how so*? Sarah Ahmed wants to reframe the question of what race *is* to a question of what race *does*. In her seminal essay "A Phenomenology of Whiteness," she explains that "[p]henomenology helps us to show how whiteness is an effect of racialization, which in turn shapes what it is that bodies can do" (Ahmed 2007, 150). Or as Michelle Wright theorizes in her book *Physics of Blackness*, "the phenomenology of Blackness" can be described using the vectors of "*when* and *where* it is being imagined, defined, and performed" (Wright 2015, 3).

Still, Blackness is not an empty category; it has within it an episteme—a way of understanding the world, born from "common historical experiences and shared cultural codes" (Hall 1993) that are acknowledged by both the group and those observing from outside as distinct and full of meanings that are dependent on both being ascribed as a member and embracing membership. Importantly, this idea of Blackness is not an essentialized, singular idea, but a multiplicity that nevertheless finds anchors and touchpoints in similar cultural practices.

Unlike the movements that characterized the twentieth century, M4BL is not making political claims based on an appeal to the sacredness of rights, the fairness of redistribution, or the imperative of recognition. Instead, #BlackLivesMatter is an assertion that Black life is a category of social being, historically and practically marked by a brutal history of specific, targeted depravation and devastation, and as such must seek remedy in the form of new social, economic, and political formations. These new political formations should serve to enable not only or primarily equality, but, most importantly, must facilitate the ability to live and thrive. Among the conditions necessary for this kind of flourishing, according to the 2020 Movement for Black Lives platform, are an end to the "war on Black people"; reparations for the historic and continuing legacy of state sanctioned murder, theft, and exploitation of Black people; investment in Black communities; local control of governance and resources; and political power.

In *When They Call You a Terrorist*, Patrisse Khan-Cullors describes the discussions that led organizers to make the political claim that Black lives matter the calling card of their efforts, though everyone understood it would cause backlash:

> There are people close to us who are worried that the very term, Black Lives Matter, is too radical to use, alienating, even as we are all standing in the blood of Black children and adults. We continue to push, to be unde- terred. . . . [W]e have to change the conversation. We have to talk very spe- cifically about the anti-Black racism that stalks us until it kills us. . . . [W]hat we need . . .is to press forward with a wholesale culture shift. (Khan-Cullors and bandele 2018, 196–197)

The movement's early understanding that to win they would have to change the way people valued Black lives is profound because it engendered a focus on what people involved valued rather than a narrow focus on what reaction or redress they could secure in the short term. This expansive thinking about how to change culture—what we value—led to the development of a political philosophy that would serve as the foundation and guide for the campaigns and policy recommendations that would come later. The early tenets of the political philosophy that I codify here began to come together in those early conversations, held in Khan-Cullors's living room, but also simultaneously in living rooms and at work breaks and in organizational meetings across the country. Khan-Cullors writes,

> In my home, we, mostly women, talk about what we deserve. We say we deserve another knowing, the knowing that comes when you assume your life will be long, will be vibrant, will be healthy. We deserve to imagine a world without prisons and punishment, a world where they are not needed, a world rooted in mutuality. . . . We deserve, we say, what so many others take for granted: decent food, food beyond the 7-Elevens and Taco Bells . . . we deserve to know life without the threat of heart attacks at 50, or strokes or diabetes and blindness because of the food we have access to and can af- ford is a loaded gun. . . . We deserve the kind of shelter that our hard work

demands, homes that are safe and non-toxic and well-lit and warm. We deserve love. Thick, full-bodied and healthy . . . in this place and in this time, when hate and the harshest version of living dominate, when even the worst assaults are blamed on victims, . . . we have come to say that we can be more than the worst of the hate. . . . We deserve to at least aim for that. . . . We say that this is what we mean when we say Black Lives Matter. (Khan-Cullors and bandele 2018, 199–201)

And this conversation about the kind of world that Black people deserve because Black people matter, because a life where thriving is possible matters, is the foundational premise of the political philosophy that I codify here.

Divergent Black Visions

Michael Dawson has detailed a range of Black American ideologies and their impact on public opinion in the late twentieth century. He notes that African American ideologies from Black Marxism to Black conservatism are characterized by the following features: they explicitly take the African American experience as their point of view, they embrace communalism, there is more likely to be a spiritual component to their philosophy and practice, and the epistemology of the movement is likely to be derived from practical activity rather than from abstract reasoning (Dawson 2003, 22). The ideology of M4BL has much in common with African American political ideologies that have come before. It shares the radical egalitarianism of Black liberalism, the commitment to redistribution of Black Marxism, the longing for Black autonomy in Black nationalism, and the distrust of the state, especially the federal government, that characterizes Black conservatism.

The founding women of M4BL understood that observers might conflate #BlackLivesMatter with Black nationalism, so they were careful to make a clear distinction from the beginning. In "A Herstory of the #BlackLivesMatter Movement," Alicia Garza writes,

Black Lives Matter is a unique contribution that goes beyond extrajudicial killings of Black people by police and vigilantes. It goes beyond the narrow nationalism that can be prevalent within some Black communities, which merely call on Black people to love Black, live Black and buy Black, keeping straight cis Black men in the front of the movement while our sisters, queer and trans and disabled folk take up roles in the background or not at all.

Black Lives Matter affirms the lives of Black queer and trans folks, disabled folks, Black-undocumented folks, folks with records, women and all Black lives along the gender spectrum. *It centers those that have been marginalized within Black liberation movements.* It is a tactic to (re)build the Black liberation movement. (Garza 2016, 25)

Instead of Black nationalism, the movement's most immediate and important ideological ancestor is Black feminism, a worldview that insists on valuing embodiment; that is, asserting that how we actually live as well as the interconnectedness or *intersection* of oppressions must be at the heart of our analysis and our political solutions. These views, most recently coined as "embodied discourse" by Brittney Cooper and "intersectionality" by Kimberlé Crenshaw, assert, respectively, that Black people's, especially Black women's, bodies are "a form of possibility and not a burden," and "a commitment to centering the Black female body as a means to cathect" to political thought, and the analytical categories of gender, race, class, and other politically relevant categories of disadvantage cannot be separated in their practical impacts and so should not be separated when conceiving their legal and political remedies (Cooper 2017; Crenshaw 1989, 1991).

As Cooper points out, "Black women's knowledge production has always been motivated by a sense of care for Black communities in a world where non-Black people did not find value in the lives and livelihoods of these communities" (Cooper 2017, 2). This emphasis on lived experience is a key tenet of the Black feminist intellectual tradition and has always animated the movement. As Garza puts it, those "most impacted" by structural oppression must be the center of the work. In philosophical terms, this means that the theory of justice that M4BL has built looks to the "margins" as articulated by bell hooks and the "periphery" as described by Enrique Dussel. Like these political theorists, M4BL rejects the notion that deducing the meaning of justice from an abstract universalism can deliver its promises to most people. This is because the inequality produced by the current dominant paradigm is constitutive of our lives in this moment, not an accidental or unintended consequence.

This insistence on specificity and aversion to abstract universalisms for theory-building locates the Movement for Black Lives outside both liberal and Marxist traditions, and instead takes the approach of philosophical pragmatism. Pragmatism is a perspective that rejects the *sub specie aeternitatis*, or abstract universalist orientation, of traditional philosophy and is instead concerned with "the problems of men" (Dewey [1946] 2007). John Dewey, the leading figure of pragmatist thought, proposed that the task of theorization was not to find eternal rules or perfect procedure, but instead to understand what people are doing and why they are doing it. Only from that perspective, he opined, could we hope to change and improve the way people live in the world.

I should be clear here that pragmatism, in my usage, does not take on any of the colloquial implications of preemptive compromise or triangulation of the middle between extremes. M4BL is radical. Participants in the movement understand their task to be addressing the *radix* (root) of the problems that plague us, and imagining and devising ways to address those root-stalk ills. That necessarily means upending our current notions of the possible. adrienne maree brown puts it this way: "What is politically possible at this moment—that's what we have to be shifting all the time. Because otherwise we're in false solution land." She goes on to clarify:

> I don't identify as a revolutionary because I think it's cool. I identify because I want . . . all the children who come from all the people I love, to have this magical earth to live on and to be in right relationship with each other on it. To me, revolution is the only way we get there so, the question is: how do we make revolution politically possible? That's what's interesting to me. (Carruthers and brown 2019)

In this way, M4BL's radicalism and its pragmatism are complimentary. The movement's understanding of politics builds in an acknowledgement that what is necessary for justice might not be politically possible at this time. The job of people who are interested in freedom, in a world that has systems that do not reproduce the current oppressions, is to create political conditions that make new things possible. However, there is no telos that names a static structuring of society and maps the movement of the path M4BL must take to reach its goals. Instead, those who seek a world where all Black people can live and thrive have to imagine, persuade, win power, and experiment their way toward a more just and flourishing world. Put differently, the political task of people in movement is *world-building*, which is why brown and one of her coauthors, Walidah Imarisha, opine that "all organizing is science fiction" (brown and Imarisha 2015, 3). This is because the arrangement of power that will deliver the *experience* of justice to oppressed peoples is neither predetermined nor proscribed. It must be imagined, plotted, and measured, all by the yardstick set down by the question: is this what it means to experience justice?

If you are thinking that this kind of process of questioning and measurement is a prescription for a never-ending pursuit, then you've got the right idea. Pragmatist politics are implicitly democratic because they posit an ever-relevant quest for progress that has no end. It is a view of politics that is built on the belief that the work of life is aligning our action with our principles, and that such work will never be complete, though we can and must certainly take account of when we do better and when we do worse.

For the pragmatist, politics simply *is* an iterative process and we should prepare ourselves (through education, cultural orientation, material support, etc.) to be able to engage in it. There is no steady state of justice and harmony, construed in thin procedural or thick substantive terms. By these lights, we are capable of invention, of enormous progress, of remaking both the cultural and material ground that we tread together, but things will always change. And so our politics will have to change as well.

In line with the movement's disinterest in appealing to notions of justice for idealized, unsituated subjects, M4BL is not primarily a movement advocating for equality before the law or in social mores. And though many of the participants in the movement are anti-capitalist and prefer socialist forms of economic organization, M4BL flatly rejects political interpretations that prioritize economic reorganization over political, social, and individual liberation. While most movement actors favor disruptive tactics and imaginatively expansive ways of living together, the central idea is not war against the state, as such, as in anarchist philosophy, nor a separatist nationalism in the tradition of Marcus Garvey. Instead, M4BL is fundamentally a political project that wishes to confront the realities of oppression and domination that unjustly constrain capabilities and life chances, or the flourishing of the most marginalized, with the understanding that if the most disparaged and maligned are free everyone would have to also be free, because "our freedom would necessitate the destruction of all systems of oppression" (Combahee River Collective 1986).

The Radical Mandate

According to M4BL organizer Mary Hooks, "The mandate of Black people in this time is to avenge the suffering of our ancestors, to earn the respect of future generations, and be willing to be transformed in the service of the work."

To have a mandate is to have both the authority and the mission to carry out a course of action. Hooks wrote the mandate for the movement in a big, bound notebook that she keeps for writing thoughts and verse, while sitting at home in 2015. She recalls,

> I can remember the train of thought. I always say our ancestors talk. And I remember thinking, there is something that Black people need to hear. There is something we need to be doing in this moment. And the words just came as clear day. (Hooks interview, 2018)

The mandate would go on to be chanted as a call and response at demonstrations and direct actions around the country. I asked her what each phrase of the mandate meant to her, specifically how the ideas of intergenerational connection, responsibility, and transformation defined the twenty-first-century Black liberation movement. She began her explanation with the first line: the reason and political meaning of Black people's need to "avenge our ancestors." She reflects,

> [W]e're clear on the genocidal attack that has happened to our people and continues to happen. We carry the history and the stories in our DNA. And I believe that our ancestors, some are proud. But I also think that some, many others, are still struggling, many of the wounds they incurred still have yet to heal. So, there is still suffering happening. (Hooks interview, 2018)

Here, it is useful to note the definition of *avenge*. To avenge is to inflict harm in return for a wrong done, but the word's root is the Latin *a vindicare*, to vindicate, which means to clear someone of blame or suspicion, to show or to prove someone right, reasonable, and justified. For Hooks, an abolitionist, *avenge* has the potential for all of these meanings, but its most important meaning is to vindicate. This emphasis in no way diminishes the fact that it is a term rich with anger and holds within it the potential for aggression. However, the primary purpose of *vindication* is not served by doing harm. Instead, vindication is accomplished by proving that the wrongs that have been done and are ongoing must be accounted for, reckoned with, and repaired. Hooks explains:

> [W]hen I think about the avenging, I think of it in two parts. The first is Black fucking joy. Black goddamn joy, Black love, Black unity, Black fun,

Black humor, you know. . . . But there is also another level, [we] have to grapple with a level of melancholy, with the fact that we are fuckin mad. Like, you damn right I'm mad about what you have done to my mother and my grandmother, my great grandmother, my foremothers. *Yeah, you damn right*, I was born with a fucking attitude. (Hooks interview, 2018)

Hooks's insistence on seeing vindication as an affirmation of both joy and anger is a nod to the humanist underpinnings of the movement's philosophy. Emotion is not regarded as antithetical to reason, and people are encouraged to bring their whole human selves into the work. In this way, people in movement reject one of the main behavioral tenets of what Evelyn Higganbotham called "respectability politics," a long African American tradition "which teaches one to deflect racial provocation and to master and contain pain" in recognition of the fact that such a stricture asks Black people to deny their humanity. This denial of humanity is a key aspect of American depictions of Blackness, whether in service of white supremacy or in an attempt to combat it. As the writer and cultural critic Ralph Ellison put it, "the full, complex ambiguity of the human," which is a "sensitively focused process of opposites, of good and evil, of instinct and intellect, of passion and spirituality," is left out of this equation (Ellison 2003, 81–82).

The emphasis on defending and cultivating Black joy is a key aspect of the political philosophy and practice of the movement. Black joy is the defiant affirmation of Blackness in spite of the material and psychic deprivation that often marks members of the group. It is a critical component of movement work for two central reasons: the first is that it is a confirmation of Black experience beyond suffering even in the midst of colossal, intergenerational struggle against oppression and domination. And the second is that this joy is a political resource. This is because joy, particularly the joy in and of the group, is a sustainable and sustaining reason to participate in collective action.

Importantly, this politicized joy is simultaneously experienced by the individual as a single individual and by all those participating in the group, as a group affect. It is what Emile Durkheim called "collective effervescence," a sensation of euphoria that one feels in the presence of others who are aligned in thought and action. Deborah Gould notes that "such happenings have an almost sacred quality to them" (Gould 2009, 209). They induce participants not only to cognitively realize, but also to feel, the potential power to affect change that they might wield, if they continue to act in concert—with and for each other. In this way, joy is both grounding and clarifying. It gives one a sense of solidarity and possibility. It is mobilizing. It draws participants into collective activity and keeps them there, reminding them that political struggle is not only what Mary Oliver calls "pain and logic,"[5] but is also affirmation in community and interdependent strength.

However, the second part of avenging the suffering of the ancestors is also critical; it is about acknowledging and accepting the sadness and anger that is the natural reaction to the systematized and intergenerational violence that has targeted Black people. As Hooks points out, "we have to grapple with this other level, this melancholy," and in grappling with it, find its uses. In her book, *Eloquent Rage*, Brittney Cooper takes us through the surprise and clarity that results from the process of grappling with the anger that arises in response to oppression, coming to understand this anger as a "superpower." She writes,

> I *was* angry. As hell. And I was fooling no one. Black women have a right to be mad as hell. We have been dreaming of freedom and carving out spaces for liberation since we arrived on these shores. There is no other group, save Indigenous women, that knows and understands more fully the soul of the American body politic than Black women, whose reproductive and social labor have made the world what it is. This is not mere propaganda. Black women know what it means to love ourselves in a world that hates us. We know what it means to do a whole lot with very little, to "make a dollar out of fifteen cents," as it were. We know what it means to face horrific violence and trauma from both our communities and our nation-state and carry on anyway. But we also scream, and cry, and hurt, and mourn and struggle. (Cooper 2018, 4)

Just as joy can be a political resource, so too can anger. Audre Lorde, one of the key intellectual touchstones in the movement, spoke about the uses of anger in her 1981 address to the National Women's Studies Association. In it, she affirmed that anger is a normal and necessary response to racism, and that it is only in acknowledging that anger and the pain lurking just

---

[5] The last line of the poet Mary Oliver's poem "Singapore" poses the rhetorical question, "If the world were only pain and logic, who would want it?"—an instructive reflection for the ongoing debate about the reasons people engage in collective action. They do so not only to achieve political and policy ends, but also for the immaterial, but no less real, emotional and psychological benefits of banding together in community for the sake of a common project.

underneath and beside it that it can become possible to perceive the depth of the harm white supremacy causes and to imagine the scope of what would be necessary to dismantle it. Lorde explains,

> My response to racism is anger. I have lived with that anger, ignoring it, feeding upon it, learning to use it before it laid my visions to waste, for most of my life. Once I did it in silence, afraid of the weight. My fear of anger taught me nothing. Your fear of that anger will teach you nothing, also. . . . My anger is a response to racist attitudes and to the actions and presumptions that arise out of those attitudes. If your dealings . . . reflect those attitudes, then my anger and your attendant fears are spotlights that can be used for growth in the same way I have used learning to express anger for my growth. But for corrective surgery, not guilt. Guilt and defensiveness are bricks in a wall against which we all flounder; they serve none of our futures. (Lorde 1981)

Here Lorde points out that anger is useful, not only for the person who is angry, but also for the people she is in relationship to and with. This is an observation that contemporary political theory does not grapple with. Anger is so tightly associated with violence that it is treated as an emotion to be suppressed and ignored in the service of a civilized and civil politics. However, this deliberate evasion is a mistake. Anger need not lead to violence. Anger can often be clarifying, leading to the only kind of understanding that motivates the changes that can underpin peace. Psychologists have long pointed this fact out regarding individuals, noting that anger can be a positive emotion, motivating change that improves relationships, particularly in instances when less confrontational strategies have been attempted but have failed to effect behavioral change. This is because anger cues people that there is a problem that must be resolved, motivating them to try to resolve it.

This response can actually *reduce* violence. For example, research on anger and political attitudes in political science has shown that race and anger are tightly linked in white racial attitudes—spurring white racial conservatives to oppose issues that trigger anger (making them more racially resentful) and making racial liberals more supportive of (perceived) racially redistributive policies (Banks 2014a, 2014b). In addition, anger that is expressed motivates self-insight, helping people to focus on the reasons *why* they are angry, and therefore clarifying how the anger might be redressed. Additionally, angry people tend to be more optimistic about resolving problems than those who are fearful or sad. The benefits of anger are not present when it is excessive or aimed at simply inflicting cruelty, but when the point of expressing anger is to draw attention to a long-standing problem, it often has positive results (Averill 1982; Hess 2014; McNulty and Russell 2010). The benefits of anger for individuals point very clearly to the possible uses of anger for groups in conflict within a polity. Lorde continues,

> Every woman has a well-stocked arsenal of anger potentially useful against those oppressions, personal and institutional, which brought that anger into being. Focused with precision it can become a powerful source of energy serving progress and change. And when I speak of change, I do not mean a simple switch of positions or a temporary lessening of tensions, nor the ability to smile or feel good. I am speaking of a basic and radical alteration in those assumptions underlining our lives. (Lorde 1981)

Joy and anger taken together are a powerful source of political emotion, and one that is essential for social movements, particularly those seeking radical change. This is because joy motivates commitment and incentivizes collective action, while anger is the catalyst for challenging status quo arrangements with both determination and optimism.

The intergenerational aspect of the mandate is already clear from its beginning in the vindication of the ancestors. However, the intergenerational responsibility of liberation is not only to those passed, but also to those yet born. The mandate means that the living generation must always be cognizant of the world it will leave for coming generations and consider what must and can be done to make it more habitable and hospitable. Mary Hooks elaborates:

> When I think of earning respect. I think we will have to really work. We are going to have to freakin' work, and we are gonna have to sacrifice some shit. We are going to have to grapple with our commitment to capitalism. To punishment. We are going to have to commit to doing things a different way. And you can decide to call it what you want, you can call it socialism, or whatever, but it is about dismantling capitalism and doing the work of living together. It is about being in right relationships with other people who don't sound like you, who don't think exactly like you, who don't talk

like you. People you're still mad at. If we're talking about abolition, then we have to be willing to resolve differences differently. That's the work of liberation. We have to be able to model what we want to be. That is the heart and soul of the work, that we have to become the thing that we are striving to be. Even though the material conditions and current content of our objective reality makes it very fucking hard. (Hooks interview 2018)

Earning the respect of future generations will require sacrifice, pragmatic imagination, and democratic experimentation. It requires the ability to give up some of the things that we know in order to create the conditions and practices that make it possible for Black people to be a bit freer from oppression and domination.

Of the last term of the mandate, being "transformed in the service of the work," Hooks explains,

The idea of transformation is familiar to me because it's a part of the historical memory of my political home [Southerners on New Ground, or SONG]. We are always asking each other that—it is woven into the culture of the organization: "are you willing to be transformed in the service of the work? Are you willing to choose courage over fear? Are you willing to choose the movement and the collective over 'the I' and isolation? Are you willing to move from a place of righteous anger, from a place of longing and desire, from a place of love?" Because that's why we must do this work, not only because we're mad but because we love Black people. It's a different posture. (Hooks interview, 2018)

To be transformed means to be changed in regard to condition, nature, or character—to become otherwise. To be transformed in the service of the work, then, means to be changed in ways that serve the process, cause, and ends that one identifies and affirms. That is, to become more capable of doing the work, not only by learning new information and skills, but also by developing a new self-understanding about the kind of person one is and wants to be. I will discuss this concept at length in chapter 4, in the context of how the notion of "transformation in service of the work" shapes the distinctive way M4BL regards organizing and the way their conception ought to inform political theorists about the significance of organizing as a unique political phenomenon, distinct from mobilization and activism.

The Intersectional Lens and the Margin-to-Center Ethic

The movement's concern with theorizing from and acting on behalf of those most impacted by systems of oppression requires an intersectional lens. Intersectionality and its theoretical antecedents—"double jeopardy," "triple oppression," "simultaneity," and "interlocking oppressions"[6]—all describe a similar social fact: oppressive institutions and dominative arrangements of power are interconnected and cannot be examined separately, especially because their effects are impossible to disentangle in people's lived experiences. If one views oppressions as intersectional, a distributive conception of justice is not enough. It's confusing rather than enlightening: if all one can account for is whether one has a just portion, the question becomes, for what part of myself? The effects of oppression and domination cannot be divvied up in this way. Instead, to combat oppression and domination, an enabling conception of justice is required. The question is thus transformed from whether I can be said to have my just portion to whether I am able to develop myself and determine the course of my life in a way we can all evaluate as just. In this way, an intersectional view of politics is incompatible with a distributive view of justice—though the movement's intersectional lens certainly yields demands for the redistribution of resources, that redistribution is in accord not with a call for rights under the principle of formal equality, but with a call for creating capacity and capabilities under the principle that freedom requires the ability to flourish.

Charlene Carruthers, the founding director of the movement organization BYP100 (Black Youth Project 100), explains that the organization's guiding commitment to using a "Black queer feminist lens" is a specific iteration of using the intersectional lens as a diagnostic and a margin-to-center orientation as a political ethic.

> The analogy of the lens is crucial and what it does is, literally, is imagine if you put on a pair of glasses, it can amplify the way you see certain things— no matter what you're looking at, it will impact the way you see things. So, the utility of a Black queer feminist lens is to impact, shape, and form the

---

[6] The phrase "double jeopardy" refers to the pamphlet "Double Jeopardy: To Be Black and Female" (Beal 1969). "Triple oppression" is attributed to Claudia Jones, a prominent member of the Communist Party in the United States (discussed in Davis 1983). "Simultaneity" is discussed in the Combahee River Collective Statement (1977), and "interlocking oppressions" comes from Collins's 1990 *Black Feminist Thought*.

way you look at all issues that impact our people. And when you do that, what it requires you to do is to make certain considerations and tell certain stories, see certain things that were hidden from view. It allows you to see certain things as necessary to assess what the problem is and to form a solution in different ways than you would with a lens that is simply one of Black nationalism or Black progressivism or whatever. It's an invitation to see things differently and requires us to think differently. (Carruthers interview, 2017)

For example,

When you put on a Black queer feminist lens and look at the issue of mass incarceration it requires you to think about how mass incarceration impacts Black trans people. Period. And you can still make the choice when you're coming up with solutions to say, fuck these people, they don't matter, but more often than not . . . it means that when you're cutting the issue and asking how are we going to approach the broad topic of criminalization, you can't just ask, how do we stop Black and brown men from being stopped and frisked, you have to also ask: How is this impacting people who are not men, who are not straight, who are not cisgender? You have to ask yourself a different set of questions. And when we ask those different types of questions in collective space as organizers, we come up with different solutions to the problems. And, in crafting more complete stories of the problems that are really facing all of us, we also come up with more complete solutions that will help us address these problems more effectively and improve all our people's lives. (Carruthers interview, 2017)

Here, it is important to emphasize that "telling more complete stories" is viewed as not only ethically imperative, but also fundamentally the most practically effective way to achieve change that is focused on the *radix*, the root of our most persistent and damaging political problems.

In her influential book *Feminist Theory from Margin to Center*, bell hooks describes the special perspective of those who are positioned at the margins of society: "To be in the margin is to be part of the whole but outside the main body" (b. hooks [1984] 2015, xvi). She contends that this marginality is reinforced daily as Black people move through the world. In the small Kentucky town where she grew up, the railroad tracks were the physical symbol of the margin. She writes that "across those tracks were paved streets, stores we could not enter, restaurants we could not eat in, and people we could not look directly in the face" (xvii). Today, the margins are marked differently, by neighborhoods that are neglected and derided by city officials; stores that offer fewer choices yet charge higher prices; restaurants that serve food that leads to obesity, disease, and premature death; police who shake down and shoot bystanders and people suspected of minor crimes on sight and with impunity; and people who deny that any of these racialized phenomena amount to more than problems of "personal responsibility."

"Living as we [do] on the edge," hooks explains, "we developed a particular way of seeing reality. We looked both from the outside in and from the inside out. We focused our attention on the center as well as on the margin. We understood both." Note the echoes of Du Bois's notion of the "double consciousness," the result of "the veil" that separates the lived experience of oppressed peoples from those who are not. In the canonical *Souls of Black Folk*, Du Bois explains:

> The Negro is a sort of seventh son, born with a veil, and gifted with second-sight in this American world,—a world which yields him no true self-consciousness, but only lets him see himself through the revelation of the other world. It is a peculiar sensation, this double-consciousness, this sense of always looking at one's self through the eyes of others, of measuring one's soul by the tape of a world that looks on in amused contempt and pity. One ever feels his two-ness, an American, a Negro; two souls, two thoughts, two unreconciled strivings; two warring ideals in one dark body, whose dogged strength alone keeps it from being torn asunder. (Du Bois [1903] 1994, 2).

Like Anna Julia Cooper before her, hooks also observes this tension, but is less prone to see this twoness as "threaten[ing] to dismember the Black self" and more likely to understand this reality as a "generative tension" (Cooper 2017, 6). That is, hooks, in the Black feminist tradition, understands the gift of "second-sight" as a "mode of seeing" that reminds us "of the existence of the whole universe . . . unknown to most of our oppressors" (b. hooks [1984] 2015, xviii).

It is not only African American thinkers who have sought to help us understand the unique perspective of oppressed peoples in conceptualizing what justice consists in and, more accurately, evaluating when gestures in its direction succeed or fail. Postcolonial political theory emphasizes the same margin-to-center ethos that guides M4BL's ideology. Enrique Dussel, for example, asserts that a key principle of justice in the world as it is, characterized by a history of colonialism and white supremacy, is one of "exteriority." Exteriority is a principle that holds that we begin all investigations of justice with the question, "Who is situated in the Exteriority of the system, and *in the system* as alienated, oppressed?" (Dussel 1996, 8). Using the principle of exteriority, it is incumbent upon those pursuing just political and social relations to do two things: (1) describe the practical reality of a system of oppression from the point of view of the oppressed, and (2) imagine a system in which "the personhood of the Other is the absolute criterion of both ethics and liberation" (10).

This is the task that M4BL takes up, and it is also why the movement doesn't see its focus on Blackness and Black people as discriminatory, isolationist, or myopic. In "A Herstory of the Black Lives Matter Movement," Alicia Garza explains this:

> #BlackLivesMatter doesn't mean your [non-Black] life isn't important—it means that Black lives, which are seen as without value within White supremacy, are important to your liberation. Given the disproportionate impact state violence has on Black lives, we understand that when Black people in this country get free, the benefits will be wide reaching and transformative for society as a whole. When we are able to end hyper-criminalization and sexualization of Black people and end the poverty, control, and surveillance of Black people, every single person in this world has a better shot at getting and staying free. When Black people get free, everybody gets free. This is why we call on Black people and our allies to take up the call that Black lives matter. We're not saying Black lives are more important than other lives, or that other lives are not criminalized and oppressed in various ways. We remain in active solidarity with all oppressed people who are fighting for their liberation and we know that our destinies are intertwined. (Garza 2016, 26)

Garza articulates a view that those seeking just political relations need to think in terms of good policy effects "effervescing up" rather than "trickling down." She explicates her point this way:

> The reality is that race in the United States operates on a spectrum from Black to white. It doesn't mean that people who are in between don't experience racism, but it means that the closer you are to white on that

spectrum, the better off you are. And the closer you are to Black on that spectrum, the worse off you are. When we think about how we address problems in this country, we often start from a place of trickle-down justice. So, using white folks as the control, we say that well, if we make things better for white folks, then everybody else is gonna get free. But actually, it doesn't work that way, we have to address problems at the root. And when you deal with what's happening in Black communities, it creates an effervescence—so, a bubble up, rather than a trickle down. (Garza, Khan-Cullors, and Tometi 2016)

The terminology of effervescence is especially interesting because it echoes the idea that justice is best served when we focus on the political problems and proffered solutions of the most disadvantaged, an observation made by radical democratic socialists like Rosa Luxemburg, who writes that

only unobstructed, effervescent life falls into a thousand new forms and improvisations, brings to light creative force, itself corrects all mistaken attempts. The public life of all countries with limited freedom is so poverty-stricken, so miserable, so rigid, so unfruitful, precisely because, through the exclusion of democracy, it cuts off the living sources of all spiritual riches and progress. (Luxemburg 1972, 246)

Rosa Luxemburg observes that what makes democracy indispensable is that it enables the polity to correct its course, providing both signal and possible solutions to political problems as they inevitably arise. But the movement takes this observation one step further, drawing on the political philosophy of Black feminism, and asserts that it is not the undifferentiated masses that provide the clues for society's greatest enlightenments, but specifically those who are most marginalized by common practices and institutional arrangements.

When asked whether the specificity of #BlackLivesMatter is exclusive, Garza asserts the same principle in plainer language:

[W]hen Black people cry out in defense of our lives, which are uniquely, systematically, and savagely targeted by the state, we are asking you, our family, to stand with us in affirming Black lives. Not just all lives. Black lives. Please do not change the conversation by talking about how your life matters, too. It does, but we need less watered-down unity and more active solidarities with us, Black people, unwaveringly, in defense of our humanity. Our collective future depends on it. (Garza 2016, 28)

She points out that this is not only a matter of acknowledging the conceptual position of the oppressed, but also about acknowledging the material history and reality of the work that Black people have done to provide models of resistance for all people:

> And, to keep it real—it is appropriate and necessary to have strategy and action centered around Blackness without other, non-Black communities of color, or white folks for that matter, needing to find a place and a way to center themselves within it. It is appropriate and necessary for us to acknowledge the critical role that Black lives and struggles for Black liberation have played in inspiring and anchoring, through practice and theory, social movements for the liberation of all people. The women's movement, the Chicano/a liberation movement, queer movements, and many more have adopted the strategies, tactics, and theory of the Black liberation movement. And if we are committed to a world where all lives matter, we are called to support the very movement that inspired and activated so many more. That means supporting and acknowledging Black lives. (26)

This centering of the marginalized extends to groups and individuals within the Black community who are generally overlooked, dismissed, or considered disposable by dominant society. Kei Williams describes the commitment of the movement this way:

> The Movement for Black Lives is for every Black life. There is no tunnel vision focus on this one type of person, which historically has been Black men. A lot of people associate Black Lives Matter with rallies in the street that center Black men and boys and that's generally been a trigger event that gets people into the streets. And, we have seen, over time, the difference—a thousand folks come out for a Black man, 10 come out for a Black woman and 5 come out for a Black trans woman. And so, we're really challenging folks to consider that when we say Black Lives Matter we mean every Black life. Not just the . . . person who was on their way to college and had their life stolen. We're talking about everyday Black girls and boys. We're talking about everyday Black people. We're talking about the drug dealer, we're talking about the sex worker, we're talking about the folks who are disposed

by society, but we welcome them in and show them love. (Museum of the City of NY 2017)

Following this argument, the only way to achieve a just politics, one that has a "sense of wholeness," as hooks puts it (b. hooks [1984] 2015, xvii), is to start building it, as with any edifice that one intends to be sound, from the exterior to the interior and from the bottom up.

Politics of Care

Politics consists of the activities associated with building and achieving power for the purposes of governing. These activities include developing the understanding, working out the preferences, arbitrating conflicts, galvanizing participation, guiding collective action, and making decisions as a group, constituency, or polity. In the dominant liberal conception, politics is the domain in which we manage competition over naturally divergent interests. And in both political theory and colloquial usage, politics derives its legitimacy (insofar as it has legitimacy) from the rational and strategic rather than from emotion and need. How, then, can we conceptualize a politics of care?

Well, what if we conceived the currency of political aspiration not as "interest," whether "real" and material or constructed from some indistinct (yet somehow naturally decisive) miasma of desire and cost/benefit, but instead in terms of dignity and flourishing? Such a change is one of orientation toward the motivation and ends of politics, not in the nature of the political enterprise. In other words, a politics of care does not take its mission to be making the process of gaining political power for governing nicer; the competition to direct the attention and resources of a polity will always remain fierce, and movement actors do not balk at hard fights. However, the politics of care sees interest disconnected from concern for the dignity and flourishing of the individual-in-context as ethically unmoored and fundamentally illegitimate, unworthy of collective engagement and action.

The politics of care is so central to the political philosophy of the movement, and such a contribution to American political thought, that I expand on it at length in the next chapter; however, in the context of the broader political philosophy of RBFP, it is important to know that the politics of care has six major characteristics: the acknowledgement of oppression as traumatic, the centrality of interdependence, the embrace of unapologetic blackness, a focus on accountability, a defense of Black joy, and a commitment to restoration and repair. In Black feminist thought, this understanding of care is often discussed through the metaphor of mothering. Alexis Pauline Gumbs notes that Audre Lorde and June Jordan, among other Black feminists, write about the practices of mothering outside the confines of biological ties or sexed roles, as specifically political because this kind of "radical mothering" foregrounds the ways that we are obligated to care for ourselves and each other as whole human beings, especially when we are subject to oppressions that denote our embodiment as always already "threatening," or "criminal" (Gumbs 2020, 184–190).

From this point of view, the first premise of political engagement is that trauma and healing must be considered not only personal but also political issues, because the ways those facts shape our experience of the world and our motivation and ability to organize and become mobilized are considered indispensable information for any political project, especially those that consider justice to be their aim. This is because a politics of care is predicated on an acknowledgement that oppression is not only unjust, it is also traumatizing.[7] Therefore, those who seek to organize and mobilize oppressed peoples in an effort to unwind and upend oppressive systems must incorporate a concern with, and a practice of, healing in their work.

This healing work is seen as not only a psychological, but also a social and political salve and, even more profoundly, it is believed that the individual has the best chance to heal by participating in the social and political work of ending oppression. Healing is thus a multidimensional enterprise; it is necessary not only for the individual but also for society, and that means the approach to attaining healing must be from the individual as they exist in and change the sociopolitical. This is where the concept of "healing justice" derives its meaning. There is an ecosystem of people and organizations

---

[7] The *Diagnostic and Statistical Manual of Mental Disorders* defines trauma as direct personal experience of an event that involves actual or threatened death or serious injury or threat to one's physical integrity. Witnessing an event that involves such threats can also produce a traumatic response, as can learning about unexpected or violent death, serious harm, or threat of death, or injury to a family member or close associate. Memories associated with trauma are typically vivid and difficult to forget. A person's response to trauma can range significantly, but usually involve intense fear, helplessness, horror, anger, and social or emotional paralysis. Oppressed peoples—those who are subject to laws, institutional practices, and social customs that deprive them of self-development by creating and reproducing conditions that decisively and often violently curtail their life chances and those of the people in their familial and social group—experience not only individual traumas, but also collective trauma that arises from the cumulative "weathering" and negative consequences of being identified with and living as a member of a structurally marginalized and socially maligned group.

that help people in movement understand what healing justice as applied to the Movement for Black Lives means, including the abolitionist and scholar Mariame Kaba, artist activists like Gina Breedlove, Spirit McIntyre, curator and organizer Cara Page, somatic practitioner Prentis Hemphill, organizer Emanuel Brown, and organizations like Harriet's Apothecary and Black Organizing for Leadership and Dignity (BOLD), among others.

Second, the politics of care is based upon an understanding that our selves are always situated, which means that to account for one's self is also to account for one's social condition, location, and connectedness. This means that in RBFP, the individual is not the basic unit of analysis, nor is an imagined unitary collectivity; instead, attention is focused on the *individual-in-context*. Structural conditions and interpersonal interdependence are thus taken as always relevant to public problems and their solutions.

The third element, a focus on accountability, is a deeply pragmatic and democratic orientation. Accountability is not only about taking responsibility for one's action, but also, critically, about acknowledging that since one's self is always situated and in-context, the actions that one takes may have unintended consequences. To be accountable is to develop a practice of checking in with those one is working with and for in order to understand the effects of discussions as they evolve, decisions as they are taken, and impacts as they are felt.

Fourth, unapologetic Blackness is the practical manifestation of a rejection of respectability politics. It is the commitment to acknowledging the whole selves, good and bad, productive and reactive, of the people in movement. While unapologetic Blackness is specific to Black people because it is a rejection of pathologizing Black people, it grows from a more general view about embracing the human. Our movements and our conceptions of justice must not be tuned to the exceptional but to the ordinary, not only to the innocent but to those who have harmed, not only to those who fulfill normative expectations but to those who do not. Unapologetic Blackness means that no one deserves to have their needs go unacknowledged, their concerns swept under the rug, or their personhood thrown away.

This may be the most radical aspect of the politics of care and, indeed, the entire philosophy of RBFP. Those involved in the movement become radical in the definitional sense: they see themselves as tasked with thinking, speaking, and acting in a way that affects the *radix*, or root, of the political problems that they understand Black people to face. That set of problems is not only a matter of rights acquisition, economic exploitation, or quasi/legal social exclusion. It is a historical problem, to be sure, but one of ontological proportions. It is about the negative way that people—including Black people—have understood Blackness since race became a legible concept and the physical, psychic, and social tortures that have been rendered logical and justified on the basis of that belief (Mills 1997; Gordon 1995).

The task of the movement, then, is to transform all of our understandings about what Blackness is and means, which brings us to the fifth component of the political philosophy, defending Black joy. The defense of Black joy is not only about making and holding space for Black people to be carefree and express unencumbered happiness, but more profoundly, this defense is also an offense—a cultural project meant to shift the set of dominant associations between Blackness and suffering to a fuller panoply that offers the many ways that Blackness is infused and characterized by a joy that is enhanced by some of the lexicons, traditions, and habits commonly found across the African diaspora. This is what it means when people in movement say they love Black people. It means they are no longer approaching the fight for racial justice (or justice of any kind) from the position of apology that usually characterizes the posture of the oppressed. This is not a project of acceptance or inclusion into dominant society, it is not about positioning the Black community as acceptable or appropriate within white supremacy. Radical Black feminist pragmatism is about what Black people deserve and demand as Black people. In this way the movement is able to flip the perspective of analyses and demands; they can ask, as one popular call and response at protests does: "I love Black people! You don't love Black people? What's wrong with you?" This perspective is how the movement has shifted the perspective from asking questions about what justice requires to designing new ways of enacting the answers that they find. As Charlene Carruthers writes, "Following the vision of BYP100 leader Fresco Steez, we made it cool and relevant to be 'unapologetically Black.' It was not popular to build an all-Black activist organization or common for a membership-based organization such as ours to be led by young, Black women and LGBTQ folks, but we did it anyway" (Carruthers 2018, xvi). And here, too, is the genius of the movement: by embracing that love of Black people as whole, unapologetic selves, they *made it popular* to be involved and invested in a disruptive, Black-led, political movement.

Finally, the politics of care is concerned with how to think through harm and its consequences from a perspective of restoration and repair rather than one that centers punishment. The politics of care is an abolitionist politics, which acknowledges that people are not only good or evil, innocent or guilty, but that all people both experience harm and are capable of doing harm. Moreover, this abolitionist perspective asks us to think first about the context in which harms are committed and, with that in mind, to craft methods of both redress and prevention of future harm. The scholar and abolitionist Ruth Wilson Gilmore writes,

> [A]bolition is a practical program of change rooted in how people sustain and improve their lives, cobbling together insights and strategies from disparate, connected struggles. We know we won't bulldoze prisons and jails tomorrow, but as long as they continue to be advanced as the solution, all of the inequalities displaced to crime and punishment will persist. (Gilmore and Kilgore 2019)

In this way, the concern with restoration and repair is a way both to care for people who have been harmed by seeking ways to repair the hurt caused or restore to them a measure of what was lost *and* to care for the person who has committed harm by asserting that even as the perpetrator of harms, they are not disposable, and *because* they will not be thrown away and are still a part of the society, they are required to be accountable for their actions by repairing and restoring, as much as possible, what they have damaged or destroyed. This impetus toward repair is not only operative on an interpersonal level or as a mediation between individuals mediated by institutions or the state, it is also an orientation that is meant to be taken up at scale. A politics of care requires us to consider what harms society ought to account for and how we should reckon with the need for reparation.

3

The Politics of Care and the Idea of Healing Justice

won't you celebrate with me
what i have shaped into
a kind of life? i had no model.
born in babylon
both nonwhite and woman
what did i see to be except myself?
i made it up
here on this bridge between
starshine and clay,
my one hand holding tight
my other hand; come celebrate
with me that everyday
something has tried to kill me
and has failed.

—Lucille Clifton

In the previous chapter, I discussed the principles of the political philosophy of the Movement for Black Lives. Their view of what constitutes justice and freedom and the means to achieve these goals is not identical to any of the twentieth-century ideologies (liberalism, communism, socialism, populism, etc.); however, radical Black feminist pragmatism still proffers an analysis that transcends the particular, offering a set of principles that can be applied in multiple contexts. The key difference between it and twentieth-century philosophies is that RBFP does not pretend universality; instead, the theory takes as its starting point the immanent relevance of people's lived experiences, centering the experiences of those who are most impacted by systems of domination and oppression.

Domination, writes Iris Marion Young, is "the structural or systemic phenomenon which exclude people from participating in determining their actions or the conditions of their actions" (I. Young [1990] 2011, 31). Domination must be understood as structural, rather than as the imposition of the directed will of a malevolent individual or class of individuals, because "the constraints that people experience are usually the . . . unintended product of the actions of many people" operating according to the laws and habits of institutions that predated their existence or intentionality. Individuals have choices, but those choices are constrained by the world as it currently exists, by the laws, customs, and common ways of understanding that characterize the way people live their lives in a particular time and place. These constraints can and do produce outcomes that are both patterned (e.g., systematic), and unintended by the individuals who are both acting independently and imbricated in rules and mores beyond their control. Take, for example, the dominative institution of law enforcement. This reality of situated individuality is true both for those who have positions that afford them relatively more power and those whose positions restrict them to having relatively less.

Oppression, Youn[g] [...] njustice some people suffer . . . because of [...] [in]tentioned liberal society." It consists of t[...] [...]s that are not necessarily the result of th[...] instead "embedded in unquestioned norms, [...] [...]tions underlying institutional rules and t[...] [follo]wing those rules" (I. Young [1990] 2011, 4[...] [...]ve ways, what Young calls the "five faces of [...] [...]lization, powerlessness, imperialism, an[d ...]

[handwritten note: Is Woolly's construction of domination give too much credit to those in power?]

In addition to its [... analysis of domi]nation and oppression, the movement values history, imagination, and vision as the indispensable, critical contexts that condition the ways they choose to build power and act. In the next chapter I will explore the theory and practice of building power or organizing as it is practiced in the Movement for Black Lives (M4BL). However, in this chapter, I expand on the most unique aspect of the movement's political philosophy, what I call a *politics of care*. The politics of care practiced in M4BL is characterized by an acknowledgement of trauma and a commitment to healing, an understanding of interdependence, unapologetic Blackness, a defense of Black joy, an insistence on accountability, and an abolitionist perspective favoring restorative justice practices that deal with harm by focusing on accountability and reparation rather than punishment.

One of the main ways this politics of care is enacted is through the practice of *healing justice*, a mode of analysis and action that acknowledges that oppression causes harm that is more than distributional, instrumental, or infrastructural, and that addressing that harm requires both personal and political action toward care. That is, healing justice recognizes that "our movements must invest time and money" in identifying how "we can holistically respond to and intervene in generational trauma and violence, and . . . bring collective practices that can impact and transform the consequences of oppression on our bodies, hearts, and minds," as well as on our politics (Page and Kindred Healing Justice Collective, n.d.). Importantly, a healing justice perspective takes participation in collective action for social change to be an essential part of the process of healing, because it is only through such activity that we can change the conditions of oppression—the context in which much of our trauma occurs and in which it will be reproduced unless we can mitigate or eradicate its causes. This approach is a radical one because its logic springs from the observation that it is impossible to resolve our socially and politically produced traumas, to heal ourselves from the damage of collective and systematic ills, while only focusing on individuals' internal processes. While therapy, self-work, and personal transformation are important, because RBFP understands individuals to always be in context, the philosophy proscribes social and political change as a part of the cure for what ails those who live under oppressive structural conditions.

In other words, for those who adhere to RBFP, care is not only an ethic or a set of moral principles, it is also a *politics*, an essential activity of governance based on the acknowledgement of the basic need for and responsibility to provide the care that is *always* required for human life, and therefore must be attended to in the arrangement, management, and maintenance of society and politics. This notion of care has a deep affinity with the voluminous literature in feminist political theory. Joan Tronto's notion of a "ethic of care," which she introduces in her book *Caring Democracy*, contends that "what it means to be a citizen in a democracy is to care for citizens and to care for democracy itself" (Tronto 2013, x). However, people in the movement do not center care because of a commitment to the idea of democracy or the duty and value of citizenship, but instead in accordance with the fundamental political claim animating the movement. That is, because they *matter* to themselves and to one another. There is no intermediary term between care and the person to legitimate the necessity of caring, and there is no appeal to abstract categories to bestow significance on the bodies, minds, and spirits in need of care. People simply matter, and that is reason enough to care.

Let us pause to consider this. To matter, by its primary definition, is just to exist as physical substance that has mass at rest. But it also means to be of importance or significance and to have content and substance that is distinct from manner and form. A matter is also an affair under consideration, the reason for distress, the pus that seeps from a wound. One does not matter because of the way one behaves or the way one's form is made or appears. One does not earn the properties of substance and significance via motivation or avocation. One is not bequeathed this ability to matter by right. There are explanations for the reasons we matter, but no justification is necessary. We simply do matter. And so we deserve care.

Care, here, is not a mere sentiment, nor does it indicate a posture of deference or coddling. Instead *care* hews closely to the dictionary definition. In its noun form, it means the provision of what is necessary for health, welfare, maintenance, and protection, and also serious attention to doing something correctly in order to avoid unnecessary damage or risk. As a verb, *to care* means to feel concern for or interest in something, to attach importance to it and provide for the needs one observes. In this way, the politics of care begins with the conviction that it matters when whole populations are hurting from harms inflicted by the ways we have structured society, whereby some people are systematically advantaged and others systematically disadvantaged. It matters that we have designed politics so that some voices are much more likely to be heard and have influence than others, though all may bear an equal claim to citizenship. It matters that in the United States, we have a grotesquely huge carceral system that consigns some people to not only be confined in cages, but also to what Orlando Patterson has called "social death," the "denial of full personhood and the mark of disposability" (O. Patterson 1982). And so *to care* means to take seriously not only the material depravation, but also the pain that accompanies these political realities, and to work to mitigate the causes and repair the devastating results. A politics of care begins with the notion that it matters if we're hurting—that we must attend to that in the conception and carrying out of our activities toward governance.

Therefore, the politics of care is a reframing of the purpose, priorities, and experience of politics. It is a way of pursuing self, community, and political governance that values feelings and somatic embodiment along with what we are enabled to do in the world as it actually exists. In this way, the politics of care acknowledges those modes of experiencing, knowing, and doing that are most devalued in dominant liberal, masculinist, and capitalist paradigms. It is because of these underlying values that the politics of care (1) acknowledges oppression as traumatic; (2) understands interdependence to be fundamental; (3) insists on the centrality of accountability; (4) affirms unapologetic Blackness, a specific instance of unapologetic human embodiment; (5) emphasizes the defense of joy and pleasure as a personal and collective necessity and political resource; and, finally, (6) is abolitionist, looking to restorative rather than punitive practices to address harm. These values are summarized in Table 2 and discussed in detail in the next sections.

Table 2. Values Underlying the Politics of Care

Oppression as Social Trauma	Effects of oppression go beyond unfair distribution of rights and resources, and constitute psychological and even physiological consequences that have measurable impacts on social groups at both the individual and aggregate levels.
Interdependence	The individual is always already in context. There is no atomistic, autonomous individual; we instead are born and develop in contexts that condition, but do not fully determine, our life chances.
Accountability	The obligation of interdependence is a commitment to being responsible to a group or community.
Unapologetic Blackness	The rejection of respectability politics and the embrace of the notion that Blackness is plural, anti-Blackness effects all people who identify or are perceived as Black regardless of performance of dominant values; the struggle for Black liberation must include all kinds of Black people, centering those perceived as variously deviant in the dominant culture, without apology.
Defense of Black Joy	Joy is a political resource that is especially essential to the mental and emotional well-being of oppressed people, as well as their capacity to organize for social and political change.
Abolition, Restoration, and Repair	The safety of Black people and other oppressed groups cannot be obtained through policing and prisons. Instead, safety is a matter of having one's basic needs met, and when harm occurs, the goal is repair and restoration rather than punishment.

Oppression as a Social Trauma

Though we often locate the political genesis of the Movement for Black Lives in police shootings, a more accurate assessment of movement motivations must consider what Audre Lorde calls the "institutional dehumanization" that plagues Black life (Lorde 2007, 39). This dehumanization is the outcome of systems of oppression anchored by histories that stretch back to before the Atlantic slave trade. This historiography is important not only because it explains the origin of anti-Black racism, but, just as importantly, because it explains the origin of what Cedric Robinson calls "racial capitalism," a tradition of racializing social orders for the purpose of economic oppression that predates European encounters with non-Europeans (C. Robinson [1983] 2000). This is worth noting because it points to a new dimension of the way that the particular lived experience and the general "order of things" are intertwined. Anti-Black racism is particular and particularly virulent, playing out via oppression and domination in various legal and practical frameworks around the world, but it is also one example among many interlocking systems that evince the tension at the heart of modernity's logic: that equality is a value to be distributed among equals, and that some must be explicitly or implicitly disqualified in order for the universal to seem to exist. This tension sharpens the edge of every difference that we acknowledge as significant (and some of those things that we acknowledge as significant differences can and do change over long periods of time), and it is the logic that gives oppression and domination sense—that is, the ability for these concepts to help us understand the ordering of the world.

What makes the political philosophy of M4BL unique and radical is that it goes after this ordering of the world, displacing the debates about rights, natural or otherwise, and citizenship, and puts people and their lived experience at the center. Oppression, then, is no longer a problem of malice, bad faith, or misapplied principles, but rather an observable fact of some people's lives. One that must be undone—not for the sake of fairness, but because people matter and should not suffer because of society's arrangement. Indeed, from this point of view, it is the chief mission of governance to (re)arrange laws and practices—political, social, and economic—so that people do not suffer, at least not in systematic and predictable (and thus, preventable) ways, because people matter, and the purpose of politics—to paraphrase Tronto, stripping away the accoutrement of citizen-talk—is to assign responsibilities for care and ensure that people are as capable as possible of participating in this assignment of responsibilities (Tronto 2013, 30).

Oppression is, in many ways, the opposite of care, and so it makes sense that this is the place where a political philosophy committed to centering the most marginalized would begin. Iris Marion Young writes that oppression is "the disadvantage and injustice some people suffer not because a tyrannical power coerces them, but because of the everyday practices of . . . society." These "systemic constraints . . . are not necessarily the result of the intentions of a tyrant," they are instead "embedded in unquestioned norms, habits, and symbols, in the assumptions underlying institutional rules and the collective consequences of following those rules" (I. Young [1990] 2011, 41). Oppression, then, is "the institutional constraint on self-development," which always operates in concert with the related social condition of domination, which is "the institutional constraint on self-determination" (37). "Constraint on self-development" means barriers to what people *can become and do* given their structural positioning amid legal, economic, and social practices that impact people in systematically unequal ways depending on the circumstances they are born into. These structural constrains are not entirely determinative (some people will beat the odds), but they do create patterns of inhibited opportunity that are empirically observable and probabilistically relevant. The collective consequences of oppression accrue in an intersectional hierarchy, with relative privilege coalescing at the top and lethal disadvantage pooling at the bottom. It is important to emphasize that this constraint on self-development is not primarily a matter of maldistribution. Oppression's harm includes but goes well beyond the unfair distribution of rights and wealth.

Young writes that if we think of people as "doers and actors" instead of "possessors of goods," then the dimensions of oppression's true harm becomes more clear: it is not only that oppression prevents people from *having* their due, it is also and more profoundly that oppression keeps people from *becoming* who they might be if not so constrained, because oppression limits people's ability to increase their capabilities and expand their capacities through exploration, education, and experiences. One of the ways this happens is via the trauma that oppressive conditions inflict on those on the wrong slope of the hierarchy of privilege. Likewise, this trauma is not only something that afflicts individuals, because individuals are always in context and systematic traumas—those traumas occurring to particular populations because of who they are ascribed to be according to extant structural hierarchy—impact the entire group. If these systematic conditions reproduce traumatic social conditions for groups over time, there are broad social and political consequences. We call such effects *generational trauma*.

Psychologists note that any group of people who suffer long-term or ongoing systemic oppression may exhibit symptoms of generational trauma. The bulk of the research on historical trauma focuses on post-genocidal societies, including the "soul wound" sustained by the Indigenous people of the Americas and the psychic strain borne by Jewish people after the Holocaust (see Brave Heart 1999; Yehuda et al. 2016; Hirsch 2012). Researchers have also "identified race-related historical trauma as a large-scale, systems-related macro-stressor that adversely impacts both the physical and mental health of the affected racial/ethnic group" (Sotero 2006, 96). Race-related generational trauma "originates with the subjugation of a population by a dominant group" (102). The public health researcher Michelle Sotero posits that to exhibit measurable effects, generational trauma must include sustained physical and psychological violence, segregation and/or displacement, economic deprivation, and cultural dispossession. For example, group-specific maternal stressors are produced by oppression, not only regarding material deprivations such as malnutrition, but also including external conditions and events that pose a particular social threat to the group (see also Williams, Neighbors, and Jackson 2008; Reid, Mims, and Higginbottom 2004; Yehuda et al. 2005; Southwick et al. 2014). For example, Black women, particularly those with a higher education, are more likely to have preterm labors and births than their white peers. A 2017 study of preterm birth among women found that "chronic worry over racial discrimination" is significantly related to the likelihood of preterm births (Braveman et al. 2017). Under these conditions, the trauma of oppression can be so severe that it is passed down epigenetically from one generation to the next. For example, "Type 2 diabetes in adults may be caused by metabolic adaptations of the fetus in response to maternal malnutrition. The disorder is then propagated throughout subsequent generations via hyperglycemic pregnancies" (99).

There is also the damage done by sequelae, which is a medical term referring to a morbid infection occurring as the result of a previous disease. The anthropologist Christen A. Smith points out that in addition to the weathering of racism, every incident of state-sanctioned violence against Black people causes potentially lethal harm to not only the person who is directly victimized, but to the whole community of people who depend on and care for them as well. She writes,

> Although state terror often results in the immediate physical death of young Black men, it is principally, yet tacitly, performed for Black women and

impacts Black women disproportionately. . . . [T]he gendered necropolitics of trans-American anti-Black violence is expansive and includes the direct, immediate death of Black people and the lingering, slow death caused by sequelae. (C. Smith 2016, 31)

Movement participants have taken in the reality of generational trauma by applying it to how they analyze politics and create spaces for movement work. They know it is impossible to organize people at the margins—those subject to oppression and its generational effects—without considering "the impact of oppressive trauma [that] creates cultural and individual wounding. . . . [Such wounding] becomes an impediment to the individual and collective's ability to transform and negotiate their conditions" (Akili 2011), unless it is addressed directly as a part of the normal practice of organizing. Nikita Mitchell, the former director of organizing for the Black Lives Matter Global Network Foundation puts the problem this way:

[A] lot of the shift in our movement, looking at relationships, power dynamics, emotions, is in reactivity to what people perceive as faults of the civil rights movement, right?. . . . [W]e are doing something magical and new. We believe that getting to a new world is not just about policy change but it's also culture change, so most of our work is in service of building a new community—repairing relationships and building a new community as the basis of our power, then I think tending to the emotions is actually necessary because of how we want to be in the future. We need to practice being now the type of community we want in the future. So I think valuing people's full selves is extremely important. Therefore, we have to be clear about our movements . . . [and] put capacity towards our being able to deal with people's full selves, which is a constant struggle to think about how do we do that. (N. Mitchell interview, 2018)

But this hasn't been easy; Mitchell goes on to express her frustration with movement work when people and organizations are not able to find a balance between the acknowledgement of the weight of people's emotional and mental loads and the need to do the political work:

I believe that Black Lives Matter is a political home for people, who in their day-to-day lives may not be able to voice trauma at home. May not be able to voice when there is an issue where they feel harmed, and so they enter the organization as I entered the organization looking for the ideal place, where they can, like, dump their emotion, and unfortunately, sometimes that comes at the cost of doing this work in a way that actually wins tangible things for our people. . . . Sometimes it's an overcorrection; [it can seem] we care more about us individually than we do about getting things done on behalf of our whole community. How do we balance that commitment between the individual and what we need to do by the collective? It's been hard. (N. Mitchell interview, 2018)

Indeed, movement _____ culty of trying to invent practices that a _____ itics of care. However, Ife Williams, a mem _____ ty Council, a team of people within the m _____ developing practices for the prevention o _____ djudicating processes to address harm, insi _____ d parcel of the experimentation that is co _____ phy. She explains that

we're creating cult _____ nsformative justice or that's what spea _____ the systems that we know do not care for us and do not serve us, because you can't just abolish something and not have a vision for what that something will turn into. I think that that's super key.

So, I think part of the work that we're doing is working through and it's very clear, let's be very clear, this is an experiment. We have never done this before and I am so humbled every day that first of all, people trust us enough to be in this work with us and to also understand to be compassionate about the ways that their challenges come up, or hiccups are part of this experiment. Yeah, so I think we're shifting culture. We're also creating culture. So, we're speaking to the visioning of alternative systems. (Williams and Roberts 2018)

Interdependence

Taking interdependence as a reality is not an aspirational but rather a pragmatic element of the politics of care. As feminist scholars have pointed out for some time, people simply *are* related, and the foundation of these relations are the needs and obligations of various kinds of care. As Bernice Fisher and Joan Tronto remind us, "survival establishes the fundamental context of caring. As a species, we have no choice about engaging in caring activities" (Fisher and Tronto 1990, 39). Whether these relations are for better or worse, resulting in oppression and domination or flourishing, is the matter for assessment and action. One of the movement's key critiques of liberalism is of the figure of the autonomous agent connected to others primarily though contract and/or voluntary association. From the perspective of feminist theories, including RBFP, this is a distortion of reality that actually harms us, with particularly pernicious consequences for those situated at the economic, political, and social margins.

The political problem that caring presents is that there is no place for this basic and universally necessary human activity in the picture of public personhood that modernity has sanctioned as valid. Bernice Fisher and Joan Tronto write that "caring has virtually no place in the description of 'the good life' that provides a focus for Western philosophy, despite the fact that caring permeates our experience" (Fisher and Tronto 1990, 35). Not only does caring permeate our experience, but, as Martha Nussbaum points out, receiving adequate care and caring for others is a crucial part of any good life. She explains:

> [T]he person is a political and social animal, *who seeks good that is social through and through* . . . the good of others is not just a constraint on this person's pursuit of her own good, it is a *part of her good*. She leaves the state of nature not because it is more advantageous in self-interested terms to make a deal with others, but because she can't imagine being whole in an existence without shared ends and a shared life. (Nussbaum 2004, 503)

Instead of acknowledging this practical truth of human existence, care has been styled as a private matter, governed by "nature," "love," and/or "choice," characteristics that were deemed by liberal political theory to be improper subjects of collective action and common governance, and have, in any case, been turned over to the logic of market rationality along with all other domains in the neoliberal reimagining of the dominant paradigm. In this way, the activities of care traditionally carried out by women and often displaced by more affluent women onto working-class and poor women of color are continuously imagined to be beyond the realm of politics, and, even in feminist corrections, care is often described as an ethic rather than a politics in itself.

This imagination of care as private and natural and coming from love, as opposed to a universally necessary set of skills and knowledges requiring labor, support, and governance like other forms of work, has been particularly disadvantageous to Black women. As Shatema Threadcraft notes,

> Black women have occupied two seemingly ironic positions throughout American history. First, they were expected to perform exploitative productive labor typically reserved for those who possessed masculine embodiment. . . . Second, they were considered suitable for a form of marginal, often backbreaking, and always exploitative women's work—work within the white intimate sphere, and work that served to meet the bodily needs of white families often at the expense of care for the bodily needs of their own. (Threadcraft 2016, 8–9)

The displacement of care from our politics is not only detrimental because it results in inequality, where care of children and elderly falls disproportionately on women and is further offloaded from middle-class women to poorer women of color, but also because the logic that banishes care from the realm of the political has facilitated the development of a culture in which we barely have time to care for ourselves. Neoliberalism has exaggerated the *homo economicus* of the Enlightenment, who nevertheless had space and time for "sentiment," to the point that the activity one is meant to value above all others is working for a wage—something we must always be available to do—and all else must exist secondarily. The organization of our lives such that waged work is supposed to supersede and engulf all else became more severe as the twentieth century turned over to the twenty-first and has, as a result, given rise to an enormous industry dictating various ways that we can individually self-help ourselves out of consequences of structural arrangements. Women, in particular, have been counseled on the ways they can "have it all"—or on the reasons why they cannot. And everyone has been encouraged to find "work-life balance," marketed individual programs for "wellness," and scolded to be more "mindful"— all attempts to offload the collective costs of the dominant political economy and the ideas that undergird it onto individuals. This creates a reality in which most people spend large amounts of time trying to ignore or manage their feelings about the displacement and devaluing of all parts of themselves that don't serve to help them labor or make choices about consumption. Ronald Purser argues that "[a]n industry has formed around the 'stressed subject,'" and as such "the dominant mindfulness narrative is that stress is all inside your own head," but "[y]ou can't separate the individual from the environment. We're embodied social beings" (quoted in O'Brien 2019).

This basic understanding and embrace of human beings as embodied and social—that is, experiencing physical needs and limitations and always in context—is the basic notion undergirding the politics of care. The literature that makes these basic understandings most explicit, combining them with practical knowledge, comes out of the disability justice movement, from which RBFP takes most of its cues.[1] A disability justice perspective adopts the feminist observations about care as a basic human function and takes them a step further, by emphasizing that care is not life-cycle specific (focused on children and elderly), nor is it predicated on othering those whose bodies don't afford them the illusion that they are fully subject to their individual wills (those with disability or chronic illness). Leah Lakshmi Piepzna-Samarasinha writes in her book *Care Work* that "a Disability Justice framework understands that all bodies are unique and essential, that all bodies have strengths and needs that must be met," and, as such, the political necessity of care is to create a polity in which people are structurally enabled to care for themselves and others instead of impeded from meeting those needs (Piepzna-Samarasinha 2019, 21). Therefore, the politics of care asks, How can we create institutions and routines that understand *care* for all kinds of bodies, abilities, and levels of health to be a basic, necessary function of governance?

The answer to this question will not be decided at the level of abstract philosophy, but will instead be realized through practical imagination and democratic experimentation that are relevant to concrete contexts. Basing a politics on the acknowledgement of interdependence requires a commitment to processes that allow us to notice, analyze, and act on the reality of our contexts and their effects on individuals. Radical Black feminist pragmatism takes the reality of interdependence to be a fact and does not try to abstract itself from that reality. However, while one is born into a context

---

[1] Piepzna-Samarasinha (2019) writes, "'Disability justice' is a term coined by Black, brown, queer, and trans members of the original Disability Justice Collective, founded in 2005 by Patty Berne, Mia Mingus, Leroy Moore, Eli Clare, and Sebastian Margaret. . . . [T]hey dreamed up a movement-building framework that would center the lives, needs, and organizing strategies of disabled queer and trans and/or Black and brown people marginalized from mainstream disability rights organizing's white-dominated, single-issue focus" (15). She adds, "Disability justice is to the disability rights movement what environmental justice is to the mainstream environmental movement. Disability justice centers sick and disabled people of color, queer and trans disabled folk of color, and everyone who is marginalized in mainstream disability organizing" (22).

that preexists and shapes the individual, one's structural context does not wholly prescribe community. For community to have meaning, it has to be the collection of people to whom one chooses to be accountable, not merely a group to which one is assigned based on ascriptive characteristics. This gives the colloquial inquiry common at Black social gatherings—"Who are your people?"—philosophical heft. It is not only a question of whom one is related to (the most literal interpretation), but also who are the people you claim and how will you represent them in this space and at this time. The abolitionist political theorist Jasmine Syedullah calls this a "congregational" model of public commitment:

> Congregating in churches, homes, and swamps for the cause of abolition was a practice in recreating the sociality of the plantation as sites of marronage within reach of the hold of slavery, but out of sight and beyond the view of those who policed the movements of the enslaved. Congregating breathed space for something new to enter the frame of antebellum segregation and was a generative way for enslaved people see each other, feel themselves, and realize opportunities to improvise on the realities that held them captive to the will of another. To know, in their bodies, that their purpose, pasts, and priorities were beyond the imagination of those who drove them, hunted them, "broke" them, and killed them was, in itself, abolition.

Syedullah is careful to make a distinction between an abolitionist congregation and other kinds of collectivities, arguing that while collectives "with fixed roles, standard issue protocols, and a pre-determined endgame" were and are present in spaces of resistance

> congregating was born in the dark, from clandestine spaces. It was an emergent, iterative, co-created practice of "flocking" to borrow language from adrianne maree brown.... During slavery the relationality of the congregational space was organized around ceremony rather than mission. It was a cumulative praxis of "prayer, preaching, song, communal support and especially feeling the spirit," which, as Albert J. Raboteau wrote... "refreshed the slaves and consoled them in their time of distress". By imagining their lives in the context of a different future they gained hope in the present. (Syedullah forthcoming 2022)

As such, the movement cultivates norms of "showing up" and "holding space," where such ceremonies for comfort, perspective, and innovation can be made. Let us examine these practices.

Showing Up

First, when a movement participant remarks about their intention or ability to "show up," they mean more than to be in attendance. In the language of the movement, to "show up" is not only to be in a particular place at a particular time, but to arrive with a certain comportment or "posture," as Je Naé Taylor, a member of BYP100's Healing and Safety Council, describes it, one that evinces an "embodied commitment" to "clarifying intentions." In this way, showing up is not only about the posture one has upon walking through the door of a shared space, it also includes the willingness to shift that posture in order to become intelligible to those one hopes to relate to. This is because "showing up" in this sense is fundamentally an action expressing commitment. The feminist political theorist Mara Marin writes that commitments "are taken on voluntarily, yet without knowing at the outset the final form of [the] obligations, which is subject to continual transformation . . . commitments take shape, over time, through chains of open-ended actions and responses" (Marin 2017, 15–16). Taylor's explanation of the reasons for and process of showing up put flesh on the bones of this definition:

> [I]t's about, for me, a commitment. BYP100 is a commitment to loving Black people. For me, I'm clear about that. And I'm clear that I want to be in relationship with loving Black people, and that requires that I show up a particular way. And what I think our big desire in our organization is, *how are we embodying that commitment?* Does that mean that if someone says, "Hey, I feel that you have harmed me in this way," even if I feel you are telling a bold-faced lie. I ain't never show up that way, my commitment is saying, "I love Black people enough that imma say, 'Aight, Tell me what part of my behaviors brought that to you, that you interpreted my intention in that way?'" That's my posture. My posture isn't, "oh, I ain't do that. I ain't never show up like that." My posture is, "okay, tell me how did you interpret my intention that way?" And then, "how do I get better at clarifying my intentions?" Because if that's not what I meant, I need to make sure I fix my

behavior so that I can articulate clearly why I'm doing certain things, why I'm here, and why I'm in relationship with you.

So, much of our organizing is centered on, "how are we clearing our intentions? How are we shifting our posture?" My friend says, "gratitude is our posture toward the things that sustain us." And loving Black people sustains me, so that means that our posture has to constantly be in a position, and in a way that it's clear that like, "Look, I love you wholeheartedly, and I'm here to show up, and I'm here to be accountable." (Taylor and Green 2018)

In this way, to "show up" is not only about a person's internal comportment and bodily presence, but also encompasses the way they appear to others, the way their posture and actions are perceived by those to whom they are accountable. This is an incredibly sophisticated and difficult line to walk in daily interaction, particularly in the pressure cooker of political activism and movement organizing. Participants are not always successful and movement spaces are still often characterized by conflict over analysis, priorities, strategy, and short- to medium-term goals. Interpersonal antipathy and harm also occur. However, the philosophical commitment to a politics of care along with the formal institutional mechanisms for preventing harm and mediating conflict create a unique set of practices that have helped to sustain organizations as well as the overarching goal of the work—making a world where Black people can expect to live and thrive.

Holding Space

Another practice that supports healthy interdependence is the activity of "holding space." Like "showing up," "holding space" is more complicated than it seems. Christina Sharpe (2016) writes that the notion of a "hold" has much to teach us. A hold is a place of departure and arrival and the container for the time in-between. The hold of a ship or aircraft is a place where one waits, suspended, even as the conveyance moves along its course. For Black people, "the hold" has often been an awful space of liminal suffering: "the hold of the slave ship, the hold of the birth canal, the hold of Middle Passage, the hold of prison, the hold of the migrant ship, the hold of the morgue, the hold of the state, and so on" (Green et al. 2019, 919). However, a hold can also be another name for a fortress, a protected place where participants prepare for actions that must be taken. Sharpe goes on to suggest that a hold can be a place where we become "beholden to and beholders of" one another (Sharpe 2016, 101). To hold space, then, is to create a protected place that gives space for stillness and preparation even as the group or organization, and the world outside, continues to move. Holding space is thus a dynamic practice that is essential to enabling reflection, accountability, and healing. As BYP100 Healing and Safety Council member Marshall (Kai M.) Green and their coauthors write,

> [W]e realized that much of what we have done, and continue to do, in the [Healing and Safety Council] is hold. In other words, we be-holdin'. We be-holdin' space. We be-holdin' meetings. We be-holdin' circles. We be-holdin' processes. We be-holdin' mediations. We be-holdin' trainings. We be-holdin' workshops. We be-holdin' names. We be-holdin' naming. We be-holdin' time. We be-holdin' pain. We be-holdin' disappointment. We be-holdin' failure. We be-holdin' trauma. We be-holdin' expectations. We be-holdin' grief. We be-holdin' anger. We be-holdin' sadness. We be-holdin' success. We be-holdin' joy. We be-holdin' affirmation. We be-holdin' love. We be-holdin' those holding on. We be-holdin' our ancestors. We be-holdin' Black people. We be-holdin' each other. (Green et al. 2019)

Like showing up, holding space is a process-oriented and practical activity, an action of care born out of commitment to both a set of ideals and the people with whom one does the work of political change.

Intergenerational Interdependence

Included in RBFP's understanding of interdependence is not only a Durkheimian functionalism, but also a sensitivity to intergenerational connection and responsibility. Charlene Carruthers notes that one of the sources of her commitment to political struggle and supporting elements of her political joy is "celebrating my lineage, the people that I come from. Me and momma, my grandmama, the 10,000 grandmothers at my back. And knowing that I'm not at this thing alone and I'm not the first to do it" (Carruthers and brown 2019). This sentiment is widely shared in the movement. For example, Jewel Cadet, the chapter chair of BYP100 New York, makes vivid this notion of interdependence when she describes a successful protest action that took place in the summer of 2017.

During 2017 and 2018, activists were demanding that Americans re-visit the history of figures memorialized in monuments all over the country whose legacies were steeped in violence against marginalized peoples. The New York chapter of BYP100 took on the publicization and condemnation of the legacy of J. Marion Sims, an American physician known as "the fa-ther of gynecology," who made his name in medicine by doing surgeries and experiments on enslaved Black women without anesthesia. Sims was memo-rialized with a statue that had stood in a position of honor in front of the New York Academy of Medicine for forty years, which seemed a denial or disregard of the violence and suffering he perpetuated against Black women who had no power to refuse. In other words, the Sims statue was a monu-ment to Black women's lives not mattering. So movement activists staged a stunning protest where Black women activists, dressed in hospital gowns splashed with red paint at the waist, encircled the statue and read from his-torical documents describing accounts of Sims's activities, made statements affirming the humanity of the women who had been used against their con-sent, and sang and chanted affirmations. This action was widely covered by New York news outlets and—added to the ongoing and intensifying advo-cacy of groups like East Harlem Preservation—would prompt the statue's re-moval by April 2018.

Cadet described the rigorous research and public education components of the Sims statue action to me in detail during our interview, but what struck me as especially interesting was the palpable idea, throughout our discus-sion, that the impetus of the action was not only to remove a present-day affront, but also to execute a custodial responsibility to the people who had come before, both the women who had struggled under Sims's knife and the people who had struggled to bring this malevolent legacy to light. Cadet recounts that she dressed herself on that day with careful attention, listening to music and wearing her hair in a way that made her feel "close to ancestors." She goes on to say,

> I feel like the people who came before me, freedom fighters who had come before me, were embodying me in that moment. And so, when I was doing it, I didn't feel like I was doing it by myself. You know, so it's like everyone was with me. Everyone from the past who was a freedom fighter was with me. It's super heavy you know . . . it was very intense. I started to cry, we all started to cry, we were there chanting and having this whole experi-ence because we all felt them in our spirit, right there. You know this isn't

something that we're doing for show. I mean you have the picture that went viral . . . [but] people don't know. It was a super heavy action that weighed on us emotionally. (Cadet interview, 2017)

This notion of acknowledging ancestors, particularly in the form of a liturgy of spoken names, is large part of movement practice.[2] This spiritual practice was often contained in the activity that participants call "grounding," a class of techniques adapted from psychology under the banner of "mindfulness" that help participants feel anchored in their bodies and in the moment—facilitating people's ability to "show up" in the posture most aligned with their own intentions and the purpose of the group.

Accountability

An essential component of healthy interdependence is accountability. Interdependence without accountability quickly devolves into codependence, a state of relation that is not conducive to imagining or implementing changes in behavior and action. In order to be in what movement actors call "right relationship" with others—that is, exhibiting a commitment to care that is reciprocal—all parties must be willing to be accountable. To be accountable is to be required or expected to justify one's decisions to some group to which one owes a duty, obligation, or commitment; that is, to be responsible to a constituency. However, accountability is not only about giving reasons for actions; it also requires that those reasons be explicable and understandable. In other words, those in healthy interdependent relations with others have to be able to give an account of our decisions and actions. Charlene Carruthers has written extensively on the importance and difficulty of accountability to movement actors and organizations. When I interviewed her, she explained this:

[W]e don't have healthy models for accountability, we have models that rely on punishment and on shaming people, and in fact, most of our models are extremely violent and perpetuate the very thing that we say we are against.

---

[2] A practice that is common in many religious traditions, but which is also uniquely characteristic of Black feminism, according to Brittney Cooper, who calls this phenomena Black feminist "citational politics" (see Cooper 2017).

And so, community accountability and transformative justice becomes an important skill set. Although many of us don't actually have that full skill set, we're trying. . . . That piece is so new. It's also exciting but it's also deeply . . . it's a painful process. (Carruthers interview, 2017)

Prentis Hemphill, the former Director of Healing Justice for the BLM Global Network Foundation, writes, "we realize that care and accountability are at the root . . . and are some of the most difficult and direct actions we can take. Care and accountability require us to reveal, to center, and more than anything, to change" (Hemphill 2017). This kind of change is meant to be transformational for individuals, but it is also an attempt to change culture by shifting people's understanding of what interdependence means and frames of reference for what relating to each other ought to entail. In order to achieve relations and build organizations and institutions capable of acknowledging the fact of independence and centering the necessity of accountability, it is also necessary to emphasize a regard for people that is grounded in appreciation for their (and our own) humanity. This kind of regard demands a rejection of worldviews that dictate that only those who are properly productive deserve respect and regard for their needs, desires, and choices. For Black people, this entails a specific rejection of stereotypes and tropes that blame supposedly pathological individual behaviors for the structural limitations placed on the group. The politics of care therefore demands challenging anti-Blackness and white supremacy with an unapologetic rejection of "respectability politics," along with public defense and private celebration of Black joy.

Unapologetic Blackness and Defense of Black Joy

The Movement for Black Lives attempts to create language, make space, and build counternarratives that make the case for cultivating and defending Black joy, thereby holding space to define, celebrate, and embrace the diversity of Black peoples and ways of identifying and performing Black culture unapologetically. To be "unapologetically Black" is not just a statement of pride. It is also a succinct way to encapsulate the movement's rejection of the politics of respectability for the purpose of earning an inclusion that is supposed to be a matter of right(s). The simple phrase holds a world of meaning, asserting that M4BL seeks freedom for *all* Black people, not only the "good" or "achieving" ones. This is because the politics of care is an antidote to dehumanization, and humans, in reality, are messy and contradictory and imperfect, so our histories and institutions and governance ought to take these facts into account. The moral philosopher Emily Townes explains that "the challenge is to resist measuring Black realities by the ideological stereotypes, the denigrating myths, of the fantastic hegemonic imagination" (Townes 2006, 21–22). She goes on to lament that "so much of Black history . . . [has] been made a social project—not the story of flesh and bone and spirit and emotion" (30). She asks, "How do we grasp hold of our identity and truly name ourselves instead of constantly looking into some strategically placed funhouse mirror of distortions and innuendos . . . ? When black identity is property that can be owned by someone else, defined by someone else, created by someone else, shaped by someone else, we are chattel dressed in postmodern silks" (45). One of the most important things that is happening culturally as a result of the movement is that Black people have been able to draw their own "unapologetic" images, first on social media, then in a thriving Black online news ecosystem, and then in pop culture. That is, the "respectable negro," the "gansta," and the "conscious" or neo-soul-inspired Black person are no longer the only easily accessible tropes of Blackness. There are Black queers, cosplayers, dapper dons and donnas, punkers, nerds, futurists, and others. Black people have claimed their humanness as authors of our own experience—authors who are not trying to prove anything to the dominant group. The culture of M4BL is the exploration of all that we are— our full, diverse, flawed, fragile, and triumphant humanity.

This is the opposite of mid-twentieth-century approaches, in which marginalized groups often attempted to police the behavior and expression of their own members as a part of their appeal for inclusion, showing that their values and actions were continuous with, even exemplary of, dominant ideals. Respectability politics aims to show that those who are oppressed and dominated do not deserve poor treatment, but instead deserve to be included in the polity on equal terms and granted rights and respect.

The rejection of respectability politics and embrace of unapologetic Blackness did not merely arise from the ether. Its emergence as a core part of movement philosophy was importantly dependent on the movement's development during the Obama era. Obama and his loving, attractive, and accomplished family are the perfect expression of Black respectability. One could scarcely imagine a better example of middle-class American values personified, with what was, for many, an enchanting dash of magical negro and Black girl magic thrown in, elevating this talented bunch from exemplary to magnetic. Still, this charismatic excellence was not enough to shield Obama from a historic backlash of racialized conspiracy and hatred, and his presidency seems to have sparked the activation of a lethally resentful and widespread white grievance politics. In addition, the example of the Obamas in the highest office in the land did nothing at all to curb racial resentment, mitigate structural inequality, or restrain state violence against Black people and other people of color. Social psychologists hopefully embarked on studies aiming to track changes in racial attitudes during Obama's campaign and presidency, only to find that the quantitatively measured mean explicit and implicit anti-Black attitudes did not change (Sawyer and Gampa 2018). In short, there could be no greater object lesson for the movement truism that "respectability will not save you" than the persistent reality of racism and the defiant resurgence of open racial animus in what was supposed to be the "post-racial" Obama era.

In the brilliant documentary *Whose Streets?* (Folayan and Davis 2017), which chronicled the uprisings in Ferguson, Missouri, after the murder of Mike Brown, one participant in the protests comments, "I waited all my life for a Black president. I still ain't had me one. Ain't he a constitutional law professor? Well, we ain't got no constitution in Ferguson. So tell that nigger to teach a new class. Or bring his ass down to Ferguson Burger Boy and help us figure out why we ain't got no constitution."

Like the simmering anger of Black people after George Zimmerman was acquitted of stalking and shooting a seventeen-year-old Black boy on his way home, the rage expressed here is closely undergirded by disappointment and surprise. No matter how common the cynical (and self-protective) refrain that America has never been good to or for Black people and nothing better ought to have been expected in the Obama era, most people *did* hope for better. To be confronted with such overwhelming evidence that no way of being Black—from the near-perfect personal comportment of the presidential family to the perfectly ordinary hoodie-clad slouch of a teenager walking through his own neighborhood—could be viewed without violent suspicion made it imperative to turn toward a new way of regarding Black people and reimagining Black politics.

So, unapologetic Blackness emerged as not only a rejection of respectability politics, but also as its overcoming. Regardless of whether one personally believed in bourgeois standards of individual comportment and educational and professional achievement, it became clear that as a political matter, the standard of respectability was not and could not lead to a world in which Black people can except to live and thrive. Therefore, unapologetic Blackness insists on an unashamed embrace of Black peoples and cultures in all their diversity, whether the dominant standards of comportment would judge them refined and achieving or deviant and disgraceful. The Blogger Charlene Haparimwi describes the sentiment thusly,

I am absolutely here for the gum popping, finger snapping, fast talking, weave wearing Black women. I am here for the basketball playing, rap loving, fashion forward Black men. I am here for nerdy Black girls and boys, quiet Black boys and girls, entrepreneurial Black boys and girls. I am here for every stereotype and every exception to the rule of Blackness the world sees, imagines, perpetuates or tries to eradicate. There is no me against them, we are all one voice, one people. (Haparimwi 2016)

Damon Young, cofounder of the popular website Very Smart Brothas, puts it this way: "[S]top crafting your thoughts and actions around what White People (collectively) might think if you thought or acted a certain way. Step outside of the White Gaze and stay there" (D. Young 2016).

BLM Global Network Foundation communications strategists Shanelle Matthews and Miski Noor characterize the organizational commitment to unapologetic Blackness this way:

We are expansive. We are a collective of liberators who believe in an inclusive and spacious movement. We also believe that in order to win and bring as many people with us along the way, we must move beyond the narrow nationalism that is all too prevalent in Black communities. We must ensure we are building a movement that brings all of us to the front.

We affirm the lives of Black queer and trans folks, disabled folks, undocumented folks, folks with records, women, and all Black lives along the gender spectrum. Our network centers those who have been marginalized within Black liberation movements.

We are working for a world where Black lives are no longer systematically targeted for demise.

We affirm our humanity, our contributions to this society, and our resilience in the face of deadly oppression.

The call for Black lives to matter is a rallying cry for ALL Black lives striving for liberation.

Every day, we recommit to healing ourselves and each other, and to co-creating alongside comrades, allies, and family a culture where each person feels seen, heard, and supported. (Matthews and Noor 2017)

As such, M4BL is a movement that actively attempts to release Black people from the "veil" of "double consciousness" that Du Bois described at the turn of the twentieth century (Du Bois [1903] 1994) and rejects the notion that an elite portion of talented race men and women ought to lead the way to freedom.

Further, M4BL endeavors to avoid what Cathy Cohen describes as "secondary marginalization," which is the practice of defining certain members of a marginalized group as "innocent and worthy of mobilization, while others [are] labeled deviant, immoral, and bad" (Cohen 1999, 346). To practice unapologetic Blackness is to reject the shaming of certain Black people in an attempt to uphold the moral rightness of others, and to refuse the idea that the admonishment of individuals to "pull your pants up" or "take off that hoodie" serves any practical or political purpose beyond perpetuating domination and oppression.[3]

In order to ensure that no apologies for any variety of Blackness enter into their politics by the default process that allows people in marginalized groups with relatively more power and privilege to set the tone and priority of movement issues, the movement insists on the necessity of theorizing and practicing politics "from margin to center," attempting to foreground the needs of those most reviled and written off in dominant society. Chris Roberts, a member of the Healing and Safety Council of BYP100 explains:

We want the people naming their truths, speaking their experiences, who historically have not been able to speak that and have not been valued, more importantly. When it's like, okay, we want this particular perspective, who are the people that are last referred to? Who are the people who are last reached? We're trying to shift that whole dynamic and say, no, that these are the voices that are most important for us as an organization and as a community. (Williams and Roberts 2018)

---

[3] Respectability politics and secondary marginalization are a common feature of the way social movement organizations prioritize issues, frame issues, and distribute resources. It is not a phenomenon limited to Black social movements. See Woodly 2015, chap. 3, on the gay respectability politics that undergirded the turn toward marriage in gay politics during the late 1990s and early 2000s.

Therefore, M4BL deliberately foregrounds issues such as violence against trans Black people, support for the incarcerated, and the abolition of police and prisons.

M4BL seeks to avoid secondary marginalization not only in its public campaigns, but also in its internal practices. This requires participants and leaders to make space for and be willing to learn from people whose voices are not often heard. The way the movement came to foreground the necessity of trans Black lives provides a telling example. Charlene Carruthers explains it this way:

> [W]e're being told, I'm being told, in this moment in Chicago, that Black LGBTQ issues—they don't even say that—that Black gay and lesbian is-sues are not Black issues. . . . In this particular moment where we're calling for the resignation of Mayor Rahm Emmanuel, cause he got to go. And we're calling for the 40% that CPD takes from our public service budget in Chicago—we're calling for that to change—we're being *pummeled* by ho-mophobic and transphobic rhetoric. And rhetoric that has turned into ac-tual physical violence as well. Both coming from the police state itself and from Black people in movement spaces. But this whole idea of being told to wait, to get in the background is unacceptable. And we know that we come from a lineage of Black folks who have said that shit is unacceptable. And we will not wait. And we cannot wait. . . . We refuse to wait. We don't have time to wait, our lives are on the line.

Carruthers goes on to say,

> [T]he difficult and heart-wrenching struggle, that when you commit to Black queer feminist values, that you actually have to struggle with and not throw things underneath the bus or the carpet and name what you don't know and go to people who do know way more than you know and we have a responsibility to actually put our values into practice and to struggle with that and not be perfect. Perfection isn't the goal but integrity and accounta-bility to our values is. (Smith, Carruthers, and Gossett 2016)

The Movement for Black Lives self-consciously understands unapol-ogetic Blackness to be not only a personal affirmation, but also a political tool that helps to change dominant frames in public discourse and culture. Another unique political tool that the movement cultivates in the rejection of anti-Blackness and the embrace of a politics of care is the explicit and emphatic defense of Black joy. To defend Black joy is not only to celebrate one's own feelings of happiness and connectedness when they are felt, but, more profoundly, it is an enactment of what Jacques Lacan calls *jouissance*, the feeling of mastery attained by being the author of one's own experience and having the authority to explode the taken-for-granted. This sense of political jouissance is what allows people to dare to imagine and create a political program that challenges and changes the terms of the American political conversation on racism and white supremacy, to have the audacity to collectively author a policy platform that is available online in five different languages, and to establish initiatives like the Electoral Justice Voter Fund (see https://m4bl.org/electoraljusticevoterfund/), which seeks to recruit and support Black candidates who advocate for those policy proposals in running for political office. The politics of joy and pleasure are regarded as necessities, because they are the only things that will make the lifelong and multigenerational work of pursuing justice sustainable, and are therefore a condition of the possibility of a radical yet pragmatic politics. adrienne marie brown puts it this way:

> For a few decades of my life I did a pendulum swing of "I'm going to work hard and it's going to be miserable and then I'm going to go have my pleasure. And then I'm going to work hard again." And part of what I'm trying to do—and I don't know if it's possible, really, but I'm trying to do it in more and more spaces—is to be like "we're in this meeting, can we, like, break out into some 90s R&B and celebrate the fact that we made a decision and enjoy each other?" . . . What are the pleasures we can bring into the work? I want to get out of the cycle of burning out and recovering, where recovering is the only place I experience pleasure. (Carruthers and brown 2019)

In the same vein, Charlene Carruthers states, "I don't believe that we have to have perfect people who are at the top of their wellness game in our movements, that's just unrealistic. We wouldn't have a movement" (Carruthers and brown 2019). Treva B. Lindsey concurs, writing, "[W]e must develop an ethics around the reality that we are often not well and how we take care of ourselves and one another. We need a co-extant practice of self and other care that accounts for our (dis)abilities to show up for ourselves and one another" (Hearns and Lindsey 2017). This is difficult to do,

Carruthers says, because "many of the movement spaces that I'm in have a shape of not celebrating—big wins, small wins, medium wins—or celebrating when someone is successful," and that is detrimental to their ability to do the work long-term to model the behavior of community healing and care. She adds,

> This past week I was at the Highlander Center [campus]. And for those who don't know the Highlander Center's [main] office was burned down by . . . some white supremacists. . . . And this was last month. . . . So, we were there, a group of us [Black women], who are holding big parts of movement across this country. From people who lead organizations for formerly incarcerated and currently incarcerated women, people who lead organizations fighting against HIV and AIDS, Black trans women-led organizations, all kinds of Black women in this room and, every single morning we were singing. Every single night we were talking shit with each other, we had a whole community care night, all these things. Because we know that we live in a world that is set up for us to fail and the way that we're actually going to do this thing, transform the world, is that we have to celebrate each other. (Carruthers and brown 2019)

The joy of connection intermixed with moments of what Durkheim called "collective effervescence," or the feeling that one is experiencing a practice or action in perfect concert with others, along with the satisfaction of commitment to a cause, has always been an important part of movement work, but M4BL's recognition of this joy as a *political resource* essential for both shaping the politics of the movement and caring for people involved in movement is unique.

Abolition, Restoration, and Repair

The final aspect of the politics of care is an abolitionist ethic. For people in movement, abolition is, at bottom, a politics of care. This is because, though contemporary abolitionists believe in the ultimate elimination of police and prisons, that aspiration is predicated on creating the material and social conditions in which most people do not harm others. This aspiration, like the rest of the political philosophy of the movement, is pragmatic, not utopian. No abolitionist believes that the American polity is close to shutting down prisons and completely defunding police forces. Instead, they do practical political work with the aim of (1) changing people's minds about what motivates people to cause harm and what constitutes safety; (2) fighting for the re-allocation of resources away from policing, arresting, and imprisoning people and toward adequately feeding, housing, educating, and finding work for people; and (3) preventing as many people from being locked up and underwriting the release of as many people as possible from jails and prisons. The abolitionist position is, in its most basic form, quite simple: policing, jail, and prison do not actually perform the functions they purport to perform—keeping people safe from violence and harm. Instead, these institutions cause massive economic, political, social, and psychological harms that are quantifiable and grossly disproportionate for Black and brown people. Given this evidence, abolitionists do not accept that the current punishment-focused approach, which is widely acknowledged to be damaging and unfair, is the best that society can do.

Importantly, abolitionists are able to make the claim that jails and prisons do not keep us safe, based on a voluminous and robust empirical literature[4] documenting, in detail, the fact that the grotesque growth of the punitive penitentiary apparatus in America since the 1970s has been completely unlinked to either the rise or fall of crime rates. As Michelle Alexander writes, "the American penal system has emerged as a system of social control unparalleled in world history . . . the primary targets of its control can be defined largely by race." She goes on to say, "this is an astonishing development . . . given that as recently as the mid-1970, the most well-respected criminologists were predicting that the prison system would soon fade away" (M. Alexander 2011, 8). This conclusion was reached because there was already ample evidence that "prison did not deter crime significantly" and that instead, "those who had meaningful economic and social opportunities were unlikely to commit crimes regardless of the penalty, while those who went to prison were far more likely to commit crimes again in the future" (8). According to the National Advisory Commission on Criminal Justice Standards and Goals report issued in 1973, "the prison, the reformatory and the jail have achieved only a shocking record of failure. There is overwhelming evidence that these institutions *create crime rather than prevent it*" (8, emphasis added).

---

[4] See Beckett 1997; Cole 1999; Davis 2007; Mauer 2006; Mauer and King 2007; Alexander 2011; Balko 2014b; Hayes 2017; and Bazelon 2019.

It is also important to acknowledge the practical truth that, as the abolitionist organizer and founder of Project NIA Mariame Kaba notes, "police officers don't do what you think they do. They spend most of their time responding to noise complaints, issuing parking and traffic citations, and dealing with other noncriminal issues." We have been taught the police "catch the bad guys; they chase the bank robbers; they find the serial killers." However, as Kaba notes, quoting Alex Vitale, the coordinator of the Policing and Social Justice Project at Brooklyn College, this is a "big myth . . . the vast majority of police officers make one felony arrest per year" (Kaba 2021, 14).

Abolitionists today, like criminologists in the era before the "war on drugs"—a project of the federal government that was spearheaded by a vast public relations and funding apparatus incentivizing racialized policing and the augmentation of local police forces—posit that most people cause harm because they are already living in a context of structural harm. This harm takes the form of poverty or other material deprivation like lack of access to healthcare, schooling, adequate transportation, mental health care, housing, etc., or sociocultural harms like discrimination, neglect, violence, or negligence. The material and sociocultural structural harms described affect individuals but characterize whole communities, and their impacts can be objectively observed. Abolitionists simply point out that these massive, long-observed patterns have a consequence: lack of safety. In order to make people safer in our society, we have to make our society safer for people.[5]

A large focus of the politics of care is recognizing and rejecting the tendency to ask individuals to take sole responsibility for conditions that are both beyond their control and systematically aimed at the ascriptive group of which they are apart. In other words, it is not a legitimate approach to safety to, for example, ask people in a neighborhood that has been almost completely divested of legal work not to work in illegal trade and commerce. The harm that arises from the high-risk and high-violence organization and execution of illegal trades occurs between individuals, but it is *caused* by already occurring and state-sanctioned harm and deprivation. The recognition of this state of affairs does not absolve the people who have perpetuated interpersonal harms, because those acts have interpersonal consequences

---

[5] See, for example, the call and response chant at the BY100 2016 National Convening: "We want living wage jobs. Not cops. We want funding for public education. Not cops. We want access to mental health services. Not cops. Sustainable food and water sources. Not cops. Affordable housing. Not cops. Free public transportation. Not cops." Accessed April 4, 2020, https://www.youtube.com/watch?v=uMTCU0G9y94.

that must be attended to, but the full weight of blame for the pattern of activity must also include the ideas and institutions that have allowed harmful structural conditions to arise and persist.

The politics of care asks what kinds of harms are already occurring at the social level that create the conditions in which harming others, by theft or violence, comes to make sense. It is the mitigation of those conditions that must be the first concern of people who wish to ensure the safety of society. Abolition is a key part of the politics of care because its primary programmatic goals are about intervention before the moment of offense. As Ruth Wilson Gilmore often says, abolition is not primarily about absence—the absence of police and prisons—it is fundamentally about *presence*, the presence of "jobs, education, housing, health care—all the elements that are required for a productive and violence-free life." It is about investing in "vital systems of support that many communities lack" (Kushner 2019).

In this way, abolitionists ask us to consider a radically different root of safety. Mariame Kaba, explains:

> Security and safety aren't the same thing. Security is a function of the weaponized state that is using guns, weapons, fear and other things to "make us secure," right? All the horrible things are supposed to be kept at bay by these tools, even though we know that horrible things continue to happen all the time with these things in place—and that these very tools and the corresponding institutions are reproducing the violence and horror they are supposed to contain. (Kaba and Duda 2017)

The question inevitably arises: But what is society supposed to do with people who commit serious and irrevocable harms like rape and murder? Kaba has a two-pronged answer for this question:

> I guess that answer won't satisfy people who want you to provide them with [an immediate] *solution*. . . . This is the question that always gets thrown at anybody who identifies as abolitionist—and my question back is "what are you doing right now about the rapists and the murderers?" That's the first thing: Is what's happening right now working for you? Are you feeling safer? Has the current approach ended rape and murder? The vast majority of rapists never see the inside of a courtroom, let alone get convicted and end up in prison. In fact, they end up becoming President. So the system you feel so attached to and that you seem invested in preserving is not

delivering what you say you want, which is presumably safety and an end to violence. Worse than that it is causing inordinate additional harm. The logics of policing and prisons are not actually addressing the systemic causes and roots of violence. [. . .]

Number two is that I always say: the answer to the question is a collective project. Your question is a good one in the sense that you're thinking about how we might address harm (which is not the same as crime incidentally)—and so let's figure out together, across our communities, what would be a just system for adjudicating and evaluating harm. That's a very different posture to take. It's a question that invites people in, that invites people to offer their ideas. It invites us to argue with each other, to say "this will work better" and "no, this is the best way," *rather than accepting as permanent and always necessary the current oppressive institutions that we have* [emphasis added].

Our current punishment apparatus are sites of terrible and incredible violence. (Kaba and Duda 2017)

Kei Williams, formerly of Black Lives Matter Global Network Foundation's New York chapter and now an organizer with the Martha P. Johnson Institute, helps people reflect on the idea of safety by conducting the following exercise:

There's this exercise I like to do in spaces really capturing the cultural aspect . . . there's a core belief for me that the cultural influences the institutional and then that flows down into the interpersonal, into the everyday lives. But until there is a culture around certain things, the institutions won't change. And we see this, for example, with the cultural belief around whether women should be able to vote. If you say that women shouldn't be able to vote now, you seem completely crazy whereas 100 years ago it was the norm.

So . . . I would like for everybody to have your feet planted on the ground. Close your eyes. Take a couple of breaths and realize where you are . . . [now] think about the safest place you have ever been in your life. Think about what's in the room. What's the environment like? What does it smell like in the room? For me, it's my bedroom. I'm a Cancer, it's my hub. I've got my blues, got my painting, got my essential oils. What is it like for you? Is there anyone in the room with you? Hold that for a minute. Who's in the room with you? Sit in that space. Keep your eyes closed. [Pause]

Now, I want you to raise your hand with your eyes closed if you pictured a police officer in the room with you. Raise your hand if you pictured a police officer in your safe space? Open your eyes and look around the room. [Everyone looks around. No hands are raised]

So there is this misconception that we believe that police keep us safe. One of the campaigns that we are all a part of which is called Safety Beyond Policing is about really shifting the ways that we think about police and the ways we think about safety in our daily lives. (Museum of the City of New York 2017)

Kaba expands on this idea that one of abolition's most important tasks is to change how people think about safety. She writes,

I believe that living in the way we live makes it difficult for most people to seriously consider the end of policing. The idea of security, the idea that cops equal security, is difficult to dislodge. To transform this mindset, where cops equal security, means we have to actually transform our relationships to each other enough so that we can see that we can keep each other safe and ourselves safe, right? Safety means something else, because you cannot have safety without strong, empathic relationships with others. You can have security without relationships but you cannot have safety—actual safety—without healthy relationships. Without getting to really know your neighbor, figuring out when you should be intervening when you hear and see things, feeling safe enough within your community that you feel like, yeah my neighbor's punching [their partner], I'm going to knock on the door, right? I'm not going to think that that person's going to pull a gun on me and shoot me in the head. I don't believe that because I know that person. I know them. I built that relationship with them and even though they're upset and mad I'm taking the chance of going over there and being like you need to stop this now, what are you doing? Part of what this necessitates is that we have to work with members of our communities to make violence unacceptable. What my friend Andy Smith has said is that this is a problem of political organizing and not one of punishment. How can we organize to make interpersonal violence unthinkable?

Kaba goes on to say, "In that way, a big part of the abolitionist project that I've been involved in now for over a decade and a half at least, is unleashing people's imaginations while getting concrete—so that we have to imagine while we build, always both" (Kaba and Duda 2017).

That imagination must include repair. Patrisse Khan-Cullors writes in the *Harvard Law Review*, "Abolition calls on us not only to destabilize, deconstruct, and demolish oppressive systems, institutions, and practices, but also to *repair histories of harm across the board*." We are to do so by not only abolishing "prisons, policing, and militarization, which are wielded in the name of 'public safety' and 'national security,'" but also by demanding "reparations" and incorporating "reparative justice into our vision for society and community building in the twenty-first century" (Khan-Cullors 2019 [emphasis added]).

According to an abolitionist perspective, if we repair the context of already occurring harm, most common conflicts and injuries would simply have less occasion to arise. However, most does not mean all. Human beings will sometimes cause harm to each other by accident or design as long as we live in close proximity. So when harm does occur, abolitionists propose a different rationale and set of methodologies for dealing with its consequences. Gilmore asks, "[W]hy don't we think about why we solve problems by repeating the kind of behavior that brought us the problem in the first place?" Should we, as a society "model cruelty and vengeance"? Most countries in Europe, for example, already make very different choices about how to deal with harm. Gilmore notes that murder is rare in Spain, but if someone is convicted of murder they are likely to get a prison sentence of about seven years. She said, "What this policy tells me is that where life is precious, life *is* precious." To her this means that "in Spain people have decided that life has enough value that they are not going to behave in a punitive and violent and life-annihilating way toward people who hurt people." Gilmore concluded that "what this demonstrates is that for people trying to solve their everyday problems, behaving in a violent and life-annihilating way is not a solution" (Kushner 2019). Healing justice is the overarching methodology that movement participants use to think through and implement methodologies for both preventing and addressing harm.

Healing Justice

Healing justice, then, is a collection of commitments and movement practices promoting the health, healing, and joy of Black people, by acknowledging

the trauma that oppression and domination cause and by trying to understand and address both the historical roots and proximate causes of the
structural violence that impacts Black lives. Cara Page and Kindred Southern
Healing Justice Collective cleared a path and told us that "healing justice . . .
identifies how we can holistically respond to and intervene on generational
trauma and violence, and to bring collective practices that can impact and
transform the consequences of oppression on our bodies, hearts and minds"
(Hemphill 2017). As a result, many of the organizations leading the work
in the Movement for Black Lives, such as the Black Lives Matter Global
Network Foundation and BYP100, have official positions for "healing justice" directors, coordinators, and councils who draw personnel, inspira-
tion, and knowledge from professional therapists, social workers, and other
healers such as members of the Kindred Collective, a group founded in 2007
to provide counseling to victims of Hurricane Katrina.

It should be noted that the healing justice framework is not an invention of the Movement for Black Lives. *Healing justice* is a term that origi-
nated in the disability justice movement that emerged in 2005, which was,
in turn, building on thinking that had come out of the fights for environmental and reproductive justice that had begun in the 1980s and 1990s.[6] That
these "justice" movements all emerged as offshoots and alternatives to the
mainstream "rights" movements concerned with similar causes is significant. "Justice" movements all arise in the late twentieth century and respond
to the same deficiencies of the mainstream organizing, and with similar insistence on the need to reframe the discussion and actions confronting the
problems facing movement constituencies. Justice movements want to step
out of the distributive paradigm that characterizes rights movements. They
know, from lived experience, that one can win the right to abortion or ADA-
compliant building access without actually being able to access those rights
in any meaningful way. Altering legal and juridical frameworks can be important for people who are suffering under conditions of domination and
oppression, but the provision of rights is *almost never* sufficient to guarantee
the ability that those rights can be exercised, particularly by people who are

---

[6] For example, the environmental justice movement, which started in 1982 (Skelton and Miller
2016), the reproductive justice movement, which started in 1997 (Sister Song n.d.), the disability
justice movement, which started in 2005 (Wikipedia 2020; Piepzna-Samarasinha 2019), and the
healing justice movement, which started in 2007 (Piepzna-Samarasinha 2016). Note that the oldest
two, environmental justice and reproductive justice, are most closely tied. Loretta Ross describes the
reproductive justice framework as addressing "the ability of any woman to determine her own reproductive destiny" and argues this is inextricably "linked directly to the conditions in her community—
and these conditions are not just a matter of individual choice and access" (Ross 2007).

not already well-connected, well-resourced, and relatively well-assimilated with individuals and within institutions that already have power. So justice movements seek to shift the focus of political fights toward issues of access and capability and away from the distribution of rights. The disability justice pioneer Leah Lakshmi Piepzna-Samarasinha writes,

> If a healing justice space is all or mostly white [people], it's no different from any "mainstream alternative" white space. Healing justice was created as a term and a movement in part because a lot of "alternative healing" was dominated by white middle- to upper-middle class people doing culturally appropriative work with nary an analysis of race and a high fee for service. (Piepzna-Samarasinha 2019, 105)

She goes on to say,

> If white healers slap "healing justice" on their work but are still using the healer traditions of some folks' cultures that aren't their own, are primarily working with and treating white middle-class and upper-class people, are unaware or don't recognize that healing justice was created by Black and brown femmes, are not working with a critical stance and understanding of how colonization, racism, and ableism are healing issues, it ain't healing justice. (106)

One of the differences between healing justice and other frameworks that promote wellness is that healing justice practitioners are quick to point out that their work is not rooted in "self-care," but is instead underpinned by "collective care." This shift in emphasis is one that is meant to highlight the importance of interdependence, commitment, and accountability to health. It is absolutely important that people have the material resources, time, and space to care for themselves, but they do so as individuals in context. People care for themselves so that they can be ready to "show up" and "hold space" in small or large ways, when their talents, knowledge, wisdom, or action are needed. Piepzna-Samarasinha writes that "collective care means shifting our organizations to be ones where people feel fine if they get sick, cry, have needs, start late because the bus broke down, move slower, ones where there's food at meetings, people work from home—and these aren't things we apologize for. It is the way we do the work, which centers disabled-femme-of-color ways of being in the world . . . where we actually care for each other and don't leave each other behind" (108).

In 2017, the Black Lives Matter Global Network Foundation published a Healing Action Toolkit that spoke specifically about the ways that Healing Justice is essential to the political work movement organizations undertake. The statement of principles opening the manual unfolds as follows:

Black Healing and Wellness Are Essential to Our Liberation—State violence and systems of oppression traumatize us and our communities, and make it simultaneously impossible for us to fully heal. We have the inherent right to access healing and be free of institutions and systems that explicitly harm and undermine our capacity to live with our full humanity, connection and purpose.

Liberation Is in Our Practice—Loosely defined, liberation is freedom from limitations. Liberation is not gained by the outcomes of a singular political event or destination, its roots live deep inside us and in all of our relationships. We know that our politic is revealed in our practice, in our intimacy and communication with one another. Through healing, we free ourselves from the oppression of respectability, and ground our interactions in love and accountability.

Black Wellness Is Self-Determination—We recognize the sacredness, brilliance, and inherent worth in every Black body. Healing justice calls us to be changed in our consciousness and transform the internalized practices of ableism, heteropatriarchy, classism and all other forms of oppression that place value and order on our bodies. We see Black self-determination as bringing our communities into our whole, varied and vibrant expressions. (Black Lives Matter 2017)

Je Naé Taylor, a member of the BYP100 Healing and Safety Council (HSC), explains the centrality and integration of healing justice into movement work: "We know that healing justice work is not in addition to political organizing or direct action. All of this work—direct action, electoral organizing— is healing justice work" (Taylor and Green 2018). Marshall (Kai M.) Green expresses how the development of the Healing and Safety Council is a challenge of both imagination and implementation, explaining:

It's a really interesting challenge because it's basically trying to create a world and a way of being and rules and regulations for that world—how do we want to treat each other? How do we want to feel? What do we need to do in order to feel the way we want to feel? What space do we need to heal? In order to create and produce this world that we want—and like Je Naé said this is a practice space for the world that we want so, how do we do it in our organization? That means really figuring out, what do we do when harm happens? Do we have a method or mode that we can implement to deal with that? How do we *not* fall into things like replicating [the approach] of the State?

Taylor explains that as the HSC has developed methods of intervention, they've had to be very deliberate about implementing core principles. She explains:

We've had to do that through multiple entry points—we have cheers and chants, we have a manual, we have multiple agendas that we've created as an organization and the thing is [you have a lot of diversity] you have Black folks who don't read English, Black folks who don't speak English, Black folks with disabilities—how do I make sure the message "I love being Black"—how do I make sure the transformative justice message is clear? . . . I have to think about all Black people. So, that means we are very intentional about creating as many platforms and forums to get our message out there and we don't limit ourselves to one form of organizing—to do that would be to fail Black people. (Taylor and Green 2018)

Conclusion

Herein I have argued that care, in the Movement for Black Lives, constitutes the backbone of the political philosophy of radical Black feminist pragmatism while at the same time serving as a politics—that is, a way of orienting and organizing governance. The politics of care is a radical departure from enlightenment theories of politics for several reasons.

First, the politics of care begins with the concrete and particular and builds to the abstract and general, identifying philosophical and political problems from the evidence of the lived experience of the marginalized in a given society. This inductive approach puts the question of what people's lives are actually like at the center of conceptualizing and solving political problems. This fundamental orientation means that the politics of care does not begin in either philosophical or juridical questions of right, but instead starts with the question, Are the most marginalized able to live and thrive, and if not, why not? How can we build a politics in which such thriving is possible?

Second, the politics of care suggests a different theory of relation than exists in the dominant modern theories of politics on both the left and right, moving away from analyses that turn on the fairness of distribution and the existence and adequacy of rights, and instead embraces the point of view that because people matter, they are entitled to care, and, as such, care must be the main subject of governance. Furthermore, the understanding of care that operates in this political philosophy is not paternalistic. It is instead grounded in the notion that people understand what they need in order to develop and fulfill their capacities and are perfectly capable of coming up with solutions to the political problems that inhibit the flourishing of their lives given the proper access to necessary resources.

Third, the resources critical to human life are considered to include material things necessary for physical sustenance, like adequate income, housing, food, and education, but also to exceed these material items and include psychological health and well-being. This notion of well-being incorporates the wisdom of healing justice, a theory of wellness that contends that oppression causes trauma, which requires both individual and community attention in order to be addressed, and further that a part of the treatment for these oppression-induced traumas must be the dismantling of the structural conditions that have allowed harms to accrue, compound, and proliferate across populations.

The political project of breaking down harmful systems and institutions and rebuilding healthier ones requires an orientation toward justice that centers the prevention of harm and an emphasis on repair when a person or group experiences harm. This emphasis on repair requires techniques of redress that focus on the restoration of relationships rather than on punishment. Such emphases make abolition a necessary aspect of the politics of care.

In sum, the politics of care offers a unique way to engage in politics because it begins in a different place than either liberalism or socialism—though it may borrow aspects of either—and understands the purpose of politics to be creating the conditions under which everyone, starting with those who have been marginalized and subject to oppression and its accompanying traumas, can have access to the care that they require to develop their capacities, secure their well-being, build communities, and determine the course of their lives.

4

The Art of Organizing

The mandate for Black people in this time!
Is to avenge the suffering of our ancestors!
To earn the respect of future generations!
And be willing to be transformed in the service of the work!
—Mary Hooks, Southerners on New Ground (SONG)

Radical Black feminist pragmatism and its key tenet, the politics of care, are illuminatingly expressed in the Movement for Black Lives' approach to organizing and organization-building. As discussed in the foregoing chapters, radical Black feminist pragmatism (RBFP) is fundamentally anchored by the notion that democratic politics has been diminished by the dominant emphasis on rights, procedure, and participation to the exclusion of considerations of capacity, political understanding, pragmatic imagination, and political change. Organizing is the political activity that brings these less-studied and less-discussed political activities into focus. In this way, the Movement for Black Lives (M4BL) takes up the concern most closely articulated in philosophical pragmatism that "the conscious adjustment of the new to the old *is* imagination" (Dewey [1934] 2005, 283), and that this kind of imagination is critical to political organizing. This point is critical because there can be no practicable solutions to pressing and long-vexing structural and political problems without pragmatic, socially intelligent imagination and the action that it can galvanize.

Political organizing, which is what leaders in social movements do, funds the capacity for political actors to recognize themselves as political subjects capable of acting, in the Arendtian sense; that is, by creating something unexpected and new (Arendt [1958] 1998). In other words, organizing is not primarily about assembling a mass of people for a political cause (mobilization), nor "turning up" in defiance of authorities though protest (activism). Instead, organizing is fundamentally the process that allows people to be "transformed in the service of the work" as Mary Hooks (2016), a lead organizer in Southerners on New Ground, puts it. I argue that Hooks's refrain gives us a framework to understand the understudied yet unique and politically powerful phenomenon that is political organizing—an activity that is distinct from either mobilization or activism in that its result is not to *do a thing* but to *become the kind of person who does what is to be done.* In this way, organizing is of critical import to democracy itself, because it is a process through which people learn what membership in a democratic polity must entail and reminds them that they have both power and responsibility in the undertaking that is self-governance.

The following proceeds in two main parts. The first contains a theory of political organizing that makes clear how it is distinct from activism and mobilization. In it, I discuss the American traditions of organizing, then describe how radical Black feminist pragmatism incorporates and exceeds these traditions, and finally explain why organizing is a crucial aspect of democratic change, as such, particularly if we understand the nature and process of democratic change through John Dewey's pragmatist lens. The second part focuses on the organizational structure of the Movement for Black Lives. In it, I detail the movement's organizational structure, organizational culture, and the interorganizational environment present in the movement.

Part 1: A Theory of Political Organizing

Political organizing is a process of meeting, engagement, education, and preparation for collective action that people undertake in the service of some public end. There are two main intellectual traditions of political organizing in America: the community-based organization (CBO) model first articulated by legendary Chicago organizer Saul Alinsky—a tradition carried on today in CBOs like the Industrial Areas Foundation—and the Folk School model developed by Myles Horton and his collaborators at the Highlander Folk School (now Highlander Research and Education Center), most notably Black organizer Septima Clarke, who served as both the school's education director and a leader in the NAACP and the Southern Christian Leadership Conference (SCLC). Out of these traditions, the Movement for Black Lives has crafted its own unique approach, steeped in radical Black feminist pragmatism, recently codified by Charlene Carruthers, the former director of

Black Youth Project 100 (BYP100), in her book *Unapologetic: A Black, Queer, and Feminist Mandate for Radical Movements*.

It is important to clarify what organizing is by being clear about what it is not. Organizing is distinct from both activism and mobilization. Activism is chiefly characterized by the activity of protest; it need not include the analysis of power, cultivation of leadership, or plans for further future action. Mobilization, on the other hand, is the assembly of people who already have the requisite understanding and skill for the completion of a public task. People are mobilized when they have previous education, experience, or training for the task at hand. One mobilizes soldiers to be deployed or registered voters to show up at the polls. Political mobilization has often been explored as though it is synonymous with organizing (Rosenstone and Hansen 1993; Green and Schwam-Baird 2016), but individuals who have not been either socialized (in early life) or organized into politics cannot be mobilized; they must first undergo a process of engagement and education that shifts their understanding of a public problem or cause and their ability to effect it.

Regardless of the tradition they come out of, organizers prepare people to relate, understand, and act. Therefore, the first activity of organizing is to develop "interpersonal and sound relationships" that can serve as the basis for social engagement, political education, and collective action (Carruthers 2018, 91). The way those relationships are constructed will vary, but most organizers agree that there can be no engagement, education, and activation of people toward public action without finding ways to relate under reciprocal conditions of trust and support. The kinds of relationships that organizers aim to establish resemble the political friendship Aristotle detailed in the *Politics*, which consists of goodwill animated and directed by common purpose. In addition to cultivating political friendship, organizers seek to develop into leaders some of the people they meet and establish political friendship with. Leaders are organizers who are responsible for helping to bring more people into the particular understanding of the world and events subscribed to by the organization and/or movement. They are also tasked with action, with initiating new relationships of political friendship, gathering resources, and executing public plans. Charlene Carruthers indicates that one of the key responsibilities of leaders is to tell "complete stories" that help people hold the contradictions of our histories together "in order to make more informed and strategic decisions as a movement" (Carruthers 2018, 45). Michael

Gecan, a noted organizer in the CBO school, describes leaders as people who are able to use "a combination of power, pressure, and patience to create the conditions that make it possible" to take action (Gecan 2004, 15). These activities of cultivating broad understanding and planning and executing public actions are key tasks of leadership in the context of political friendship.

The question remains: What does it mean to take action, to act and act effectively? Organizers take a broadly Arendtian view of action. That is to say that action, for an organizer, is not just the activity of protest, but is also the process by which those who are in a relation of political friendship work together to make claims, develop their means, and secure their ends. For Arendt, activity is judged to be action when "it disclose[s] the identity of the agent, affirm[s] the reality of the world, and actualize[s] our capacity for freedom" (d'Entreves 2019). The action we take shows who we are, what we understand, and what we are willing to do, to author (imagine), to change, in order to bring those things into alignment in the world we share. We exhibit our capacity for freedom not by making choices between given alternatives, nor merely through the exercise of our will, but instead by utilizing our natal ability to begin. Arendt writes, "[I]t is in the nature of beginning that something new is started which cannot be expected from whatever may have happened before. This character of startling unexpectedness is inherent in all beginnings. . . . The fact that man is capable of action means that the unexpected can be expected from him, that he is able to perform what is infinitely improbable" (Arendt [1958] 1998, 171). Action, then, is what Lorella Praelli, president of Community Change Action, calls "the art of the possible." She explains:

> I came into this work because I was undocumented and I was afraid and I was ashamed and I lived with a tremendous amount of fear. And before I understood that there was a policy fight that needed to be had and needed to be won, I needed to go through my own liberation and my own transformation. And that's why policy alone is not possible, that's why policy fights alone are not enough because doing the movement building, the deep organizing work on the ground, and having that be felt in D.C. and driving and shaping our national politics is [about] what really moves someone from a state of hopelessness into a state of hope and power and fearlessness and possibility. And so, I believe that organizing is the art of the possible. (Praelli 2019)

When one says organizing is the art of the possible, it means that it is the method by which people relate action (new and unexpected) and consequence (outcome). This is not a plainly causal relationship but is instead a pragmatically imaginative one. What becomes possible when I see myself differently, when I hear my name differently, when I cannot be hailed in the old way? What becomes possible when I see the context of my community differently, when I see my fellows differently, when I perceive the world differently? What is possible is certainly constrained by material and structural realities, but possibilities are only *foreclosed* by our inability to perceive how to get from here to there. This perception is not only about apprehending, but also about acting (and acting in concert) to create the conditions that will allow new possibilities. Organizing is meant to induce an experience of the kind of socially intelligent "reconstruction" of the self in the world that can make possible today things that were not possible yesterday and that can push the horizon of political possibilities farther than we are accustomed to perceiving.

It is important to note that while all organizers do the work of cultivating political friendship with and between people as well as developing and preparing leaders (who are members of the communities effected by some common problem) to act, and most organizers agree that building power is at the center of their work, the notions of what counts as right relationships of political friendship, power building, and action can and do differ.

The CBO Style and the Folk School Way

Those who organize in the Alinsky tradition exhibit a hyper-localism and an allergy to ideology that is quite distinctive. In this tradition, relationships conducive to organizing are "public relationships"; power-building is purposely devoid of historiography, ideology, or expansive vision; and action is strictly about demanding concrete results from decision-makers who can deliver them. Public relationships are those that are genuine and interpersonal, but are aimed at orienting people to "to step out, not to be consumers or props or spectators but to be players in the unfolding drama of public life" (Gecan 2004, 22). For Gecan, the organizer's main tool is *meeting* (not meetings, he's careful to note). Organizers "take the time to meet one to one with others, to hear their interests and dreams and fears, to understand *why* people do what they do or don't do what they don't do" (21).

This approach to organizing is widespread and practiced by CBOs all over the country, constituting a wide field of civic and political activism. However, the organizations that make up this sector are often invisible to the general public (Swarts 2008). This inconspicuousness is not accidental: CBOs often remain locally focused with decentralized decision-making apparatuses on purpose. Even long-established CBOs with dozens of small affiliates in cities and towns all over America, many with impressive accomplishments under their belts, such as Gecan's own Industrial Areas Foundation, PICO National Network, and Gamaliel Foundation, do not publicize themselves and have no agendas outside their local communities. Those who organize in this tradition believe that political organizing must be unrelentingly local in its focus in order to be effective: addressing practical local problems rather than larger structural issues and "building power" block by block (Alinsky [1971] 1989).

Along with this localism, Alinsky promulgated a deep suspicion of the usefulness of ideology to achieve concrete objectives, refusing to define his goals in abstract, normative terms. This aversion to ideology as a basis for organizing often translates, in Alinsky-inspired groups, to an organizational culture characterized by distaste for the abstract notion of social movement and the expressive protest tactics that sometimes accompany them. Michael Gecan vividly illustrates what he takes to be the pitfalls of expressive demonstrations by describing an anti-globalization protest he witnessed in 2001 this way:

> Five people stood [ ] tor Street. Two had splashed black pai [ ] lack paint on their faces. They writhed [ ] nonstrator pounded a drum and a you [ ] crowd. Twenty-five cops eyed the scen [ ] ing and stairs, their nightsticks in their [ ] heir nightsticks.... [W]hat was their [ ] a hastily painted sign: "Save the U'[ ] to Fidelity Capital. The woman with th [ ] derstood.... For all their choreographed movement, the demonstrators seemed remarkably static. Still life: *Activists on a Manhattan Street....* What crystalized for me that day in Manhattan was this: what I was observing was not an action at all, but a reenactment. (Gecan 2004, 50–51).

[handwritten note: Don't you need both Alinsky-style movement and protest collaboration? public private]

Gecan thinks activists are ridiculous—that they are mere "high minded" critics with "rational analysis, supporting data, and six enlightened recommendations" who refuse to really "enter the arena" and "be held accountable, not just hold others accountable" (9). Activists, for Gecan, don't build power or take action, they "reenact" protest to feel morally virtuous, not with the intention of "acting effectively," which must involve getting a *reaction* or response from decision-makers authorized to deliver what organized people demand. In an Arendtian vein, in order to count as action, the activity has to produce or provoke something new. Action must declare the identity of the organized group in such a way that they cannot be ignored because they are bringing the reality of the world into focus and underlining their human capacity for performing and producing the unexpected and "infinitely improbable" (Arendt [1958] 1998, 178). Or, in Dewey's terms, action is different than re-enactment because it is something that people *experience* in that it involves a reconstruction of the perceived relationship between thought/speech/action and consequence, rather than something people can *recognize* as fitting a category they already understand and can compartmentalize and ignore. Re-enactments don't make observers think, because they feel they've seen it before and already have a heuristic that allows them to set it aside. "To have an experience," on the other hand, "[t]he action and its consequence must be joined in perception. This relationship is what gives meaning" (Dewey [1934] 2005, 46).

Gecan, unlike Dewey, is not convinced of the significance of meaning, but values action because it has the potential to build power by inducing the respect required for reciprocity. Outside these conditions, "[t]hey don't even see you. They never learn your name. . . . there's not even a 'you' to respond to. . . . Without power, you can only be a supplicant, a serf, a victim, or a wishful thinker who soon begins to whine." He goes on to say, "Power in the new millennium is the same as power when Thucydides was writing about the Melians and the Athenians. It is still the ability to act. And it still comes in two basic forms—organized people and organized money" (Gecan 2004, 36).

The Alinsky school views ideology as suspicious in the same way it disdains activism. According to this thinking, ideology does not engage "the world as it is," but instead gets unproductively hung up on what ought to be. Gecan writes, "[Y]ou can't get near what *should* be, not even close, unless you build and use power, unless you manipulate that power so that you can slog through the mud of the world as it *is*, unless you're willing to push and tug the teachers and mayors and pols and cops and yourself and your own institutions in the direction of what ought to be" (Gecan 2004, 36). He adds, "It's not a question of right or wrong. It's a question of what is, what reality is, and what happens to you when you meet this reality. . . . You're going to have to have enough organized people and enough organized money, enough discipline and enough luck, to *make it happen*. That's the way it works in the world as it is" (36, 37).

Gecan and others who organize in the CBO tradition can afford this distance from ideology partly because of the scale at which they are committed to engaging: discrete, local, practical. Employing transcendent principles, imagination, and vision are not important because it is assumed that ordinary people's "real interests" are commonsensical and their goals are moderate. What organized power is for, in this view, is to signal "dissatisfaction with the way the two other major sectors in society—the private and public—are handling certain matters. And . . . present an implicit challenge: you are ready and willing to show other sectors how to tackle those matters more effectively" (Gecan 2004, 8). To that end, organizers are to use their skill sets to "create the conditions that make it possible for people to move from the margins into the social and economic mainstream" (15). This kind of organizing utilizes no particular political philosophy, discounts vision, and does not hold imagination in very high esteem.

Myles Horton, a contemporary and friend of Saul Alinsky, saw this approach as short-sighted. Horton scholar Mie Inouye writes,

> Horton thought that movements thrived when they were directed toward ends that transcended concrete objectives and could never be fully achieved. Setting an impossibly ambitious goal enabled participants to transform beyond what they could currently imagine. This was one key difference between Horton and his friend Saul Alinsky, who thought that participants in social movements were motivated by the experience of attaining concrete goals. Horton argued that it was dangerous to motivate people with the prospect of winning because this allowed narrow self-interest to creep in and take the movement in undemocratic directions. He thought this tendency accounted for the fate of Alinsky's Back of the Yards community organization, which began discriminating against black residents after Alinsky left Chicago. By contrast, if people were motivated by unreachable goals, like democracy and brotherhood, they would become committed to the unending work of transforming themselves, which

would guide them away from narrow self-interest and toward increasingly inclusive social ends. (Inouye 2019, 19)

So Horton's organization, the Highlander Folk School, took a different tack than Alinsky. He believed society had to be transformed economically (abolish capitalism), politically (decentralize participatory government), and socially (forge a culture of brotherhood/solidarity), but that this could only be done "if those who were most oppressed by existing institutions sought to transform them" (Inouye 2019, 12). They would only do so if they received a kind of education that could make them less dependent on established authorities and more confident that their own experiences could generate knowledge worth acting upon. Horton had a specific conception of what characterizes experience as a source of knowledge that was influenced by John Dewey. Horton knew Dewey only slightly but was deeply familiar with his scholarship, and the two men admired each other's work.[1] So it stands to reason that Horton developed his notion of liberatory education taking into account Dewey's idea of growth through experience (Dewey [1934] 2005). Dewey defines experience as the meaning people make from their active encounters with the world. Experience that leads to growth must, in Dewey's estimation, involve "an element of undergoing, of suffering in its large sense . . . otherwise, there would be no taking in of what preceded. For 'taking in' in any vital experience is something more than placing something at the top of consciousness over what was previously known. It involves reconstruction which may be painful." He goes on to distinguish experience from what he calls "recognition," which is a more frequent process in which we "fall back, as upon a stereotype, upon some previously formed scheme" (54). Experiences that lead to liberatory learning involve the active reconciliation between what one thought they knew and what they have newly discovered through an encounter with the world. This process is essential for liberation for two reasons. First, and most obviously, it allows people to learn new things, but second, and more importantly, this kind of experience teaches people how to become intelligent. Intelligence is the factor that allows people to vary their actions in response to new situations and requirements or past experience. The kind of education that encourages intelligence helps people learn how to navigate the tensions between what they

---

[1] This is evidenced by their correspondence in the 1930s. Mie Inouye unearthed a letter dated September 27, 1933, in which Dewey refers to the Highlander Folk School as "one of the most hopeful social-education programs I know of" (quoted in Inouye 2019).

thought they knew, what they have undergone in order to learn, and how they should act given new knowledge or circumstances. The role of teachers in this tradition is not that of an expert but instead that of chaperone. They are to hold the space, ask questions, and affirm the participants/students' experiential expertise.

With the background understanding informed by Dewey, Horton came to believe that showing people how to engage in this kind of liberatory learning was the best way to help them regard themselves as efficacious political actors, and that such education would help people learn to be self-governing in the way that democracy requires. It is in this way that education is transformative—not in the sense of a single metamorphosis from passive individual into democratic citizen, but in the sense of an *inculcation into an active way of being in the world* that opens and attunes people to how knowledge should be derived from experience. This provides them with a continual source of education that they can draw from to analyze their circumstances, solve problems, and invent solutions as needed.

Having experienced what Horton called "yeasty education" (Inouye 2019, 14), people would also be able to share their way of learning and experiencing with others, seeding a dynamic capacity to learn from experience and act on that knowledge rather than encouraging them to rely on a set of edicts derived from doctrine. This kind of education became the basis of the Folk School way of organizing. Its aim was to empower people to trust their own experience-based learning as the basis for action that could address the needs and affect the conditions that impacted their lives.

Organizing in the Tradition of Radical Black Feminism

Organizing in the Movement for Black Lives shares more with the Folk School way than the CBO style, but traces of both traditions can be found in the contemporary movement. This is in no small part because Highlander still exists as an active education center that trains organizers across several different movements, including the Movement for Black Lives, to engage people in liberatory education. This infusion of ideas is evident in the thinking of members of M4BL. For example, Charlene Carruthers writes that "being in movement work taught me how to take information, put it into context, and produce my own knowledge to understand current conditions and to create a vision for the future." She goes on to say, "[O]ur movement taught me the value of study, rigorous thinking, and discipline to take action. . . . My journey has been mentally, physically, emotionally, and spiritually challenging," and "[m]y beliefs today have evolved because I made a conscious choice, often as the result of direct agitation, to see through different lenses," a process that "continues today" (Carruthers 2018, 8, 11). Nevertheless, M4BL infuses the values of radical Black feminist pragmatism into the twenty-first-century approach it has developed. The key elements of RBFP that give organizing in the movement a distinct flavor are the centrality of imagination and the necessity of proceeding according to a politics of care.

Liberatory projects require both concrete campaigns to win better conditions in the world as it is and the employment of pragmatic imagination, which is the ambition and vision to "dream a world," as Langston Hughes put it, in which the most marginalized can live and thrive. Pragmatic imagination is imagination toward action: it is the activity of imagining what a world that ensures the safety and supports the flourishing of those who have been systematically oppressed would look like, and imagining the possible practical pathways from the world as it is to the just world that is imagined. The sharing of this imagination and the possible pathways to make it manifest is what constitutes vision. Carruthers writes that "[i]t is within the spaces of imagination, the dream spaces, that liberatory practices are born and grow, leading to the space to act and to transform" (Carruthers 2018, 25). Organizing toward liberation is necessarily an imaginative process that is shared with the goal of inducing a collective commitment to a common vision. The place of imagination in organizing in the movement tradition should not be understated; this is because both those who are doing the organizing and those being organized are understood to be systematically marginalized by white supremacy, patriarchy, and capitalism, not merely improperly left out of the procedures and privileges guaranteed to those who are centered as proper rights-bearers. This is because marginalization is understood to be purposeful, not accidental, with the many marked by non-normative race, gender, class, and/or sexuality made to bear the cost of relative prosperity for the few white, cis male, upper-class individuals who are unconditionally regarded as unmarked universal humans. Under such conditions, it is necessary but insufficient to target discrete policies and practices. Instead, what is required is the rethinking of how we ought to understand ourselves in the world and, correspondingly, how we ought to remake the world for the selves that we are not yet. For Carruthers, "the Black imagination lives . . . in our ability to create alternatives," and "those organizing political education programs [need to] reimagine what is essential and foundational" because to do otherwise would be to "stop believing in a world where we live with dignity" and instead content ourselves with the lethally damaging notion that "the social order will not change" and "it is okay to just keep holding on to the bottom rung" (Carruthers 2018, 39, 51, and 38).

Therefore, in the Black feminist tradition, pragmatic imagination and the vision(s) it gives rise to are critical to the practices of meeting, sharing stories, mutual education, and ongoing agitation that constitute the activity of organizing. It is important here to distinguish vision from ideology. Ideology is a system of ideas and ideals that make up a coherent whole that constitutes a canonical set of beliefs that is resistant to change. Movement organizers avoid indoctrinating people into any one particular ideology, just as those in the Alinksy tradition do, but for different reasons. Gecan and those in the CBO tradition believe ideology is inauthentic and that the things ordinary people want to fight for are material and will always be self-evident.

M4BL organizers, on the other hand, know that the value of the lives of Black people are not self-evident or universally legible in the hegemonic culture of anti-Blackness that has characterized modernity. It is not even always legible to Black people themselves, hence the deep culture of movement promoting unapologetic (rather than "respectable") Blackness. Rather, organizers in the movement and in the tradition of Black feminism have a philosophy that is both radical and pragmatic; that is, a way of thinking together that is based on the principles of care and questioning, but that also assumes that the understanding, ideas, and goals of those participating will and should change over time.

Building relationships in the M4BL tradition of organizing includes the cultivation of public relationships but is also characterized by what I have discussed in this book as a *politics of care*. Let us briefly review the characteristics of the politics of care as they relate to organizing. First, those practicing a politics of care commit to centering the most marginalized. A common refrain in the movement is that those who are closest to pain should be closest to power. That means that the people that are most impacted by deprivation due to their position at the intersection of multiple social and economic hierarchies that ignore, discipline, criminalize, discriminate against, dominate, and/or oppress them ought also to be the people whose diagnoses, critiques, and imagined solutions should be given priority. Second, the politics of care is based upon an understanding that our selves are always situated, which means that to account for one's self is also to account for one's social condition, location, and connectedness. Structural conditions and interpersonal interdependence are thus taken as always relevant to problems and their solutions. Further, the ways those facts influence our experience of the world and our motivation and ability to organize and become mobilized are considered indispensable information for the political project. Third, the politics of care acknowledges that oppression is not only unjust, it is also traumatizing. So attention to healing—personal and collective—is a requisite for effective political organizing. This view is often referred to as "healing justice." Healing justice is an acknowledgement that oppression causes harm that is more than distributional, instrumental, or infrastructural. Instead, healing justice acknowledges that "our movements must invest time and money" in identifying how "we can holistically respond to and intervene in generational trauma and violence, and . . . bring collective practices that can impact and transform the consequences of oppression on our bodies, hearts, and minds" (Carruthers 2018, 75). A fourth characteristic of the politics of care is a conception of justice that is reparative and restorative rather than punitive or carceral. Fifth, and finally, this politics is characterized by a commitment to the defense of joy as a personal and collective necessity as well as a political resource.

The formation of interpersonal relationships under the rubric of a politics of care takes place in a register that is explicitly both emotional and political. Deborah Gould has referred to this kind of relationship-building as "emotion work," which comprises the practices of "authorization" and "incitement" that create the "emotional habitus" of a movement (Gould 2012, 109). Gould explains that, "in a world where impersonal, abstract forces" of oppression "shape daily lives and can generate sentiments of being out of control, of inefficacy, of helplessness and hopelessness, social movements are often a space that engenders rich and textured counterfeelings" (210). One of the ways that organizers do this is by telling stories. Carruthers writes that "the crux of grassroots organizing" is sharing stories about our "challenge, choice, and outcome," because "our stories are the mediums for us to understand ourselves and understand other people" (Carruthers 2018, 94). Organizing is "rooted in relationships between individuals working toward the same goal, often with various tactics" (89).

The work of organizing is political, but it should also be noted that organizers can work within any domain—cultural spaces, issue-based campaigns, civic clubs, etc.—and they can also work from left or right. Indeed, "some people organize to *restrict* access to human dignity for others";

however, organizers in M4BL explicitly work to "dismantle systems of oppression and replace them with systems designed to allow collective dignity and power" (Carruthers 2018, 89). This focus on systems is important because it marks an important divergence from the CBO model of hyper-local focus on discrete and concrete problems that can be addressed by individual decision-makers. For the movement, the goal of organizing is liberation, not just building power. Carruthers writes that there is a "distinction between freedom and liberation" because individual freedom does not necessarily correspond to "collective access to our full humanity" (25). Further, liberation is an ongoing project and cannot be fully secured by the granting of rights or winning a particular policy fight. Liberation is, therefore, "a perpetual project of creating and maintaining right relationships between people and the land we inhabit. And our articulation of how we get there—how we liberate ourselves—matters" (102).

In sum, bringing people together to act is not merely a matter of convincing them that their interests are in accord. Interests are a matter of perspective. One of the major downfalls of the political Left has been the belief that material interests are somehow self-evident. This is empirically not the case. Not only do people interpret material reality differently, especially when causes are complex, but people also use motivated reasoning and prioritize decision-rules differently based on how they are used to making sense of the world (Jones 1994; Taber and Lodge 2006; Nyhan and Reifler 2010; Jones and Baumgartner 2005). In addition, the current political economy has caused the pace of life to be increasingly incompatible with civic pursuits, and the expectation that everyone should be working or available to work at all times leaves precious little time for civic engagement (Temin 2018). As a result, acting together is something that often goes not only undone, but *unthought*.

That is why organizers insist on the importance of meeting people where they are. This is the only way to build relationships and develop the capacity to act. The capacity to act involves several things: basic knowledge, ability to analyze, confidence in assessment, and assurance in the group authorization to act. The process of cultivating these capacities is what Charlene Carruthers means when she insists that organizers must be in the business of developing leaders. I argue that developing this capacity for public political leadership is not only a matter of giving people the right information, but is also and more fundamentally about socializing people into a new kind of subjectivity—one in which they think of themselves as efficacious political actors who are both capable of acting and responsible to act in concert for political change. That is, organizers are not only charged with convincing people to act, in the vein of those who mobilize, but are also charged with the incredible task of convincing people to *become the kinds of subjects who think to act politically* and, further, think to act *together* in solidarity.

The question is, how do organizers accomplish such lofty goals? The answer is complicated. Organizers' chief function is to prepare: to prepare people to relate, and especially to relate across difference; to prepare people to develop and trust in their own power analysis; to prepare people to imagine, plan, and execute collective actions that will have political impact. All these activities of preparation require a variety of distinct aptitudes and skills. These skill sets are not static but adaptive, because the organizer must "meet the people where they are." That is, prefab scripts and predetermined goals will only get the organizer so far, because their true goal should be to develop a relationship with those being organized—such that they learn through listening and providing guidance that is responsive to the concerns expressed, while at the same time adding the value of experience, further analysis, challenge, and expertise. Put differently, the organizer cannot fathom at the outset what will be required to organize people as they enter a particular setting, even when they are native to that setting. Therefore, organizing requires a talent for deep listening, patience, flexibility, toughness, persistence, and finesse. Done well, it is an art.

Organizing 101: Sound Relationships, Structural Analysis, Building Power, Public Action

The first activity of organizing is to seek "interpersonal and sound relationships" with both other organizers and those being organized (Carruthers 2018, 91). The way those relationships are constructed will vary based on the group, but most organizers agree that there can be no engagement, education, and activation of people toward public action without finding ways to relate under reciprocal conditions of trust and support.

Organizers most effectively build relationships through one-on-one meetings—the essential building block of developing civic relationships that can become politically potent. During one-on-one meetings, organizers aim to make initial connections by learning what the participants care about. The professional organizer is trained to ask questions and listen in an attempt to understand the interests, values, and motivation of their conversation partner. These one-on-ones are not task-based—they are not about convincing people to join an organization or advocate for a cause—but rather are meant to probe what folks' public interests and troubles are, and to share the story, motivations, and values of the organizer.

Paraphrasing Aristotle, Michael Gecan calls these kinds of relationships "public friendship." Friendship of this sort is not based on interpersonal intimacy, but is instead a relationship of utility, based on mutual respect and recognition, good faith interactions, and the implicit intention to come to concordant understanding so that the friends can act together or for one another as circumstances require. Those who are not formally trained organizers may establish these kinds of relationships as a part of their normal disposition and mode of interaction with people. These sorts of people are what organizers call "organic leaders," and they are invaluable for the strength and scale of organizing activity and the actions that may result. Indeed, the cultivation of leaders is central to organizing.

Leaders are key people in the population being organized who are able to take responsibility for helping to bring more people into the particular understanding of the world and events that are subscribed to by the organization and/or movement. They are also tasked with action; that is, with initiating new relationships of political friendship, gathering resources, and executing public plans.

Michael Gecan describes leaders as people who are able to use "a combination of power, pressure, and patience to create the conditions that make it possible" to take action (Gecan 2004, 15). It is part of the organizer's job to identify and cultivate such leaders, because they exponentially increase the depth, scope, and scale of the relationships that can be built in the community, group, or organization that will attempt collective action. The veteran union organizer and sociologist Jane McAlevey (2016, 39) underscores this point, arguing that the quality and capacity of leaders in the organized group is the decisive factor in whether the organized will be able to win, not the magnitude of material resources available to the group. This is because leaders give the group the deepest access to what the social movements scholar Doug McAdam calls "indigenous resources," the interpersonal and institutional connections, interest, physical space to meet, and time for curious and considered conversation. McAlevey points out that "systematically structuring their many strong connections—family, religious groups, sports teams, [social] clubs ... into their campaigns" is the best method for ordinary people to challenge the powerful (McAlevey 2016, 29). It is through these multilayered connections that people develop a sense of solidarity, which is simply the political friendship of an avowed group committed to struggling together for a collective good or common cause.

Although political friendships are not private, interpersonal affairs, they are (and must be for their utility) emotional. The formation of political friendships takes place in a register that explicitly refuses the dichotomy between cognition and emotion. Instead, there is acknowledgement of the fact that our understanding of the world and our judgments about our place, purpose, and possibility are the result of the interaction between emotional and analytic information.

Developing relationships of political friendship is not only an end in itself but is also the basis for the activities of preparation that the organizer seeks to undertake; namely, cultivating the capacity for power analysis and "building power." As Charlene Carruthers notes, "not everybody comes into the organization . . . [a] radical and revolutionary. Through engaging in the work that we do people become more politicized and they get clearer reads on the situation at hand and the role that we have in transforming it" (Carruthers and Denvir 2017). That is, people develop an analysis of the conditions that led to the grievances that they have come to recognize as attributable.

However, this is a complicated process because structural oppression does not have easy, linear causal stories with clear individual masterminds. The villains that M4BL is confronting are police who murder and prosecutors who turn a blind eye, yes, but these villains cannot be eradicated without taking on the hegemonic logics of white supremacy, patriarchy, and capitalism as it exists today. This is because the perpetrators of these wrongs are not the originators of the practices that lead to and reproduce oppression (Armacost 2020). Devising ways to combat an opponent that cannot be vanquished by removing a single player or institution from public life requires a theory of power rooted in an understanding of the concept of structural relation.

A structural relation is the connection between the individual and all those elements in society—including other individuals, institutions, law, social norms, and cultural practices—that provide the context for the arrangement of the individual's life in ways that are both independent of and affected by the individual's actions (Woodly 2015b). Power analysis, then, is the ability to perceive and understand structural relations in general, and to develop a theory (or set of theories) about the way the group being organized is related and separated—to each other and to the rest of the world—by those relations.

In order to develop these analyses, participants study together. One of the things that is underappreciated about organizing in social movements is that it creates spaces of constant study. "Political education" is not a stand-in for ideological indoctrination or public relations. Political education in the organizing traditions arising from the civil rights movement is very literal: it means to research, to read (alone and together), to hold seminars and reading groups where ideas are discussed and debated. Movement organizing is an intellectual endeavor. In my interviews with M4BL participants, they would often cite works they had read and speakers they had seen or conversed with who had expanded and illuminated their thinking. Mary Hooks recounts,

> I grew up under the impact of the war on drugs—we didn't know that language, but grew up under that, saw what was happening. And I always grew up thinking it was our fault—that we did something wrong. Like, why is my mama running down the street in her addiction like this? So anyway, . . . all of these different watershed moments happened. One of them happened to me during college. Elaine Brown came to speak at my school. She was the first woman to head up the Black Panther Party. . . . She came to speak in fucking Kenosha, Wisconsin, at Carthage . . . College where the population of Black students was like 4 or 6 percent. And I remember her talking about her book *The Condemnation of Little B*. And she just begun unraveling my mind! And I remember the political climate on this Lutheran campus shifted completely for weeks. White folks was mad, writing shit on the walls, you know, vandalizing, putting "nigger" everywhere. Alumni calling. Parents calling. "Why you got this woman coming?" It was a whole thing. I remember, she crewed up the Black students there and told us, "every generation has their work," and I didn't quite get everything, but I did more studying [after that] and really learned about . . . the war on drugs. And I was like, "Oh, Reagan had something to do with all this shit? These were the laws that were being passed? It ain't our fucking fault?" And, I didn't have the language of systemic racism [at the time] but I just began to understand the political moves. (Hooks interview, 2018)

From its inception, the movement has been deeply intellectual, relying on a vast array of thinkers to help activists make sense of the world as it is. Organizers have sought to learn from the literatures amassed by Black scholars at the same time that they seek to exceed common expectations about what is politically possible. Barbara Ransby, a historian and movement elder, reports, "In 2017, members of M4BL participated in workshops/ think tanks in Chicago with presentations by Black scholars and writers, including Donna Murch, Lester Spence, Leith Mullings, Cornel West, Beverly Guy-Sheftall, Robin D.G. Kelley, Michael Dawson" in addition to "Ruth Wilson Gilmore, Cathy Cohen, Beth Richie, [and] Brittney Cooper" (Ransby 2018, 118).

In addition, public syllabi related to Black and other POC freedom struggles were a very prevalent movement tool between 2014 and 2018 (see appendix E). Reading groups on classic texts of Black radicalism like W. E. B. Du Bois's *Black Reconstruction* or Audre Lorde's collected essays and recent releases like Charlene Carruthers' *Unapologetic*, Darnell Moore's *No Ashes in the Fire*, Alicia Garza's *The Purpose of Power*, and Patrisse Khan-Cullors and asha bandele's *When They Call You a Terrorist*, hosted in online meeting forums like Zoom, remain common.

Another important aspect of organizing is the imperative to "build power." It is the element of organizing that sounds the toughest and most concrete, but while building power is high impact, it is a complicated, multistep, and often delicate process. To build power means to create a base of organized people and resources from which they can act in concert, and effectively, toward a mutually recognized goal. This requires people coming together and gathering their resources and skills in service of a common cause. Strong political friendships and thoughtful and ongoing power analysis are the practices that enable such a muscular coming together in associations and organizations that can be relied upon to facilitate action in public and political circumstances. That's what it means to *get organized*.

Power, here, can be understood to be three-faced, in the tradition of Steven Lukes and John Gaventa, which is to say that it includes (1) decisive bargaining and decision-making power; (2) "mobilization of bias," or agenda-setting power; and (3) ideological power, or the power to shape common sense by influencing language, deploying myths, and controlling information (Lukes [1974)] 2005; Gaventa 1980). But envisaging power in this way is only an analytical convenience. These three observable areas help us to operationalize power, which is a beneficial practice for assessment, both by people in movement and scholars studying movement. However, power is a relation, not an object, and as we learned from Michel Foucault, it can be wielded, whatever its visage, by people anywhere in the social hierarchy.

Still, the way people create, access, and utilize power relations is asymmetrical, so it will look different depending on their structural positioning and the resources, respect, official authority, and reputation that accompany that set of positions (Woodly 2015a). Those whose social positions afford them less advantage must "build power" before they can wield it to challenge status quo structural arrangements. They will know they have built power when they can "reward or punish . . . targets, control what gets talked about in public debate" (Speer and Hughey 1995, 732), and shape "conceptions of the necessities, possibilities, and strategies of challenge in situations of latent conflict" (Gaventa 1980, 15).

It is important to note that power in a movement does not derive from charismatic individuals or the prestige and resources of any one influential organization (even when it appears so to outsiders). Instead, movements must construct what Paul Speer and Joseph Hughey call an "ecology of power" (Speer and Hughey 1995). M4BL uses a similar analogy to refer to the consortium of individuals and organizations involved as an "ecosystem." In an ecosystem, power can be assessed by noticing whether interconnected organisms can effect desired change in and on their environment.

A style of organizing pioneered in the Movement for Black Lives favors organizing for depth rather than breadth; the proliferation of leadership nodes; and the reliance on flocking together like birds in a migratory pattern, rather than hierarchal management, for the diffusion of analysis and tactics. Movement theorist adrienne maree brown talks about this framework as "emergent strategy" in her book of the same name. This kind of strategy is based on a concept of emergence borrowed from the natural sciences in which "complex systems and patterns arise out of a multiplicity of relatively simple interactions" (brown 2017, 3). She writes,

> [W]e have lived through . . . half a century of individualistic linear organizing (led by charismatic individuals or budget-building institutions), which intends to reform or revolutionize society, but falls back into modeling the oppressive tendencies against which we claim to be pushing. . . . Many of us have been socialized to understand that constant growth, violent competition, and critical mass are the ways to create change. But emergence shows us that adaptation and evolution depend more on critical, deep, and authentic connections, a thread that can be tugged for support and resilience. (brown 2017, 14)

This view of organizing aligns with Gilles Deleuze and Felix Guattari's use and elaboration of the idea of rhizomic organization as a way to both analyze extant complexity and model social relations. A rhizomic perspective allows for multiple, nonhierarchical entry and exit points in data representation and interpretation. In the model they advance in their work *A Thousand Plateaus: Capitalism and Schizophrenia*, they point out that the natural formation of the rhizome, a unique root structure found in certain plants, defies the linear path of causality that comes to mind in a root-tree system, instead carrying nutrients and other stuff of life through "ceaselessly established connections between semiotic chains, organizations of power, and [relevant] circumstances" (Deleuze and Guattari [1980] 2004).

To lead, under a rhizomic model, is all about creating and proliferating connections that themselves can yield new, fruitful connections independent of the direction of a central decision-maker. Brown writes, "So many of our organizations working for social change are structured in ways that reflect the status quo. We have singular charismatic leaders, top down structures, money-driven programs, destructive methods of engaging conflict, unsustainable work cultures, and little to no impact on the issues at hand" (brown 2017, 52). As an alternative, she believes movements must strive be like "flocks of birds" and cultivate "underground power like whispering mushrooms" (23). In this vein, "organizing is a multilayered and institution-proliferating activity, not an expression of popular power that tends inevitably toward unmediated popular voice." Organizing is not merely a precursor to activism and mobilization; it is instead "a means for building relations and bridging institutions across lines of difference, rather than reinforcing them with a vision of a homogenous and unified people" (Pineda 2019, 17).

The last tenet of organizing is to take action. Action is not just the activity of protest, but is also the process by which those who are in a relation of political friendship work together to make claims, develop their means, and secure their ends. As discussed above, an Arendtian view of action also understands action to be an identity-disclosing activity. That means that people not only reveal but also shape who they are in the world by what they do in the world. When an individual or group takes action, they are bringing the reality of the world into focus by delineating their place in it and underlining their human capacity to change it by beginning something new.

It is in this way that organizers work to undo what I have called elsewhere the "neoliberal common sense" that characterizes the modern understanding of the subject in society (Woodly 2015b). Neoliberal common sense is the widespread reification of the individual such that it is nearly impossible to conceptualize or acknowledge that social forces beyond any one person's intention or control can be decisive in shaping the choices and life chances of individuals. Because this belief is a part of the American *doxa* or background understanding of the way things are, or, as Clifford Geertz put it, "the doctrine of the self-evident," organizing is a critical first step to developing any kind of political action in which people participate together, particularly when that action is outside the boundaries of activities we acknowledge as matters of individual right, such as voting.[2]

Part 2: Organizational Structure, Organizational Culture, and Interorganizational Environment
Organizational Structure and Interorganizational Environment

The Movement for Black Lives has developed a new organizational form. From that form, a unique organizational culture and interorganizational environment also arise. In terms of structure, M4BL operates as a semi-federated network of independent individual organizations that come together at "tables" to share information, deliberate about movement-wide policy objectives, administer collaborative campaigns, distribute resources, and arbitrate disputes. Among these tables are those focused on organizing, resource distribution, policy development, media and communications, healing justice, and more. New tables can be convened based on new issues that movement participants wish to address, combined as areas of work converge, or disbanded when the scope of work within the movement changes. It is an ingenious and highly flexible structure for movement work in that it combines the need for a decision-making infrastructure with the recognition that local knowledge and autonomy are key to developing effective and resonant campaigns.

While the networked organizational form shares a great deal with those of the "new social movements" of the late twentieth century in that it eschews centralization, it improves upon those models by exhibiting an agreed-upon founding mythology, a shared set of foundational principles, unity of

---

[2] Even voters need to be organized, particularly people who have never voted or seen a reason to vote before. Black women organizers are at the forefront of this kind of voter organizing, which is distinct from the more common, though also necessary, voter mobilization that consists in targeted contact, reminders, and advertisements reminding people who regularly vote about when to vote and who to vote for depending on their party identification. For a summary of studies, particularly experimental data, see Green and Gerber (2019).

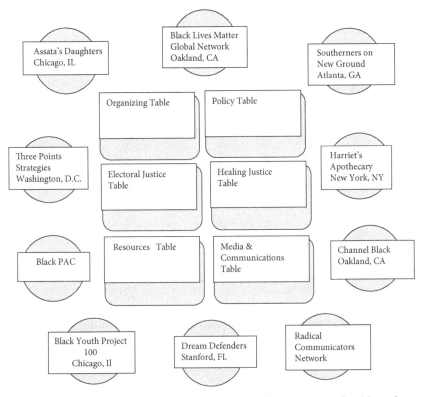

Figure 1. M4BL table structure (example). The table structure is flexible and may contain more or fewer tables depending what participants determine is required to coordinate activity and meet movement-wide goals. Affiliated organizations in this example figure show only a small fraction of the dozens of organizations that make up M4BL's network.

purpose (though with ample diversity of method and the conflict that can engender), robust and routine communication practices, and a fruitful mix of professional movement actors and grassroots organizations.

This unique form, which I call a *table structure* (see Figure 1), serves as a container for an organizational culture that seeks, but does not always attain, ways to facilitate people "showing up" as their "whole selves" in organizing and political work. In addition, the interorganizational environment (See Figure 2) is preoccupied with questions of how to mediate and resolve conflict. It is important to emphasize that mediation and resolution are explicitly opposed to conflict avoidance. The view in the movement is that conflict is not only inevitable, but also generative, because it is the normal result of

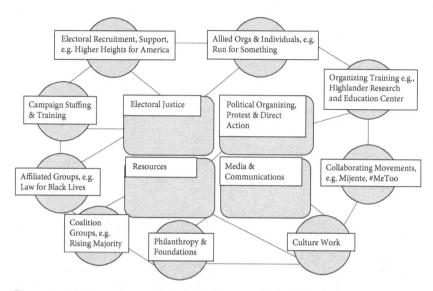

Figure 2. M4BL ecosystem (example). This is only an example ecosystem, showing how the relationships work. The actual organizations in the M4BL ecosystem may change over time as affiliated organizations spring up or fade away. Alternatively, organizations may remain affiliated while frequency of contact changes over time.

people relating to one another across their individual and group differences. It is in this way that the principles of healing justice are taken up in both the structure and culture of the racial justice social movement sector that M4BL exemplifies.

At its best, the movement functions as a set of autonomous, networked organizations practicing cooperative solidarity. However, the many organizations are resourced differently, and that can lead to conflict. All organizations have their own distinct sources of funding, but there are also several combined pools of funding both under the banner of the Movement for Black Lives and from the various coalitions of subsets of those organizations that form for specific purposes and are housed in the movement's interorganizational environment. This means that individual groups like the Black Lives Matter Global Network Foundation or Southerners on New Ground have their own legal and financial organizational structures while also being a part of the Movement for Black Lives, the broadest-based umbrella organization in the movement, and additionally each is involved in the Rising Majority, a coalition of allied organizations that include both M4BL-affiliated groups and groups from outside the movement who are interested in promoting "radical democracy."

The organizations involved are largely nonprofits with 501c3, 501C4, and sometimes L3C (social impact, or "low profit" LLC) legal structures. These organizations often win grants from traditional foundations like the Open Society Foundation and the Ford and MacArthur Foundations, but money from these sources can be slow to come in and often comes with strings attached. For this reason, movement organizations have also tried to cultivate a robust direct appeal fundraising operation, particularly through subscription services that allow donors to contribute small amounts at regular intervals. This method of funding has been especially popular with the various bail funds associated with movement, like the Chicago Community Bond Fund or the Minnesota Freedom Fund. This model allows flexibility at moments when there is a need for extra monies or when there are efforts to fundraise for discrete campaigns.

There is quite a range of funding resources between organizations in the movement. Some organizations, like the Ella Baker Center for Human Rights, BLM Global Network Foundation, Black Alliance for Just Immigration (BAJI), and Southerners on New Ground (SONG), have budgets in the millions. In 2016, the Ella Baker Center for Human Rights had a budget of $4 million, according to tax filings. In 2019, the BLM Global Network Foundation had $3.3 million in donor-restricted assets. BAJI had a budget of $3.1 million in 2017. Southerners on New Ground (SONG) had a budget of $2.4 million in 2017. This puts these organizations in the top third of nonprofits by budget size.[3] By contrast, most organizations have more modest budgets. For example, BYP100 had an operating budget of $219,111 in 2016, the latest year for which filings are available.

Regardless of size, all organizations in the movement have a chance to access resources through politically progressive funding consortiums that sprang up in the 2010s, especially Funders for Justice, which is a group of philanthropists and foundations that seek to move resources to groups with causes aiming toward equity for those living under conditions of oppression due to the intersection of race, class, gender and LGBTQ status. Funding groups include Solidaire, established in 2012 to support the efforts

---

[3] See the Influence Watch website, https://www.influencewatch.org/non-profit/, for data on the Ella Baker Center for Human Rights, BAJI, and SONG. See also https://zipsprout.com/how-big-are-most-non-profits/.

of the Occupy movement; Resource Generation, a group of wealthy young people who "utilize their resources for transformative and equitable shifts in power" (Cordery 2016); the Women Donors Network, which contributes to causes for "progressive change"; and the North Star Fund, which supports "grassroots organizing by communities of color" (North Star Fund, n.d.) and its subsidiary, the Let Us Breathe Fund, which specifically supports Black-led organizations. These groups, among others, gave the organizations in the Movement for Black Lives access to resources that allowed new organizations to be founded, existing organizations to continue and sometimes expand, and some ability to weather the abeyance after the Trump election, when the cry of Black Lives Matter receded somewhat from the top of the public's mind. It also laid the groundwork for the movement to begin learning about managing resources—a skill that they would need in the summer of 2020 when millions of Americans took to the streets with the movement slogan on their lips and millions more opened their wallets to donate more than $90 million to organizations in the movement (Goldmacher 2020). The deluge of donations in May and June of 2020 was so massive and unexpected that many organizations were overwhelmed despite having some experience with large dollar donations. The *New York Times* reported that "the outpouring has been organic, viral, and immense" (Goldmacher 2020). The rush to support the movement was so intense that an organization grifting off the movement's name took in $4.35 million in donations before it was found out and the monies frozen (Albrecht 2020). Understand also that these numbers are not just of money, but, as importantly, lists of supporters—people who can be mobilized and asked for donations at other critical moments.

The huge influx of money led some people to become confused and suspicious about where the millions of dollars supporters donated were going as protests again waned by late summer. Activists who had broken with M4BL organizations and had long been critical of the way money moved in the movement aired their concerns. On June 18, the Ferguson activist Ashley Yates tweeted, "26.1 million dollars to WHO and for WHAT? whew [*sic*] we need to have a conversation on non-transparent brand-building and the susceptibility of Black movements' toward empowering them."

In response, organizers in M4BL took to social media to plead for patience. On June 16, Charlene Carruthers wrote on Twitter, "I implore anyone here to say with great confidence that you'd know how to handle several million dollars in a situation like this . . . in a few weeks—with principle." The same day, Mervyn Marcano a cofounder of movement capacity-building firm Blackbird, in a series of tweets, argued,

> If you see some sort of "gotcha" story that all of a sudden pops up, consider for a moment what it hopes to achieve. Narratives about shadowy figures "behind" movements are made to make you feel powerless & that change is impossible. They imply we can't do it ourselves. There's no question there's a flood of resources moving in right now. Give your movements the GRACE and benefit of the doubt to get it right. The money started flowing last week. And it's, across the board, magnitudes higher than folks were prepared for. We can handle it. But it will take a second to figure it out. And this is especially true for local orgs who were operating on shoe-string budgets before. Are there conversations to be had about money and movements? Absolutely. Just be mindful of who benefits from painting a false narrative of Black led movements as shady in a time of crisis. When we are winning together.

However, by September, movement organizations had figured out what to do with all that money. Bail funds, which had received a large proportion of donations, figured out both their priorities in funding people's release and the possibilities of getting people released and on what timetables as well as what legal latitude they had in contributing to post-bail and family support (Toussaint 2020). And the best-resourced organizations in M4BL established funds of their own. The BLM Global Network Foundation announced $6.5 million in unrestricted operational funds for its chapters (Black Lives Matter Global Network Foundation 2020) and an additional $12 million fund to support other organizations that fight institutional racism (CBS News Staff 2020). Even with these developments, conversation and conflicts about how resources are distributed are ongoing and are often a source of tension.

Organizational Culture and Interorganizational Environment

The organizational culture of M4BL is heavily shaped by the politics of care and ideas grounded in healing justice. That means there's a lot of attention both to the postures, or attitudes, with which people approach conflict and to procedures that allow people to deal with conflict in ways that are not destructive. This means that organizations try to develop norms and rules both internally and intergroup that prevent doing harm as much as possible while also making sure there are processes of accountability when harm is done.

However, that is easier said than done. Sometimes hurt feelings can be presented as trauma, and the work of movement can be repeatedly set aside to process emotions. Nikita Mitchell, a former director of organizing for the BLM Global Network Foundation, reflects the delicacy and friction of the movement's approach:

> How do we balance that commitment between the individual and what we need to do by the collective? It's been hard. In our organization what that meant was we spent two years reacting to our members' emotions. . . of all things from "I don't want [paid] staff in this organization, because of my experience in the nonprofit world" to "I don't like [the tone of] how you presented this idea, therefore I'm going to block it." Or "I feel hurt because you didn't bring me in at the beginning." Or I think about how private situations between members that have nothing to do with our organization can start to take up a lot of space. People begin to act as if all of their emotions, hopes, dreams, insecurities, trauma should give them access to that private conversation, which just stops us from talking about what we actually have a role in. Sometimes there's an overcorrection that comes at the cost of actually doing this work in a way that wins tangible things for our people. So what I think I'm saying is that people are trying to find home in this movement and sometimes have a hard time delineating between what our movement is actually accountable to for the individual and the collective. It gets in the work sometimes. It stops us from thinking about all of our people. But if we believe that getting to a new world is not just about policy change but is also about culture change, then it makes sense that most of our work is in service to building a new community, and that repairing relationships and building community must be the basis of our power. So tending to the emotions is actually necessary. We have not yet figured it out. What capacity does it take to experiment together about what it means to be a better community? We're in constant experimentation. We're constantly trying to interrogate how our guiding principles live in our work. Do our values show up in how we actually move? I think we've made a commitment, both staff and in the coalition networks, to not striving to be a perfect organization, but when conflict happens, to build our toolset to deal with it. (Mitchell interview, 2018)

When activists and organizers are taught and expected to bring their whole selves to movement spaces rather than a professional self that is supposed to be stripped of feelings unrelated to work, people will sometimes bring pettiness, ego, selfishness, and narcissism with them. Or they can expect all movement spaces to be appropriate for every kind of self-work they need to do. It is for this reason that "self-care" is often recast as community care—or, as Melissa Harris-Perry (2017) put it, "squad care"—within movement spaces. Community care differs from self-care in that its central idea is that the individual is always in context. We must take care of ourselves, of course, but that care is not and cannot be isolated from our relationships, our obligations, the need to be accountable to our people, and the imperative to try to be in healthy relation to those around us. Harris-Perry writes,

> Ultimately, self-care encourages women to rely solely on themselves rather than to make demands on anyone or anything else. Self-care validates as good and noble all of those women with sufficient resources to "take a break" from the hustle and bustle while it censures those who seek relief from the collective care of the state—through child care subsidies, food assistance, low-income or subsidized housing, or health care. In so much of our political language, the black, brown, and poor women who seek care in these ways are still represented as bad, fraudulent, lazy, and wasteful.
>
> And so instead, we turn to squad care, a way of understanding our needs as humans that acknowledges how we lean on one another, that we are not alone in the world, but rather enmeshed in webs of mutual and symbiotic relationships. Sometimes our squads are small, intimate, and bonded by affection. . . . Squad care reminds us there is no shame in reaching for each other and insists the imperative rests not with the individual, but with the community. Our job is to have each other's back. (Harris-Perry 2017)

Commenting on Harris-Perry's intervention, Charlene Carruthers explains that the concept of squad care "presented a dilemma for many activists. On the one hand, we are taught and encouraged to sacrifice to no end. Our ancestors and living comrades have made sacrifices beyond what most of us today have made. Who are we not to give our lives to the movement? On the other hand, we are human" (Carruthers 2018, 73). Carruthers acknowledges that there is no easy formula to resolve the conflict that may arise from trying to sort out the contours of the care that is necessary for the work of social and political transformation. She argues instead, "Our movement should live with the tension between self-care and community care. Individual activists should commit to self-care on whatever level they are able to, and communities should commit to creating a culture of care . . . the movement should allow and create spaces for healing, with the recognition that we can not do it all" (73–74, 75).

In addition to the genuine complication of bringing whole selves to movement spaces, there are also the maladies that affect all kinds of association: rumors, information asymmetry, jumping to conclusions, and bad faith. All these things are exacerbated by the fact that so much movement-related communication happens via social media. Carruthers laments that "we live in an age . . . where simply expressing disagreement can lead to a public dragging" (81). "Dragging" is a kind of public shaming that can be used either separate from or in conjunction with "canceling," or the shunning, disassociation, or delegitimating of an individual or group. These unhealthy tendencies are present in the movement alongside the genuine commitment to try to enact and move toward a culture where these counterproductive impulses are less prevalent because people have learned good habits around harm prevention and reparative conflict resolution.

Another positive way that the movement culture prevents and mitigates inevitable conflict is by building relational bonds through joyful practices. In this way, the movement uses joy as a political resource, because it shores up the relations of good will that are necessary for people to give one another the benefit of the doubt and to remind them, when the pressures of political work make it easy to forget, that they are a part of the same community. One that is united not only by struggle, but also by celebration. As Christopher Paul Harris, an academic and organizer in BYP100, writes, Black joy is "one of the movement's most salient and consequential features." He goes on to say,

Black joy: celebrating blackness and each other as Black. Over time, as I became more deeply engaged in the work of BYP100, this was what stood out above the rest. . . . The chants, the songs and rituals. The adlibs and improvised movements. The culture.[4] These communal practices enliven our

---

[4] Here we ought to consider culture both in terms of behaviors, beliefs, and aesthetics in a broad sense, as well as the ways in which "the" as an article denotes a specific "Black" culture. At least in the United States, if not elsewhere, notions of "the culture" have become popular among Black youth, evidenced in phrases like "do it for the culture." In my reading, this is both an etic and emic position, insofar as it simultaneously articulates a shared, even if contested, understanding of what Black culture is, while also naming an action that would affirm and therefore constitute this culture. In the main, statements like this tend to represent the ways in which understandings of Blackness among Black people have expanded and become more flexible.

meetings, convenings, and workshops, be they within BYP100 or the larger M4BL ecosystem. They also facilitate—along with singing, dancing, and other forms of "turning-up"—an embodied sense of ourselves as catalysts of transformation; a sense of ourselves as capable of (un)making worlds. (Harris 2019, 109)

Conclusion

In this chapter, I have argued that political organizing is an understudied yet crucial component of democratic politics, one that we see most readily illustrated in the activity of social movements. The key feature of political organizing is that its aim is the transformation of political subjectivity rather than the engagement of interests and capacities that are already developed. The Movement for Black Lives has apprehended the American traditions of organizing emerging from both the Alinsky school and the approach Horton assembled with colleagues at the Highlander Folk School. From these knowledges, the movement has developed an approach to organizing that is avowedly rooted in the notion that in order to change politics, they have to be willing to not only imagine the world as it might be, but also to imagine themselves as they must be in order to bring the new world into existence. This transformation in the service of the work of bringing forth a new politics is not understood to be miraculous—at least not in the sense of bringing about something out of nothing in an instant—but is instead understood to be an *undergoing* or struggle that one commits to with other people. Importantly, this struggle is envisaged not as a substitute for life, but as a part of it. And, as such, attention to care, health, and joy is woven into every aspect. This kind of politics is not easy and is certainly not always successful, but it guides the building of intra-movement practices and organizations that are built with both longevity and flexibility in mind. In the next chapter, we will see the changes that this approach, and the organizations that have been built under its auspices, is already changing the public understandings and political possibilities that exist in the world we share.

PART THREE
DEMOCRATIC POSSIBILITY

"If what we need to dream, to move our spirits most deeply and directly toward and through promise, is discounted as luxury, then we give up the core—the fountain—of our power . . .; we give up the future of our worlds."

—Audre Lorde,
"Poetry is not a Luxury," in *Sister Outsider*

5

Movement Means Changing Politics

Discourse, Tactics, Policy, and a New Political Ecosystem

The broad movement in defense of Black lives has contributed to a repoliticization of the public sphere and has been successful at gaining political acceptance. Through its efforts, the movement has changed the common ways we talk about race, inequality, policing, and well-being, and inserted a commonplace understanding of structural racism and anti-Blackness into mainstream American discourse. This incorporation of new concepts into the political lexicon has opened possibilities for redress that did not exist prior to the movement's work. The movement has done this crucial work by revealing the connection between political concepts like systemic racism and governmental functions that systematically disadvantage Black people and other people of color, thereby revealing what Suzanne Mettler calls the submerged state. It has been able to do so because participants in the movement have always taken seriously the need to communicate with multiple audiences and understand that social movements can be radical, challenging, and contentious while remaining legible in public discourse.

g, I show the multifaceted impact of the Movement for Black movement has changed American politics in multiple ways, mporary conceptual terrain regarding race and racism. It large, measurable shifts in political attitudes regarding the :emic racism in governing institutions and American life, ecarceral trends, directly impacted the incidence of police ere protests took place, and developed tactics, policy, and n that has already achieved notable and concrete wins.

Changing the Conceptual Terrain of American Politics

In less than a decade, the Movement for Black Lives (M4BL) has catalyzed a public opinion realignment that has reshaped the American political landscape and the electorate itself. Although it can be hard to fathom amid the continued suffering of Black people and the backlash of white grievance politics, this shift has taken place with astonishing speed. Note here that the movement is doing what many have begged the Left to do for years, mirroring the build-up of ideas, policy proposals, and political infrastructure that the right wing built in the mid-twentieth century, while they were in a wilderness of political defeat at the national level. Victoria Hattam and Joe Lowndes offer an account of how right-wing intellectuals seized "*the* ground of politics, *the* site of change in which otherwise disparate elements are recombined into apparently coherent political positions" (Hattam and Lowndes 2007, 204). They write:

> Scholars and popular writers have generally located the origins of the rise of the modern Right in the late 1960s. These accounts rest on a story of backlash against the excesses of liberalism endemic in that decade, excesses that naturally played into the hands of conservatives generally and the Republican Party in particular. But the major themes of the national Republican message in 1968 and thereafter, including law and order, opposition to civil rights advances, federalism, and a commitment to economic conservatism, did not come together naturally, reflexively, or organically. They had to be combined into a coherent discourse and form of political subjectivity. Such combining was a long-term, contingent process that had to be worked out by political actors on the ground." (205)

In fact, the alliances that were made among conservative white evangelicals, segregationists, and economic conservatives during the mid-twentieth century were not natural; they were contingent and constructed, and the process began as early as 1948, thirty-two years before the alignment bore national electoral fruit in 1980, with the election of Ronald Reagan.

The reconstitution of the Republican Party and the idea of conservatism was anchored by the ideas of Charles Collins, a prominent attorney and intellectual from Alabama. He proposed that it was possible to unify southern Democrats, who were committed to racial segregation but also loved the benefits of economic liberalism of the New Deal, with the northern Republicans, who were not very concerned with preserving Jim Crow–style legal segregation (de facto segregation worked fine in the North) but hated the expectation of governmental largess that Franklin Roosevelt had ushered in during his years as president. It was not a self-evident proposition, and the project of constructing a shared subjectivity under the banner of "conservatism" demanded ideological foresight, social intelligence, and persistent practical politics. All of these capacities were anchored by what turned out to be the correct belief that racism could be the fulcrum on which this realignment turned. Under the auspices of reclaiming America's traditional values, Collins argued that the central importance of the individuals' rights and states' rights were the only things that could preserve both the sacredness of private property and the white-supremacist racial order. The degradation of either, he argued, would lead to the obliteration of both.

As the Black civil rights movement became more visible in the late 1940s and early 1950s, with some indications of sympathy and gestures toward further exploration from Presidents Truman and Eisenhower, these new conservatives began to coalesce and formed a third party called the States' Rights Democratic Party, nicknamed the Dixiecrats. But they didn't win. Strom Thurmond, who ran for president in 1948 on the Dixiecrat ticket, was resoundingly defeated, and the Democratic Party punished politicians who had participated in promoting the new party.

Nevertheless, the Dixiecrat ideas lived on, and Collins argued that the way to change the politics of the South would be through culture, language, and opinion first, with the ballot box following after. "Building such a political alliance . . . would necessitate not just a sense of political expediency on behalf of northern conservatives, but a deeper identification with the white South—its perspectives on race and state sovereignty, but also its heritage and cultural values" (Hattam and Lowndes 2007, 208). To this end, Dixiecrat thinkers began building a political infrastructure meant to not only support candidates, but also, and more importantly, to clearly articulate and spread ideas. This necessitated the establishment of nonprofit think tanks in Washington, DC, along with grass-roots organizations, first in the South, but later wherever the notions of white racial superiority and irritation with federal government policies found willing audiences. Thus, the creation of what is now mainstream conservatism was a long-fought battle of ideas that had deep roots in civic life and culture before it became a dominant force in electoral politics.

In the early decades of the twenty-first century, we are again at a turning point in which people's understandings of political identification and alliance are shifting, and again, as is American tradition, the fulcrum is race. However, the story of this moment's realignment is not a straightforward one about support or aversion to M4BL marking a dividing line in American public opinion. Rather, it is a longer-running story, the telling of which might properly begin after the election of the nation's first Black president.

Perhaps because of America's ethnic diversity combined with the history of chattel slavery marking the nearly uncrossable racial divide between Black and white, the nation's politics have always been organized around lines of racial and ethnic identity above those of class (Katznelson 1981; Dawson 1994). However, racial identity and/or one's opinions about racial equality are only intermittently determinative of people's party identification. From the 1970s through the 1990s, only African Americans' party affiliation and views on issues that had been racialized could be reliably predicted based on racial identity, and even that predictor was thought for a time to be an artifact of class politics. The political scientist Michael Dawson, an expert on race and public opinion, hypothesized when he set out to write his first book, *Behind the Mule*, that he would find that apparent racial divides in public opinion were the result of not properly disaggregating the data and controlling for the class background of Black respondents. What he found instead, despite his skepticism, is that Black Americans, regardless of socioeconomic status, believe themselves to have a "linked fate," the idea that regardless of individual accomplishments, the status of the group will have a great impact on one's life chances (Dawson 1994). As an empirical matter, this is simply true. Structural racism acts as a constraint (though it is not fully determinative) on the life chances of Black people. Of course, this is and has always also been true of those Americans considered white. The difference is that most white Americans, even during the height of de jure segregation, did not believe this to be true. And after the revolution of common sense wrought by the civil rights movement, most white Americans began to condemn overt expressions of white identity politics, welcoming racial appeals only when "coded," usually in language quite similar to the rhetoric of "traditional American values" invented by Collins and his political allies in the late 1940s (Bonilla-Silva 2003; Haney López 2015).

However, during the Obama presidency, these truisms of late twentieth-century American politics began to change. The first thing that began to happen was that white people, especially those without a college education, began fleeing the Democratic Party. For those white people who left the Democratic Party during this period, it was not their income, job status, or feelings about their own economic position that predicted whether they would exit stage right. Instead, it was their views about race. Specifically, it was whether they perceived white Americans to be discriminated against and whether they believed Black people and immigrants to be getting more than their fair share of resources. This "racialization of partisanship was underway even before Obama became a national figure. . . . But eight years of an African American president accelerated and intensified" this trend (Sides, Tesler, and Vavreck 2018, 25). By the end of Obama's two terms, white Americans were much more likely to identify as Republicans than Democrats. In 2008, 46 percent of white registered voters identified as Republican and 44 percent as Democrats. By 2016, 54 percent identified as Republican and 39 percent as Democrats (Pew Research Center 2016b). By contrast, Black, Latino, and Asian voters have exhibited party affinities that have been stable over this period, with 87 percent of Black people, 63 percent of Latinos, and 66 percent of Asians identifying as Democrats or Democratic leaners.

In this context, we can better understand the significance of the Pew Research Center finding, in an August 2016 survey, that 43 percent of respondents viewed the Black Lives Matter movement favorably, a percentage that slightly exceeded the favorability ratings of either of the presidential candidates at that time (Horowitz and Livingstone 2016). By 2017, support for the movement had risen, with 55 percent of Americans reporting that they strongly or somewhat support the movement and only 34 percent opposing it (Neal 2017). It should be noted that majority approval of a social movement is extremely rare, and #BLM enjoys more support than the twentieth-century civil rights movement did during its height. As many have noted, the nostalgic hagiography of certain aspects of the twentieth-century movement is a social construction of the 1980s and 1990s and not a view that obtained while political challengers were making demands for change in the 1940s, 1950s, and 1960s. Though the Movement for Black Lives is careful to correct whitewashed recitations of the mid-century civil rights movement that deny its radical ambitions, it has nevertheless been able to use the retrospective positive evaluation of that movement to its advantage, even as it updates and changes some of the earlier movement's core political claims (Edwards-Levy 2018).

Since the Ferguson uprising after the police killing of Michael Brown, the movement has influenced opinion about the significance of race and racism in American life, changed policy, contributed to the reduction of police violence in major cities, and reshaped the politics of social justice. And in the summer of 2020, amid the first global pandemic in one hundred years, the Movement for Black Lives reshaped the political terrain. The 2014 uprisings had received surprising support from the public, but the massive wave of protests taking place in 2020 achieved a startling consensus of support. A Quinnipiac University poll (released June 17, 2020) found that 67 percent of registered voters supported the protests that had coalesced all over the country, and a Pew Research Center poll (released June 12, 2020) found that the same percentage of people supported the movement (Sparks 2020). A *New York Times*/Siena College poll (released June 27, 2020) found 59 percent of voters, including 52 percent of white voters, believed that George Floyd's murder is "part of a broader pattern of excessive police violence toward African Americans." The same poll found that 54 percent of voters said the way the criminal justice system treats Black Americans was a bigger problem than the incidents of rioting seen during some demonstrations (Herndon and Searcey 2020).

Stunningly, in the two weeks between May 26 and June 10, support for the Movement for Black Lives, which was already historically high for a social movement, increased by 28 points (Cohn and Quealy 2020). A Monmouth University poll (released July 8, 2020) found that 76 percent of Americans consider racism and discrimination a "big problem," up 26 points from 2015, and 78 percent of respondents to that poll declared the anger behind the demonstrations either fully or somewhat justified (Monmouth University 2020). Overall, polls show that "a majority of Americans believe that the police are more likely to use deadly force against African Americans, and that there's a lot of discrimination against black Americans in society." Back in 2013, when Black Lives Matter began, a majority of voters disagreed with all of these statements" (Cohn and Quealy 2020). However, here is the most astonishing part: in a political culture in which nearly every institution is mistrusted by the American people, a 55 percent majority expect that this movement will create positive, long-term political and institutional change (Monmouth University 2020).

The potential for political realignment lies in these shifts in political attitudes and understandings. The share of Americans who say race is a big problem almost doubled between 2011 (28 percent) and 2015 (50 percent), and the percentage of people worrying more about race and racism has continued on an upward trend, as seen in a Monmouth University poll released July 8, 2020, which showed that more than 65 percent of Americans declared that racial and ethnic discrimination is a big problem in the United States (Pew Research Center 2017; Arenge, Perry, and Clark 2018; Monmouth University 2020). That 2020 survey appears to mirror other recent reports on the topic. According to a July 10, 2020, report in the *Washington Post*, "Nearly 60 percent of those surveyed recently told Gallup that they were somewhat dissatisfied or very dissatisfied with the state of race relations in America. And more than 60 percent of Americans say race relations in the United States are 'generally bad,' according to a recent CBS news poll" (Scott 2020).

In 2014, 46 percent of Americans believed that we need to keep making changes to achieve racial equality; by 2017, that number had increased to 61 percent (Pew Research Center 2017). The most dramatic change has been among white Americans, particularly white liberals and/or those who identify as Democrats. The journalist Matthew Yglesias dubbed the marked shifts in opinion in this group "the great awokening." Between 2009 and 2015, the year when protests in defense of Black lives were most frequent, the share of white Democrats declaring racism a "major problem" increased from 32 percent to 58 percent, and it climbed to 76 percent by 2017, almost matching the concern of Black Americans (81 percent) for the first time. In another first, the majority of white people surveyed in 2020 were persuaded that Black people are treated less fairly by police and the judicial system (Horowitz, Brown, and Cox 2019).

At the same time, and somewhat counterintuitively, reported racial resentment toward Black people decreased among white people during the period of M4BL's activity. Data from a panel study conducted between 2007 and 2018 showed that while anti-Black prejudice is high, there has been a measurable overall decline since 2014, with a sharp decline in reported belief in anti-Black stereotypes among whites, from an average score of 8.1 to an average of 5.4 (out of 10), regardless of party, between 2016 and 2018 (Hopkins and Washington 2019). More provocatively, whites in counties where movement groups held protests have average scores on racial resentment measures that decreased significantly more than those of whites in counties where no protests took place. In addition, in counties where protests took place, the Democratic Party's share of the vote increased on average 4 to 6 percentage points (Mazumder 2019). The small pile of studies documenting these effects is a critical body of evidence showing that contrary to the assumptions of many traditional political professionals, bringing attention to racial inequality through protest has important and measurable *positive* impacts on political attitudes regarding racial equity. These kinds of shifts in attitudes make space for new ways to address existing problems, making more expansive policy change possible.

Unearthing the Submerged State

One of the most effective ways social movements disrupt things is by revealing the workings of institutions that were not generally known before and then helping us connect the dots from those newly visible occurrences to our values, attitudes, and lives (Mettler 2011). M4BL has been able to show how state power is used to shape, reinforce, and then naturalize patterns of racial inequality. This ability to render the submerged state visible and traceable to governing institutions has been a critical element of the movement's success. After all, patterns that are invisible are difficult to contest. In revealing how structural racism constrains the lives of Black people and other people of color, as well as how the intersecting ideological systems of patriarchy and neoliberalism constrain and order people's lives in a way that perpetuates and maintains ascriptive hierarchy, M4BL has found a way to repoliticize public life. The first step toward reconnecting with the idea of ourselves as democratic citizens is to be able to see the impact of the workings of social and political forces on the public. The "neoliberal common sense" that underlies our institutions and social practices often prevents us from perceiving these effects, because it is a doctrine that refuses to admit that social forces beyond luck might thwart the individual's will or constrain voluntary association in significant and systematic ways (Woodly 2015b).

The political scientist Chloe Thurston points out previous social movements have also exercised this democratic function: "[C]ivil rights organizations and social movements have long labored to lay bare the uses of state power against racial minorities, as a way of contesting it." M4BL's "activities have illustrated this form of politics, and not only in areas involving police violence" (Thurston 2018, 163). For example, the Vision for Black Lives, the movement's 2016 and 2020 policy platforms, points to specific, concrete ways to address the ways that federal policies advantage white households while leaving Black households without access to publicly funded benefits and opportunities. These differentially advantageous policies include tax breaks for homeowners, healthcare linked to certain kinds of employment, and taxing capital gains at a dramatically lower rate than wage-based income. In these platforms and other policy statements, the movement consistently makes the case that institutional and legal advantages "allowed white households to gain economic stability, amass wealth, and then to transfer it across generations," which is why the average white household has nearly eight times the wealth of the average Black household. In addition to being excluded from benefits that skew aid to those who are more likely to be white, Black Americans have also been denied opportunity through direct, government-sponsored systematic discrimination, most devastatingly through the practice of redlining. Thurston concludes that, "[b]y pointing out such disparities, [M4BL] offers an alternative perspective on material inequality that was tied not to individual merit in a fair capitalist system, but to the state's role in creating what Ira Katznelson has referred to as affirmative action for white Americans" (Thurston 2018, 167). The carceral apparatus is only one of the systems that has a long and brutal history of destroying both individual lives and entire communities, changing the way that people perceive and enact citizenship (Lerman and Weaver 2014). It is important to understand "political mobilization as an effort by marginalized groups to render the state's role in their lives visible and legible" (Thurston 2018, 163).

In other words, for Black and brown people, the state has never been submerged. Communities of color have long been aware that the "federal government has used its coercive powers to control the settlement, movement, and life chances of marginalized groups within its borders" (Thurston 2018, 166). The blatant, malicious interference of the state has been especially apparent to marginalized people involved in protest politics—from COINTELPRO in the mid-twentieth century to the FBI declaration of a totally made-up category, "Black Identity Extremists," in 2017 (Speri 2019). There was also state-level interference from law enforcement groups such as the NYPD, which admitted to infiltrating and surveilling M4BL movement participants' phones and organization meetings (Morales and Ly 2019).

In my interviews, movement participants expressed concern about being surveilled by state agencies, and some people who declined to be interviewed did so because they had become extremely cautious, even paranoid, concerning new people. They were aware that they could be charged with very severe crimes, up to and including terrorism, for civil disobedience. This made recruitment and integration of new people into activist roles and planning large actions difficult and dangerous. The FBI was using the "Black Identity Extremist" guidance for months before the memo establishing the fictional category was leaked to the press. Immediately there was an outcry from activists, civil libertarians, and civil rights organizations; even the National Organization of Black Law Enforcement Executives put out a statement condemning the designation, warning, "This assessment resurrects the historically negative legacy of African American civil rights leaders who were unconstitutionally targeted and attacked by federal, state, and local law enforcement agencies for seeking full U.S. citizenship under the law" (NOBLE 2017). Even so, this "threat guidance" continued to be used and a memo leaked from the Justice Department in 2019 revealed that despite copious conflicting evidence, the Trump administration considered this fictive group to be a bigger threat than white supremacists or al-Qaeda (Winter, Francis, and Naylor 2020).

Social movements in general, and M4BL in particular, make a critical democratic intervention into public understandings of state power while at the same time enduring repression in the form of surveillance, threats, interference, and retributive punishment by state actors. This state repression is part of the reason for the decline in street and other disruptive protests in the years immediately following the 2016 election, and yet another reason to be astonished at the size and scope of the massive demonstrations that reemerged in American cities throughout the summer of 2020.

Shifting Political Attitudes by Changing Public Meanings

One reason for the ability of the movement to weather state repression after 2016 may be the fact that media coverage of events associated with #BlackLivesMatter in 2014 and 2015 was relatively sympathetic by historical standards (Elmasry and el-Nawawy 2017). That means that people who learned about movement activity from non-right-wing news sources were more likely to hear the voices and perspectives of activists and organizers than is usual in protest coverage, and that coverage was more likely to be positive in tone. There is not one definitive answer as to why media coverage of the Black Lives Matter movement evinced these tendencies, but there are several contributing factors to consider.

First, by 2014 the world was amid a global pro-democracy cycle of contention that was being self-reported and mobilized online. In 2009, the "Green Movement," a pro-democracy movement in Iran exploded into the social media sphere, gaining worldwide attention. In 2010, what came to be known as the "Arab Spring" was in full bloom, with peoples across the region contesting the legitimacy and authority of their governing bodies, demanding more responsive governance, and, in some cases, ousting longstanding regimes. In 2011, the United States joined the fray with Occupy Wall Street. By that time, media had developed a narrative habit of treating protests demanding representation as credible.

Second, coverage of these twenty-first-century uprisings began on Twitter and proliferated across social media. This means there was a wealth of first-hand accounts framing the political problems and narrating the protest action authored from the point of view of people who were involved, so that journalists' views were first shaped by activists and ordinary observers rather than by authorities. This way of learning about what is significant about politics is an inversion of the usual path reporting takes, which starts with the word of officials and then explores contrasting opinions afterward, creating a bias toward official accounts and against political challengers.

As a result of both the standing narrative sympathetic to twenty-first-century pro-democracy movements and social media's impact on reporting routines, news stories used *dramatically* more quotes from protestors than from law enforcement or government officials during the Ferguson uprising. Mohammed Elmasry and Mohamad el-Nawawy analyzed coverage of the 2014 protests in the *New York Times* and the *St. Louis Post-Dispatch*. They noted that in contradiction to expectations based on previous findings of media coverage of protest, "both newspapers directly quoted protesters more than they quoted police officers and government officials combined, and police officers were directly quoted the least" (Elmasry and el-Nawawy 2017, 869). Specifically, they found that in the *New York Times*, protestors were quoted on average 4.38 times per article, while government officials were quoted 1.8 times and police only 1.3 times. In the *St. Louis Post-Dispatch*, the pattern held, with protestors directly quoted 4.76 times, on average, compared with government officials (2.1 times) and police (1.16 times). Elmasry and Mohamad el-Nawawy concluded, "The fact that protesters were sourced so regularly and so prominently may offer the best clue as to why articles ultimately tended to frame protests as 'peaceful' (rather than as 'riots')" (869).

The regular use of protestors as sources for news stories was not mere happenstance, nor was it only a product of the social media zeitgeist. Three further circumstances contributed to the inversion of authority-bias that usually characterizes news coverage: (1) Ferguson police abused reporters along with protestors during the uprisings, and the images—both those taken on cell phones and those captured by professional photo journalists—showed a shockingly militarized police presence, with law enforcement officers repeatedly caught pointing guns at or threatening to kill the people who had assembled to call attention to their mistreatment; (2) the cascade of widely circulated and highly publicized videos of police murdering Black people continued to stream unceasingly and highlighted the discontinuity between the reality that Black people and many other marginalized groups experience at the hands of police and the discordant narrative that these forces were made to "protect and serve"; and finally, (3) trained communication and visual media staff within the movement often had experience connecting to and building credibility with journalists.

The fact that there were trained people vested with the task of communicating movement stories to media has made a difference in the perception of the movement from its inception. One instance early in the life of the movement illustrates the decisive importance of the movement's respect for public discourse.

On July 7, 2016, dozens of contemporaneous protests were organized to call attention to the fact that police had murdered Alton Sterling in Louisiana on July 5 and Philando Castile in Minnesota on July 6. One of those protests was organized by Next Generation Action Network in Dallas, Texas. The demonstration was one of the largest taking place across the nation and, like the overwhelming majority of mass actions associated with the movement, had been wholly peaceful (Chenoweth and Pressman 2020) when the night suddenly erupted with the sound of rapid gunshots. Micah Xavier Johnson, a Black army veteran, had climbed to the top of a parking garage, armed with an assault weapon and a handgun, and opened fire. Johnson was unaffiliated with any organization associated with the Movement for Black Lives, but he was nevertheless a Black man who expressed animus toward white police and killed four officers during a protest. The Pew Research Center found that news coverage changed in the wake of the sniper's actions in Dallas, with news stories becoming more likely to portray the movement as a source of dangerous division. However, BLM was able to win back positive coverage in a relatively short span—not by chance, but because of the efforts of a dedicated and skilled communications apparatus.

M4BL condemned the ambush and killing of police while emphasizing that the shooter had no affiliation with the movement and, utilizing their brilliant ability to connect specific instances to larger political and social patterns, insisted that the gunman ought to be just as eligible for the "lone gunman" trope as he would have been if he were white. An article in the Guardian noted, "It was a type of angst familiar to many people of color, and perhaps best encapsulated in a tweet by the writer Ijeoma Oluo: 'We are all awake, waiting for news, because we know: if the shooter is white, he pays. If the shooter is black, our entire movement pays.'" The article further reported that "[t]he BLM organization responded . . . head-on, calling the attack 'the result of the actions of a lone gunman' and calling it 'dangerous and irresponsible' to 'assign the actions of one person to an entire movement'" (Lartey and Felton 2016). The same article quoted the Washington, DC–based activist Lauren Allen as she explained that the movement would not be cowed by baseless accusations. She pointed out that "Black Lives Matter [is] the simplest affirmation out there. Anyone against affirming that Black Lives Matter simply thinks they don't. The events in Dallas don't change that" (quoted in Lartey and Felton 2016). In this instance, one that could have easily been the undoing of the movement's largely positive public image, those affiliated remained undeterred from this simple, profound anchor—Black lives, all Black lives, matter, and the movement would not curtail this demand even in the face of attempts to blame the group for one unaffiliated individual's actions.

Displacing the Colorblind Narrative

This foundational belief is the place from which all discursive battles in the movement are waged. Through sustained effort, M4BL has ushered in a new understanding of why frank acknowledgement of anti-Blackness must be at the center of efforts toward social, political, and economic equity in the United States. It is a stunning accomplishment, and it was gained through persistent and persuasive arguments that reframed the nature of the problem as one of combatting white supremacy rather than combatting instances of discrimination. It is perhaps no surprise then that the movement fought so hard to prevent the phrase Black Lives Matter from being co-opted or changed to All Lives Matter in the early days of the hashtag's popularity. In so doing, the movement convinced people who consider themselves allied not to deploy that phrase and, further, exhorted them to educate others about why that lingual substitution is unacceptable. A Pew Research Center report quotes one respondent, who explained:

> Black lives matter vs. All lives matter: I'm white. Initially, I saw nothing wrong with saying "All lives matter"—because all lives do matter. Through social media I've seen many explanations of why that statement is actually dismissive of the current problem of black lives seeming to matter less than others and my views have changed. (Anderson 2016)

The movement worked to displace the dominant colorblind narrative that had reigned as the standard of liberal fairness in the late twentieth century with one that used systemic racism as its main lens. Using this method of confronting the dominant mythologies of race neutrality or blindness as standards for justice, the movement has been successful at changing the political conversations as well as some people's attitudes.

For example, one study by the social psychologists Jeremy Sawyer and Anup Gampa, which examined the racial attitudes of 1,369,204 respondents between 2009 and 2016, found that the social movement had a significant impact on reducing "pro-white" racist attitudes in the population at large. Indeed, the authors posit that social movements are the *only* phenomenon that has been successful at changing society-wide attitudes. Lab experiments and prominent non-stereotypical exemplars (like Barack Obama) appear to have either no effect or short-term effects on public attitudes that revert to the mean after a matter of days (Sawyer and Gampa 2018).

By contrast, social movements create new associations with the group making claims, and this repeated exposure can change people's implicit evaluations of the group because it changes the underlying associations that shape their impression of the group. Further, exposure to social movements not only changes the concepts that people associate (consciously or unconsciously) with the group protesting, but can also *cause them to alter their own identity*. In the case of M4BL, this means that people who support the movement come to think of their moral and political duty as one characterized by an active anti-racism rather than by the passive non-racism indicated in the fictive ideology of colorblindness. Though there are valid critiques of the limits of certain kinds of "anti-racist" approaches to politics and social life, the fact remains that this change in self-perception leads to changes in both political attitudes and behaviors.

In addition, movement rallies, interviews, and media coverage have given Black people the opportunity to directly voice their experiences and analyses of racism and its effects. This is potentially significant because listening to opinions expressed through speech seems to increase the likelihood that individuals will attribute nuanced, human qualities (rather than dehumanizing stereotypical ones) to those expressing the opinion—even if they do not currently share that opinion (Schroeder, Kardas, and Epley 2017). Furthermore, the millions of non-Black individuals who attend demonstrations in defense of Black lives or who come to politically identify with the movement may create new associations between themselves and Black people; such associations with the self are thought to produce more positive evaluations of the attitude object (Walther and Trasselli 2003). Furthermore, through participation in or identification with the social movement, there is the possibility of creating a common in-group identity (e.g., as anti-racists) that includes a multiracial coalition, which evidence suggests can reduce racial bias (Gaertner and Dovidio 2005).

It is crucial to underline this point: exposure to social movements can change people's attitudes in a way that exposure to individuals in the group who are deemed exceptional do not. For example, Barack Obama may activate specific preexisting associations with him, in particular (e.g., powerful, accomplished), which do not translate to the group. In contrast, a social movement that repeatedly pairs Black people in general with positive concepts and words ("joy," "magic," "unapologetic," "care"), images, and traits (honest, courageous, determined) can change the underlying valence of associations that observers have with Black people in general, thus causing more fundamental and lasting change in people's perceptions at the aggregate, societal level. This means social movements can change the common public associations about what membership in a group means. This is a profound effect of social movements. Admittedly, such changes in attitudes do not guarantee immediate changes in the actions of the powerful or the adoption of policies favored by the group, but it does reshape the field of political possibilities available to political challengers, giving them space to make their case in the public sphere and increasing the possibility that they may persuade majorities and decision-makers to their side (Woodly 2015a).

Finally, although systemic racism is a seemingly intractable problem, a mass movement like M4BL can stimulate the political imagination, raising hopes that there are things that can be done to solve long-standing problems. This increases the sense of political efficacy in the polity, combatting the politics of despair. Such an increased sense of efficacy has been found to not only increase whites' engagement in anti-discriminatory action but also to be associated with an increase in explicitly positive attitudes toward Black people (Stewart et al. 2010). Further, Sawyer and Gampa's (2018) study shows that since the emergence of the Movement for Black Lives, the trend among white people toward increasing anti-Black attitudes, which accelerated during the Obama administration, has begun to *reverse*. And unlike public opinion data, which shows this shift away from anti-Blackness only among liberals, this measure of implicit and explicit bias shows that liberals and conservative whites were all affected—with the highest-magnitude changes among liberals, and less dramatic, but still statistically significant, changes among conservative whites.

Interestingly, among Black respondents the changes were different: Black people's explicit attitudes have become more race neutral since 2014, but their implicit attitudes have not changed, remaining neutral to slightly pro-Black. At first glance, these appear to be opposing trends in Blacks' and whites' explicit attitudes, but they can also be viewed as a mutual shift toward an egalitarian, no preference position. Such a shift in explicit attitudes could be considered consistent with the movement's egalitarian underpinning (Sawyer and Gampa 2018, 1056). This is a noteworthy finding. Apparently, the implied "also" in Black Lives Matter was readily apparent to Black people, who experienced all the movement's pro-Blackness as *egalitarianism* in the face of what Edward Bonilla-Silva has called colorblind racism.

Communicating the Movement

Remember, this push toward awareness of both Black humanity and the white supremacist ideology that denies it did not happen because of a natural political evolution; instead, it has been the result of public discourse and political action initiated by people involved in the movement. This kind of public education through discussion and participation is, in part, what movements do simply by taking to the streets and articulating their positions, but M4BL has been very deliberate about embarking on the communicative and educational aspect of movement work, making an effort to deploy consistent and resonant framing in a variety of different modalities and mediums.

Professional communications people in movement spaces, like Shanelle Matthews and Fresco Steez, understand their jobs in very expansive terms. Movement communicators must not only be prepared for rapid response in the face of crisis, but must also understand their ultimate purpose to be the facilitation of widespread changes in general attitudes. In a 2017 interview, Matthews explained her job as the

> eradication of existing harmful narratives that are deeply insidious and rooted oftentimes in our subconscious, so it requires a particular kind of approach . . ., to eradicate those and to create new narratives but it's also think[ing] about how people in America understand Blackness, Black people, and so it's redefining for ourselves in this current iteration of the

Black Liberation Movement what Blackness looks like and in creating narratives that [are] not about just hearts and heads, and not just Black people but [about] people of all races and ethnicities [and] about how Black people exist in the world, who we are, how we construct our families, how we identify—you know, on our very real humanness. There is a pervasive dehumanization around Blackness and it leads to both implicit and explicit prejudicial policing, vigilante violence, death, deportation, and interpersonal violence between everyday people which makes even the most simple of interactions undignified. The work from where I come from is about changing people's behavior so that Black people can live free full lives in this democracy.

It is important to understand that not only is the Movement for Black Lives a consortium of individuals and organizations whose concerns are much broader than police violence, but likewise that the hashtag #BlackLivesMatter became the anchor for a wide-ranging online conversation that spawned additional hashtags, and attendant attention, information-gathering, reporting, and frame development for topics from Black women's often overlooked deaths at the hands of police (#SayHerName) to Black men's mental health (#YouGoodMan) and celebrations of Black culture (#ThanksgivingWithBl ackFamilies). These nested arguments created an expansive frame relating the idea that Black Lives Matter to many aspects of life in a way that was both plural and coherent, giving the discussions that took place under the banner of the hashtag texture and gravitas. People could find many spaces in movement discourse where they could locate themselves. Because there was so much space for people to see themselves and their various lived experience, there was a multitudinous proliferation of conversations on themes, problems, and solutions inspired but not controlled by movement organizations. Indeed, one study of social media accounts that self-identified as (and produced content) supportive of the Black Lives Matter Movement found that 44 percent of such accounts had no explicit organizational links (Mundt, Ross, and Burnett 2018).

For example, the hashtag #IfTheyGunnedMeDown served as a contemporaneous critique of media coverage perpetuating anti-Black troupes about victims of police violence. The hashtag was not initiated by a movement organization; instead, it was authored by ordinary Black people who flooded their social media timelines with two dichotomous pictures of themselves under the hashtag—one that, through the lens of white supremacy, could be considered "respectable," such as a graduation photo, and another that, through the same lens, could be considered "thuggish," with the subject in hip-hop fashions with a red Solo cup in hand. These side-by-side images created a powerful space for highlighting how white-supremacist stereotypes function to deny Black people's humanity and negatively impact their life chances even when no one individual is acting the part of the racist villain. Social media hashtags like this one created a space where people could express their personal fears—in this case, the fear of being murdered by police—in a broader context that illuminated the systemic practices and structural relations that render Black life expendable. Importantly, this hashtag and others like it created a context in which Black people could share the personal fear and pain that results from simply existing in a Black body in the world as it is. This way of sharing personal experiences—while explicitly connecting those experiences to a cultural and structural context—created a sense of community, reframed debates about the impact of race on daily life in America, and launched a trenchant critique that was immediately legible to both sympathetic non-Black people observing the conversation and to decision-makers in media who were being called out.

When I say that these hashtagged conversations create a sense of community, I mean they foster a sense of "membership, influence, integration and fulfill [the] need [for] shared emotional connection" (Schuschke and Tynes 2016, 27). Communities are often created and nurtured in private, but social media communities manage to create a sense of intimacy while existing entirely in public view. It is a peculiar and marvelous phenomenon. It not only allows people to build connections, cultivate group identities, and signify (a term describing the display cultural competence through wordplay), but it also allows those outside the group to witness this process, following along, adapting, and, sometimes, appropriating (and being criticized for appropriating) as their own inclination and context warrants. This, of course, is the normal process of colloquial language, but social media makes the genesis vivid and increases the speed of linguistic and idea-formation and diffusion exponentially. For example, "Black Twitter" is such a community. It is the colloquial name for Black users of the social media platform who are frequent participants in discussing various topics through a Black cultural lens (Brock 2012; Florini 2014; Sharma 2013). The denizens of Black Twitter frequently discuss both politics and pop culture, celebrating and critiquing mainstream phenomena (like the HBO fantasy epic *Game of Thrones*, discussed under the hashtag #DemThrones) and works created by Black artists (lush debates about the relevance of Beyoncé's #Lemonade). This combination creates an intimate atmosphere that is full of challenge, amusement, and analysis, which can be witnessed by anyone, and has therefore become influential in shaping American cultural understandings and public meanings, particularly on topics that are understood (or come to be understood) as racialized.

In interviews conducted with the managers of social media pages associated with M4BL, Marcia Mundt and her coauthors found that M4BL organizers explicitly identified three main uses for social media engagement. First, social media helps to mobilize resources, including both human and material capital. Second, these platforms are useful for building coalition between different movement organizations and potential allies outside the movement. Finally, social media is key for shaping and controlling the narrative of the movement (Mundt, Ross, and Burnett 2018; Yang 2016).

Another important aspect of the massive yet discursively coherent social media presence of the movement is that a lot of different kinds of people engage with it. The Movement for Black Lives is first and foremost for Black people, but it occupies an influential place in a multiracial social justice space peopled with both organizations whose focus is complimentary but distinct, such as #MeToo and the Environmental Justice Movement, and individuals who simply consider themselves and/or aspire to be anti-racist. Estimates of BLM-branded email lists and Facebook groups often include up to 40 percent non-Black members unless they are explicitly restricted to participants who identify as Black (Olteanu, Weber, and Gatica-Perez 2016). Though no movement is fully able to direct the ways its message is taken up, the social media environment adds a level of complexity, since parties outside the movement may use hashtags to index thoughts and link ideas according to their own interpretation, in a way that amounts to what Jelani Ince and his coauthors call "distributed framing" (Ince, Rojas, and Davis 2017).

Distributed framing has advantages and detriments. On the one hand, it allows a wide swath of people who are learning about or supportive of movement goals to participate in and shape the conversation about the ideas, problems, and issues that might be fruitfully discussed under the banner of movement-originating hashtags. This is a positive element of social media discourse because it increases the number of arguments nested under one narrative frame. As I showed in the *Politics of Common Sense*, movements that are able to sustain broad and nuanced public conversations that are nevertheless coherent are more likely to change public meanings about their struggle. M4BL has been remarkably successful in this regard. Disparate users deploy multiple related hashtags to describe different experiences and observations while all are still able to connect their analysis to #BlackLivesMatter.

On the other hand, distributive framing allows people who wish to challenge the motivations and veracity of the movement to argue, mischaracterize, or co-opt hashtags for contradictory or malicious interventions. However, counternarratives to movement framings have been less successful. For example, the detracting hashtags #AllLivesMatter, #BlueLivesMatter, and #TCOT (top conservatives on Twitter) were less tightly correlated in co-occurrence, making counterarguments less coherent than the movement frames that were anchored by #blm and #Ferguson, and, in any case, were dwarfed in the overall frequency of Twitter discourse and fell in circulation more quickly (Ince, Rojas, and Davis 2017; Ray et al. 2017).

The broad movement in defense of Black lives has had such success communicating its message because it has focused not only on changing policy, but also, and more fundamentally, on changing how we think about what justice requires. The movement has done this by taking anti-Blackness straight on, not only refusing to use colorblind frameworks but also challenging would-be allies not to either. This challenge is accompanied by an explanation that is repeated via multiple mediums and across venues from social media to conventional news and in creative projects. Those involved in the movement understand that what needs to change is not only policy but also public meanings.

Jennifer Hochschild writes that "changing meaning is changing the measure of value" (Hochschild 1996, 67). If you change the measure of value, outcomes can be different even when the formula or underlying principle remains the same. This is what we have to learn about the significance of public meaning (the commonplace assessment/measure of value) and political understanding (the formula or principle that the value ought to be plugged into: results norm, ascriptive norm, etc.). Speech is the action that changes the relationship between these terms: it is through speech that we come to understand and communicate the relevant measure of value of certain things (e.g., regarding the death penalty, is it more important to kill the guilty or refrain from killing the innocent?). And it is through speech that we plug these value measures into existing principles (e.g., justice as repair not retribution).

Decarceral Trends and Decreases in Police Killings

During the time that the Movement for Black Lives has been making claims in the public sphere, there have been several notable decarceral trends. Since 2014, the movement has added urgency and gravitas to the ongoing prison reform and abolitionist work that has been taking place in the country since the late twentieth century. There is no evidence that M4BL's activities directly caused the beginning of a larger-scale decarceral tendency, but the wide circulation of decarceral arguments in mainstream public discourse, which is attributable to the movement, created a common-sense justification for attempting to shrink the incarcerated population.

In the year after the uprising in Ferguson and the formation of the movement, the number of incarcerated people dropped dramatically, continuing a trend that goes back to 2009. From 2014 to 2015, the US prison population shrank by 2.3 percent, or 35,716 people. Each year thereafter, the prison population has shrunk by about 1.2 percent, or around 18,000 people. This rate of decarceration, while painfully slow, represents a reversal of the trend of greater incarceration that occurred every year from 1980 to 2009, when the first small drop (0.1 percent or 1,684 people) was followed by fluctuating increases and decreases until 2014, when protesters took over the streets in support of preserving Black lives in cities and towns across the nation. While police violence has not decreased overall nationally, police killing of Black people, particularly in cities, has decreased significantly (see Figure 3).

In addition, a 2021 study by Travis Campbell found that between 2014 and 2019, cities and towns where BLM protests had been held had as much as a 20 percent decline in police killings. This means that protestors may have saved an estimated three hundred lives during the period (Daley 2021). While these findings are stunning, it is important to note that the mechanisms causing the decarceral trend and the decline in police homicides remain unclear. And while police killings decreased across the nation, police killings in four cities—Minneapolis, Portland, San Francisco, and St. Louis—actually increased. What is clear is that there is a significant correlation between the emergence of the Black Lives Matter movement, less incarceration, and fewer homicides of Black people by police.

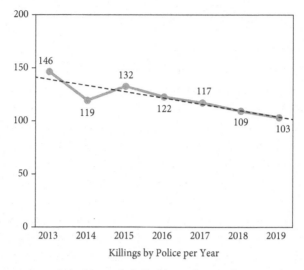

Figure 3. Number of Black people killed by police in the United States, 2013–2019.

Source: *Mapping Police Violence: National Trends* (data science project of Campaign Zero), https://mappingpoliceviolence.org/nationaltrends.

Tactical Diffusion

Another effect of the movement has been the diffusion of tactics that aim to decrease civilian contact with police and the resultant violence and incarceration. There are two main tactics that have been popularized by M4BL: the electoral removal of corrupt or regressive district attorneys and sheriffs, and the promotion of bail-out funds and actions. The former tactic has been the most widespread, bringing attention to the astonishing latitude and almost unchecked power of prosecutors in the juridical process. Early on, the movement and affiliated organizations began targeting elected prosecutors with records of overzealous criminalization of Black and brown youth combined with histories of never holding police accountable for violence against civilians and, in some cases, helping them cover up particularly troubling incidents. The first of two high-profile prosecutors removed by movement campaigns were Florida's notorious Angela Corey, who was the State's Attorney during the George Zimmerman trial, and Illinois's Anita Alvarez, who presided over the police cover-up of the murder of a mentally ill teenager, Laquan McDonald. Both prosecutors were handed crushing defeats in

2016, the first elections held after the notorious incidents and the formation of M4BL.

In Florida, a progressive coalition, including members of Dream Defenders, worked to oust Corey, dubbed "the cruelest prosecutor in America" (Pishko 2016a) due to her penchant for charging preteen children as adults, her eagerness to seek the death penalty, and her pattern of prosecuting victims of abuse for offenses committed during the course of that abuse. Her reluctance to charge George Zimmerman for the stalking murder of Trayvon Martin, and her eagerness to shut Marissa Alexander behind bars for firing warning shots at her abusive husband, are only two examples of a history of seemingly malicious prosecution. Before those cases, she made herself infamous because she charged twelve-year-old Christian Fernandez as an adult after the boy pushed his two-year-old brother into a bookshelf, causing the toddler to sustain a fatal skull fracture. She moved forward with murder charges even though medical experts testified that the toddler would not have died had the children's mother taken him to the hospital after the injury. The mother, Biannela Susana, was not home at the time of the incident and did not take the younger boy to the hospital until nine hours later because she hoped the boy would wake on his own and was afraid that child protective services would take her children from her.

This tragic series of events does much to not only illuminate Corey's pattern of cruelty, but also to highlight the recurrence of the themes I have emphasized regarding the politics of care. Think about the facts of this case and observe what could be gained by a politics of care. Imagine a child welfare system in which poor and working mothers could be supported instead of threatened when they find their children injured or endangered. Imagine a politics in which we recognized that living wages and affordable childcare for parents go a much longer way in providing for the safety of all children than the separation of families and punishment of the neglected after the fact.

While the tactic of removing regressive DA's is widespread, it is not always a straightforward fight of good versus evil. The way that prosecutors are structurally positioned, their job is to punish, even when they intend to wield that power in a less harmful way. In addition, the electoral conditions surrounding races for district attorney are not always favorable to movement demands or preferences. For example, the fight to oust Corey was not straightforward. Not only did organizers have to make certain that people understood that prosecutors are elected and could therefore be voted out; they also had to grapple with the fact that Corey's only credible opponent,

Melissa Nelson, was a conservative Republican endorsed by the NRA. However, she was also one of the attorneys who defended 12-year-old Christian Fernandez. Those in coalition to oust Corey could not in good conscience campaign for Nelson. Instead, they could only campaign against Corey, a polarizing figure who had earned enemies on all sides of the political spectrum. As such, their victory could only be partial. Nevertheless, organizers understood that removing Corey would be an important first step for both forwarding an argument about rampant and cruel overprosecution and significantly reducing harm to people subject to the authority of the district attorney's office.

In addition to the ethical complexities organizers faced, they also had to wrestle with practical challenges associated with the laws surrounding DA elections. Those working to remove Corey from office had to deal with deviously creative election chicanery that had echoes of the Jim Crow era, which were perpetrated by Corey's campaign. This is because, in Florida, party primaries are open to all voters if there is no one running from another party. Republicans dominate the northeastern part of the state, and Corey's opponent was also a Republican. However, Corey directed her campaign manager to file paperwork for her to run as a third-party candidate, thus technically making the election a competition between two parties and therefore artificially creating a closed primary. This cynical ploy (which was deemed legal) meant that only registered Republicans would be able to vote, and nearly all the Black folks who organized to have her removed had been expecting to vote in an open primary, but would now be locked out of the election unless they changed their party affiliation (Piskho 2016). Nevertheless, working in coalition, those who had stood up for Trayvon Martin stood against Angela Corey. When Election Day came, Melissa Nelson, won the primary, beating Corey by 38 percentage points. This was a remarkable achievement, as no incumbent prosecutor in this district had *ever* lost a contested election before.

In the same year, a coalition of groups under the banner of the movement, led by BYP100, unseated Chicago District Attorney Anita Alvarez. Alvarez had presided over both the police cover-up of the murder of Laquan McDonald and the maintenance of an off-the-books interrogation center in Homan Square, where seven thousand African American arrestees were abducted and held in secret detention facilities for months or years (Ackerman 2015). Black youth in Chicago organized the #ByeAnita campaign that would not only unseat the two-term incumbent prosecutor, but also handed her a bruising defeat in which she lost every majority Black ward in Chicago and won less than 30 percent of the vote in a three-person race for the office (Grimm 2016). In her place, movement organizations supported the successful bid of a progressive young African American lawyer, Kim Foxx, who campaigned on the need for a special prosecutor to examine all police-involved shootings, sentencing reform, and transparent and accurate data collection by the Chicago Police Department (Uetricht 2016). However, the #ByeAnita campaign had even further-reaching consequences. The movement's work to expose the deep corruption of the Chicago Police Department and the district attorney's office in covering up the murder of McDonald had also implicated the city's mayor, Rahm Emmanuel, who announced shortly after Alvarez's resounding defeat that he would not seek a third term in office.

In Houston, the movement helped unseat another district attorney, Devon Anderson, who had a history of mysteriously losing evidence and turning a blind eye to the abuse or death of arrestees in jail. Movement organizations and their collaborators and allies have fought and won similar victories in St. Louis, Missouri; rural Mississippi; Henry County, Georgia; several counties in Florida; and numerous locales in California, New York, and more (Alcindor 2016; Smith 2016). As Figures 4–8 show, except for the Rocky Mountain states (excluding Colorado), there is no region of the country untouched by this movement tactic. Since 2014, a wave of progressive or reform prosecutors have been elected all over the nation. While the definition of "progressive" prosecutor is hotly debated, and many public defenders will argue with you about whether such a designation can ever be accurate, seventy-three prosecutors who claim the mantle "progressive" have unseated more conservative incumbents since the events in Ferguson.

The second major tactic that has diffused more widely since the movement popularized their use is the creation of bail-out programs. These programs are aimed at bringing attention to the injustice of the cash bail system, in which defendants who are charged with crimes but have not been convicted are held in jail rather than being allowed to go home to await trial simply because they do not have the ability to pay. The most common use of bail funds previous to being taken up by the movement was to get people out of immigration detention. Although bail funds were occasionally used to free people charged with domestic criminal offenses, especially in large coastal cities like

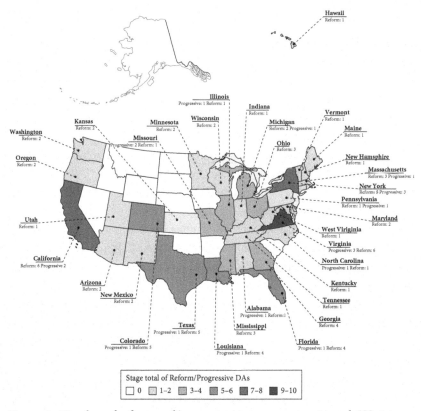

Figure 4. Number of reform and/or progressive prosecutors in each US state.

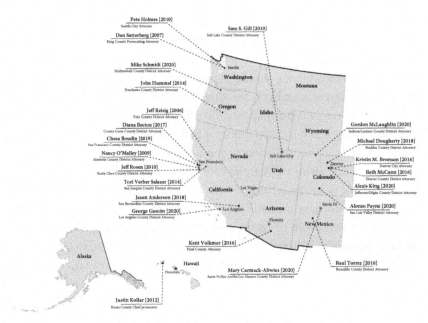

Figure 5. Western regional map of progressive and reform prosecutors.

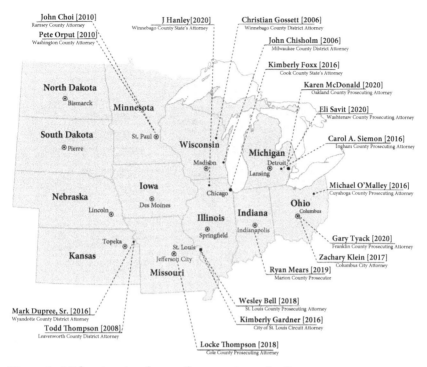

Figure 6. Midwest regional map of progressive and reform prosecutors.

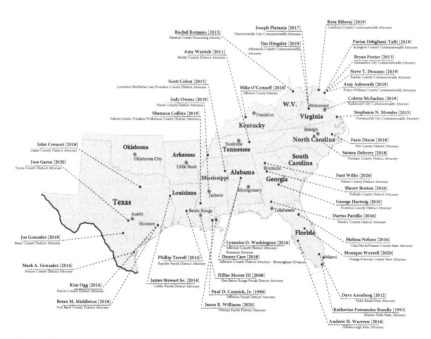

Figure 7. Southern regional map of progressive and reform prosecutors.

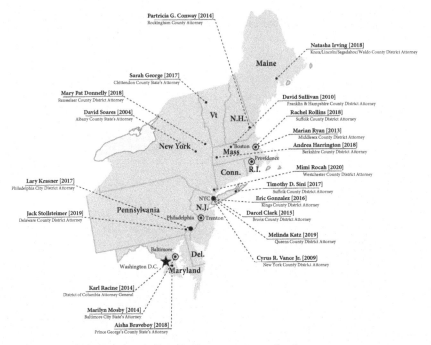

Figure 8. Northeast regional map of progressive and reform prosecutors.

New York and San Francisco, such programs were small and disappearing before the movement-driven revival of interest in criminal justice reform in 2014 (Pinto 2020).

The largest bail-out action taken by M4BL, the Black Mama's Day Bail Out, was the brainchild of Mary Hooks. Explaining her reasoning for launching the national action (which first took place the week of Mother's Day in 2017 and has continued annually), Hooks says, "Black people have a tradition of using our collective resources to buy each other's freedom. We have an opportunity to do that when we understand how the cash bail system works. The sooner we can get folks out, the ability for them to mitigate their cases increases and the less collateral damage they are likely to incur" (quoted in Patterson 2017). That first year, the Black Mama's Day Bail Out Action grew to involve dozens of organizations in eight cities and raised over $500,000, which it used to bail out over fifty women. By 2019, it had become a cornerstone action of the new organization National Bail Out, a consortium of community, city, and faith-based bail funds, which raised well over 1.5 million dollars and freed three hundred women (Evans 2019).

New Policy Initiatives

The movement's policy achievements (beyond the election of new DA's that set new criminal justice policy in their jurisdictions) have been won largely at the state and municipal levels, and they are numerous. Since M4BL introduced its demand to "defund the police" in 2020, nine states and dozens of localities have attempted to answer that call by developing programs that divert resources from armed law enforcement to unarmed support professionals (O'Connor 2021b). These programs are a patchwork and aim to reduce the resources of police departments as well as their contact with ordinary citizens. As of March 2021, Washington, Indiana, Oregon, Utah, and Maryland have moved to implement programs that divert 911 calls regarding mental health and substance use issues to civilian support staff rather than police. Illinois and Oregon have legislation that would keep police out of schools, and Hawaii and Maryland have legislation pending to disentangle police from traffic enforcement. Additionally, New York, New Jersey, and Maryland have legislation pending that would discourage or ban traffic-ticket quotas, which some police departments use as measures of officer performance, leading to excessive contact between police and citizens. If taken up nationwide, the removal of police from traffic enforcement would *dramatically* reduce civilian contact with police, as traffic stops are by far the most common way people encounter police.

Reducing contact between police and civilians by cutting departmental budgets and reducing the number of police is, as Mariame Kaba reminds us, the only proven way to reduce police violence (Kaba 2021). Measures that have sought to make police less violent through retraining have consistently failed. In point of fact, in Minneapolis, where George Floyd was suffocated to death by police in 2020, had adopted many reforms in its policing policies after police murdered Philando Castile in front of his family in 2016. These included instituting a new automated tracking system that flagged police officers with too many use of force complaints, instituting "coaching sessions" to serve as retraining for such officers, narrowing the circumstances under which officer killings would be considered justified under department policy, and rewriting their use of force policy to include the requirement that police must intervene when their fellow officers became abusive (Lartey and Weichselbaum 2020). However, none of those policies prevented four police officers from either participating in or standing by while George Floyd was brutalized and killed.

Cities have also shown an interest in reducing police budgets, shrinking police forces, and decreasing contact between citizens and armed law enforcement. The most complete step toward removing police from civilian encounters is taking place in Ithaca, New York, where Mayor Svante Myrick has proposed abolishing the police force. The proposed new configuration would "replac[e] the city's current 63-officer, $12.5 million a year department with a 'Department of Community Solutions and Public Safety,'" which would include mostly unarmed "community solution workers," along with a smaller force of armed "public safety workers," "all of whom [would] report to a civilian director of public safety instead of a police chief" (Lowery 2021). Myrick reports that he came to the conclusion that such a large-scale reimagining was necessary because after conducting focus groups with community members and police officers, he found that

> the officers are stressed and need a new model and the community is fed up with the current situation . . . it became clear we need to build something from scratch. They say that systems give the results that they're designed to give. And we built police departments and have been nibbling around the edges ever since. It's like trying to turn a refrigerator into an air conditioner and you can do it, but it won't work great. . . . You need to build from the ground up. (Favreau 2021)

Elsewhere, in 2019 and 2020, Denver, San Francisco, and Oakland developed mental health responder programs to eliminate the role of police in answering 911 calls for those experiencing a mental health challenges. This is a critical intervention given that since 2015, police have killed at least 1,400 people in the midst of mental health crises. A 2021 study by Mapping Police Violence found that removing police from mental health calls and traffic enforcement could prevent nearly one in five police killings. Further, if police were removed from calls where no one involved had a gun, police killings could decrease by 55–60 percent (Sinyangwe 2021).

In Denver, the city's Support Team Assistance Response (STAR) program is designed to provide a "person-centric mobile crisis response" to community members who are experiencing problems related to mental health, depression, poverty, homelessness, or substance abuse issues (Hauck 2021). Early data shows that these programs are phenomenally successful, competently addressing the needs of those in difficult circumstances without the threat of arrest or other violence. Additionally, San Francisco has revoked a law passed in 1994, at the height of the "tough-on-crime" era, that arbitrarily designated a mandatory level of full-time staffing for the city's police department. Now, the police department will be subject to the same rules as other city departments and will have to submit requests and rationales for annual funding (Weill-Greenberg 2020).

Berkeley, California, has pending legislation to remove police from traffic enforcement. Seattle cut $30 million from its police budget and will now enter a participatory budgeting process to allocate the savings to other social support services (Kaur 2021). In Austin, Texas, the city council cut $6.5 million from the police budget and plans to use that money to supplement the budget of the locality's Housing and Planning Department to create permanent housing for the city's unhoused (O'Connor 2021a).

This assortment of policies springing up like mushrooms all over the country may seem small in their impact, but they are the signs of initial acceptance of the fundamental logic that animates modern abolitionism; that is, if we, as a society, want to make individuals and communities safer, we need to directly invest in them and the provision of basic needs rather than in the apparatus of punishment. Christy Lopez, a Georgetown Law School professor, puts the matter succinctly: investing in social support rather than law enforcement is not "taking anything away from public safety . . . it's more directly addressing the root causes of a lack of public safety" (quoted in O'Connor 2021a). Likewise, Melina Abdullah, cofounder of Black Lives Matter Los Angeles, expresses this sentiment clearly, characterizing these shifts in policy and priorities as "a commonsense response," to the lethal failures of policing as it currently exists, pointing out that "you should have the appropriate professionals respond to the appropriate issues" (quoted in O'Connor 2021a). These efforts to divest from policing and punishment and invest in social support also indicate the first measurable diminishment of what had been an unassailable police power. They are the first, concrete, democratic experiments with what it means, in practice, to "defund the police" and begin implementing what Kaba has called "non-reformist reforms" as intermediate steps toward abolition (Kaba 2021).

Additionally, movement organizations around the country have fought for and won the creation and/or granting of new powers to 131 police oversight boards in forty-two states. The most powerful of these was created in Los Angeles County, where Black Lives Matter Global Network Foundation cofounder Patrisse Khan-Cullors has run the organization Dignity and Power Now since 2012. This organization was developed for the express purpose of supporting the incarcerated and their families, as well as pushing to curtail police power and decrease the criminalization of Black and brown peoples, especially the mentally ill. Though the creation of the civilian review board was a big win, as it creates a place where reports of abuse can be lodged and evaluated with mandatory public reporting, Dignity and Power Now was not able to secure subpoena or disciplinary power for the citizen panel, nor was it able to secure spots on the board for formerly incarcerated people. Dignity and Power Now is still organizing for these further victories under their campaign End Sheriff Violence.

The fact that this variety of policy experimentation is widespread, popular, and, in cases where changes have been implemented, are working well, bodes well for political challengers seeking to decrease and eventually abolish the role of police and prisons in American life, and also speaks to the astonishing influence that the Movement for Black Lives has had on our political sensibilities in a startling short amount of time.

Electoral Wins and New Political Ecosystem

As impressive as the movement's policy wins to date are, more important over the long term is the fact that M4BL has seeded and is supporting a vast ecosystem of new political infrastructure where progressive Black young people are being organized, trained, and mobilized for a variety of different political functions. Much (though not nearly all) of this work has taken place in the realms of political communication and electoral politics. This is somewhat surprising given that these aspects of the movement, while always present, were seen between 2014 and 2016 as the least pressing and important parts of movement work. During the run-up to the 2016 election, when the Democratic Party tried to claim allyship with the movement, M4BL posted (on August 30, 2015) the following statement on their Facebook page:

> A resolution signaling the Democratic National Committee's endorsement that Black lives matter, in no way implies an endorsement of the DNC by the Black Lives Matter Network, nor was it done in consultation with us. We do not now, nor have we ever, endorsed or affiliated with the Democratic Party, or with any party. The Democratic Party, like the Republican and all political parties, have historically attempted to control or contain Black people's efforts to liberate ourselves. True change requires real struggle, and that struggle will be in the streets and led by the people, not by a political party. . . .

While the Black Lives Matter Network applauds political change towards making the world safer for Black life, our only endorsement goes to the protest movement we've built together with Black people nationwide—not the self-interested candidates, parties, or political machine seeking our vote.

Radical movements often deride electoral politics, and M4BL was no different. While no one prohibited electoral work and its value was deeply appreciated on the local level, particularly regarding DAs, sheriffs, and judges, some participants report being dismissed in meetings when they tried to put electoral work on organizational agendas. That was especially common before the election of Donald Trump.

When I asked people in the movement about the effect of Trump's election, many were quick to point out that the core problems that M4BL seeks to address are bigger than one occupant of the White House and are instead rooted in the fundament of white supremacy augmented, as it ever has been, by patriarchy and capitalism. BYP100 organizer Jewel Cadet's comments are typical:

I don't like talking about Donald Trump. I don't. I think that what has happened is a lot of people who were blind to the messed-up stuff in the world because it doesn't impact them—like the people who were like "racism doesn't exist" are now like "Oh. This is now impacting me and now I must speak up." But the impact of that is twofold for me. Part of me is really excited because we have so many people on chapter emails saying "I want to be a member, I want to do something." That's great, but then I go to rallies and I feel a greater sense of this microwave activism—people who feel like they can just pop in and pop out. Like, I went to this one rally and now I did my duty. And, that's disturbing to me as an organizer, and really, just as a Black person because—listen—ever since I was a little girl my mother told me, "You are going to have it hard in this world." And I was like, whoa, I just started! So, it didn't take a [new] president for me to feel marginalized. And it didn't take a [new] president for me to stand up and fight for the most marginalized. . . . That has been the foundation of my organizing. And so I wonder, for the people who are like "Oh, this person is in office, now let me be an activist." Does that mean when Trump leaves, you're going to leave the work? . . . I feel a little bit critical, because I think too many people are really driven by this person and not the issues of marginalization we've been dealing with from the beginning. (Museum of the City of NY 2017)

The criminal justice journalist Donovan Ramsey, while on a panel with NYC-based movement activists, put things even more bluntly:

> Donald Trump has not changed the landscape of this country at all. Many of the things that we have seen brought to the fore with the Trump presidency were things that were always there under the surface, and certain segments of our population—Black people, Latino people, queer people, vulnerable people—have always been right up against. It just wasn't mainstream. (Museum of the City of NY 2017)

Even so, there is no doubt that the organizing environment changed with the election of Donald Trump. Movement participants were as surprised as anyone when they discovered they would be organizing not to agitate against and reveal the hypocrisy of a centrist Clinton administration but instead would be fighting for the lives of more people who were suddenly in greater danger. Importantly, these threats were personal—with the FBI designation of Black activists as Black Identity Extremists, who could be charged with terrorism—as well as shocks to the conscience. The frank, white supremacist logic of the "Muslim ban" and the separation of immigrant children from their parents at the southern border were not being perpetrated in secret, but brazenly, in full public view, with no justification beyond violent xenophobia and few checks from the federal legal apparatus. And that legal apparatus was being quickly populated by judges who seemed to condone atrocity. There was little recourse in federal oversight agencies because the Trump administration preferred to leave those posts vacant or people them with individuals who held loyalty to the forty-fifth president's regime above any other duty.

For these reasons, Trump's election made at least three things come front and center that had been lurking in the background of movement work. First, mass protest and direct action became more dangerous and more difficult. Not only had some fatigue set in among organizers and activists after three years of almost constant street protests, but now the risk of state repression for protest actions had increased exponentially. While the Obama administration's police oversight under the leadership of Attorney General Eric Holder was slow, bureaucratically complicated, and too easily thwarted, it was also not overtly hostile to protestors and did not give local departments carte blanche. While the decommissioning of police departments under the Civil Rights Act was extremely rare, civil rights investigations were forthcoming, and the hassle for police departments that came with such scrutiny may have restrained some of their worst instincts. Under the forty-fifth president's administration, Attorney General Jeff Sessions and later William Barr ceased "pattern or practice" oversight of police departments and reinstated broad powers for civil asset forfeiture, a controversial and possibly unconstitutional practice that allows police to take the property of individuals they deem persons of interest, even when no one is charged with a crime.

Second, coalitional work with non-Black people, particularly non-Black immigrants, became more important. The movement's ties to Latino organizations like Mijente became stronger and more direct. In 2017, the Movement for Black Lives, with Mijente, cofounded the organization Rising Majority, which describes itself as "a coalition that seeks to develop a collective strategy and shared practice that involves labor, youth, abolition, immigrant rights, climate change, feminist, anti-war/imperialist, and economic justice forces in order to amplify our collective power and build alignment across our movements" (Rising Majority, n.d.).

Third, electoral politics emerged as a key arena for movement work. The inclusion of electoral work as a key aspect of movement work was neither easy nor inevitable. Even after Trump's election, some activists and organizers continued to chafe at the thought of spending resources and time on parties and candidates whom they felt had never delivered for their communities. In March 2018, the Cincinnati, Ohio, chapter of Black Lives Matter Global Network Foundation broke with the national organization, changing their name to Mass Action for Black Liberation and leveling a scathing critique of BLM, emphasizing their dissatisfaction with a "shift towards electoral and liberal Democratic Party politics and away from revolutionary ideas" (Jackson 2018). Shanelle Matthews, who was communications director of BLM Global Network Foundation at the time, responds to criticism like this by acknowledging the diversity of ideas within the movement, saying, "Atop many others, one undue burden for Black organizers is to repeat again and again, we are not all the same. We are not the same . . . but we each bring unique contributions that are necessary and critical to realizing a world where Black people live free of state violence and police terror" (quoted in Morrison 2016).

Despite these consequential disputes, there was a critical mass of organizers in the movement who had come to believe that even though electoral politics could not be the only path toward social transformation, it had to be among the tools in the movement's repertoire. Shanelle Matthews put it this way: "M4BL came to articulate its unique perspective on the place of electoral work in social movements through the development of a framework called 'electoral justice,' pioneered by Jessica Byrd, a movement organizer and director of Three Point Strategies, a firm specializing in running Black women's campaigns for elected office" (Matthews, n.d.).

In a 2018 interview, Jessica Byrd explained how she first came to understand both the tension and the possibility of electoral work in a social movement framework. It was a realization brought on by the contradiction she felt in her own professional life. In 2014, when the protests in Ferguson began, she was an Obama administration alum working for Emily's List. She recalls that when Michael Brown was murdered, she got really involved with Black activists in Washington, DC, where she was living at the time. Byrd recounts: "I would literally walk into my office and take my activist hat off, try to figure out how to recruit more women to run for office, and then walk out into the streets putting my activist hat back on and organizing protest and risking arrest. It started to be this double life that was very confusing to me." She goes on:

> Yeah, it was jarring. I mean it really changed everything for me because I've always been this person who felt like I was contributing in a meaningful way. I was working on campaigns, and it was just . . . I was watching all the activists around me be really unapologetic and draw very clear lines about what justice was and what it wasn't. Then I'm sitting in meetings [at my job] where they're like, "Well, aren't we lucky that Claire McCaskill leads Missouri" and I'm like, "Not really." If she was going to eradicate racism, then sure. But she's not. And then to have white women in the organization really look at me quizzically like, "Wait, what do you mean?" So that just really fucked me up. It shifted everything. So yeah, I decided to leave. . . .
>
> I started interviewing for positions and really thinking OK, what would it look like? How can I do racial justice movement work in electoral politics? And what I was finding was that nothing existed. And what I was learning was that I could either do racial justice work with no electoral politics or electoral politics work with no racial justice. And there were people who were like, "Yeah! Let's elect Black people," but still without the meat of the values. . . . All I wanted to do was to feel better about what I was contributing, so I just decided to take on a few projects for the movement that involved electoral aspects. I decided to train some folks to be campaign managers. Then I worked with a few activist organizations to conduct get

out the vote programs and the next thing you know, people were coming out of the woodwork saying, We want this! . . .

. . . that first year when I was, like, hustling for my rent, saying no to hundred-thousand-dollar contracts, saying no to even Black people who wanted me to work with them, who I liked but who weren't on board with the values of the movement. . . . It was really a lot of discipline. Like, I literally spent a lot of time saying to people, you gotta get your politics together, and this is what I mean by that: . . . you said you want to up the police budget in the face of, like, a shooting—let's talk about why that doesn't make sense for what movement wants to achieve. So, we ask the candidates we work with about fighting mass incarceration, demilitarizing the police . . . and ending cash bail. We talk to them about what decriminalizing Black people means—including thinking through the physical and mental barriers to health and well-being that exist in many of our neighborhoods. . . . We talk about fighting for access to equal education and reimagining benchmarks for students as well as workers' rights to a living wage and to form a union. . . . We want our candidates to go the boldest route. And so, we have really clear boundaries. And what was helpful was that at the end of 2015 the Movement for Black Lives put out the Vision for Black Lives [policy platform]. So I started to really get clear on what this ecosystem's vision was and at Three Point Strategies we have taken the Vision for Black Lives [platform] and have really underlined and underscored some public policy possibilities and we don't work with people outside of those. That, for me, is what movement electoral politics is. What it isn't is just representation without any sort of values. I think that we do that at our own peril. (Byrd interview, 2018)

In October 2017, Jessica Byrd and her friends Rukia Lumumba, an experienced campaign manager, and Kayla Reid, a talented organizer in St. Louis, launched the Electoral Justice Project as the official electoral arm of the Movement for Black Lives. The Electoral Justice Project describes itself as a coalition that "seeks to continue a long legacy of social movements fighting for the advancement of the rights of Black folks through electoral strategy." However, they are careful to note that electoral politics is one of many political pressure points that must be used to achieve movement goals, saying, "We recognize that voting alone will not change conditions plaguing Black communities, but we understand that with strategic political actions we can make immediate interventions as we move toward full, safe and healthy lives" (Three Point Strategies, n.d.). In the video announcing the launch of the project, Byrd explains:

Just when we've wrapped our minds around one harmful decision from our government, there's another right around the corner. Much has been said about the white nationalists with taxpayer-funded salaries in the White House, but there are other big boulders in our road. . . structural barriers like access to voting, redistricting and gerrymandering, political gatekeepers, and skyrocketing campaign costs keep us from building the power we need to transform our communities and to fight back. . . . . Our state and local policy makers are passing legislation that's harming our families and its criminalizing us for the color of our skin. It's going unchecked because people are intentionally being blocked from voting. . . . But imagine what's possible. How about the political home we deserve? With fairly drawn voting maps, with a clear respect for everyone's voices, without barriers? What about a political home that says, I love you, your life is important and your elected leaders and public policy should reflect that? Just like any other system in this nation, we can disrupt these barriers by seeking justice—electoral justice. Not because any one party or institution or candidate wants us to, but because we deserve it—because our lives and our Black futures require it. And we're building that home. The Movement for Black Lives has launched the Electoral Justice Project, a collaboration of more than fifty Black organizations that will weave a web of Black civic power in every corner of our communities. (Movement for Black Lives 2018)

Byrd, Lumumba, and Reed are all experienced political professionals. Notably, in 2018, Jessica Byrd would go on to run Stacey Abrams's historic campaign for governor of Georgia—a race that she lost by less than 2 percentage points and under uniquely suspicious circumstances, as her opponent was also overseeing the election in his official capacity as Georgia's sitting secretary of state. Rukia Lumumba is the executive director of the People's Advocacy Institute, an organization that partners with small community organizations to increase their capacities in whatever area they deem necessary by providing "education, training, coaching, investigation, research, advocacy and legal services to assist in defining the structural inequities that cause harm, and together we develop new policies and practices that reduce oppression, and foster self-determination and a more unbiased system" (People's Advocacy Institute, n.d.). She is also the sister of two-term

Jackson, Mississippi, mayor Chokwe Antar Lumumba, and cochaired his campaigns. Kayla Reed is the cofounder of Action St. Louis, an organization founded in the aftermath of the uprising in Ferguson to "build political power for Black communities in the St. Louis region" (Action St. Louis, n.d.). Reed organized the ouster of St. Louis prosecutor Bob McCulloch in 2018, who had occupied that position since 1991. Reed is particularly famed for her unique and fun approach to electoral organizing. Though the motivation for removing McCulloch from office was intensely sad—"with tears in my eyes, I left the house and joined thousands in the streets to protest this injustice. I never forgot [McCulloch's] face on the TV screen that night, nor his half-hearted apology to the family for their loss," she wrote for the *St. Louis American*—Reed's #ByeBob campaign was full of celebration and joy. She initially began organizing the campaign through "Woke Voter STL" brunches, in which she fed volunteers while they talked, laughed, and planned next steps (Germain 2018). Reed was also the mastermind behind a 2018 campaign of the Electoral Justice Project called #WakandaTheVote, where teams of volunteers in over fifty cities registered people who had headed out to see Marvel's first Black superhero in the movie *Black Panther* (Rueckert 2018). Together, these women lead a constellation of organizations that support candidates and draft policy that align with the Movement for Black Lives.

A Theory of Political Engagement

Within the Movement for Black Lives, electoral justice is regarded as one tool among many to fight for a world in which Black people can expect to not only survive but thrive. This means working to build social and political structures that will allow Black people to live freely —without the burden of "the talk" about how to avoid being brutalized or murdered by police, without the fear of dying in childbirth because Black people who give birth are exponentially more vulnerable, without the dread of premature death that shadows the vibrant lives of Black trans people, and without the injustice of the racial wealth gap created by discriminatory state and federal laws that cannot be closed through individual bootstrap strategies.[1] The disruption and challenge of

---

[1] On maternal deaths, see, for example, ProPublica's Lost Mothers series, at https://www. propublica.org/series/lost-mothers. On violence against Black trans people, see, for example, Donaghue 2020 and Human Rights Coalition 2020. On the racial wealth gap, see, for example, Martin 2019 and McIntosh et al. 2020.

protest and direct action are indispensable ways to press demands, but electoral politics remains essential for achieving these goals.

Like all other important aspects of the movement, electoral justice is deeply theorized by those who do the work, which is to say it is not just a slogan or an umbrella term for a set of political tactics—it is also and most profoundly a theory of democratic engagement. Each word holds explanatory power. *Electoral* refers to essential values that ought to be the foundation of representative democracy. These values of reflection, dialogue, voice, and participation can only result from a long-term process of mutual education, shared analyses, and community care. Proponents have observed that these democratic values are not nurtured in the world of robocalls and micro-targeted political ads. *Justice* expresses a particular conception of politics that centers marginalized voices and commits to an ongoing process of accountability and co-governance that far exceeds the moment when a ballot is cast. Justice is a practice of freedom derived from listening to and heeding the call of people suffering the deprivation and indignities of oppression and domination.

Under the umbrella of the Electoral Justice Project, launched in October 2017 (now called the Electoral Justice Voter Fund), M4BL is building an ecosystem of organizations that aims to organize Black voters, many of whom have felt shut out of or disinterested in the electoral process; recruit progressive Black candidates for all levels of government; and support both these endeavors with money and expertise that are independent of the Democratic Party. That last element is essential. The necessity of developing a political apparatus focused on Black progressive politics that is separate from the Democratic Party is the only way to create and preserve an electoral space for Black people beyond what Paul Frymer has called "electoral capture": the Democratic Party's historical and habitual disregard for a loyal constituency that has no other reasonable alternative for representation.

Therefore, electoral justice cannot be reduced to simply voting for candidates or advocating for policies, and it is not expressed via loyalty to a political party. Instead, it is the championing of an *ongoing practice toward freedom* that uses organizing strategies to help people understand themselves as agentive members of the polity who are not only called to periodically choose between candidates, but are, much more importantly, also the people who ought to set the political agenda. This means that electoral justice is not only a plea for representation but also a demand for ongoing accountability and co-governance. *Co-governance* here means meaningful engagement with stakeholder constituencies as political concerns and possibilities arise.

In this conception, electoral politics must be about more than temporary wins; it must also be about the development of the political environment in a way that makes transformative change both more possible and more probable. That means engaging constituents in a long-term and mutual process of political education, analysis, relationship-building, and mobilization. It is crucial to the project of electoral justice that Black people and those in other marginalized communities can meaningfully participate in imagining and implementing bold solutions for improving the conditions of their daily lives.

In 1965, Bayard Rustin argued that when organizing Black people around electoral politics, "more than voting is involved, here. A conscious bid for political power is being made." Electoral justice embraces this notion, and its proponents understand that gaining and holding political power requires organizing people long-term and building community institutions capable of both electing new people with political visions that align with movement goals but also, imperatively, holding those representatives to account as they carry out the duties of governance.

Unlike the assumption that underpins traditional politics, electoral justice understands that political transformation toward freedom takes an investment of time and care, of which mobilizing people to vote is only a small piece. Just as fundamental is the necessity of changing people's minds about what is politically possible. Such a feat requires both an abundance of imagination and a patient determination that is sorely lacking when the only measure of success is whether a candidate has won or lost the vote count in a particular moment.

Electoral justice, then, is what is required for electoral politics to be able to do what we hope it will, but which it rarely does—change politics, policy, and our lives for the better. The framework of electoral justice causes one to act from the understanding that political change can only result from the deep work of listening to the lived experience of those least privileged, analyzing the conditions that cause their oppression, and defining bold, practical solutions that organized people will fight for. This is a way of building power that is fueled not with passive constituents but by active democratic citizens who remain engaged with their own governance long after the moment of election.

In addition, electoral politics can be useful to social movements *as movements* not only in service to increasing democratic access and power for the people whose concerns they represent. This is so for at least two reasons. First, electoral politics can serve as a benchmark, a way to measure the breadth and effectiveness of movement organizing. Elections are a moment when organizers can see if the people are with them and figure out where efforts have been successful and where they have fallen short. Second, elections can act as a gauge for where the general public is in relation to movement goals. This is extremely important for liberatory movements because their goals, like the abolition of police and prisons and creating economies of care, require societal transformations that cannot happen overnight and will not be achieved in one election cycle. Put simply, elections show social movements where they are on the path toward building the world they want and what steps may enable them to get from the world that is to the world they envision.

It is also important to note that the Electoral Justice Project is just one part of the political infrastructure that the movement has built. It is not possible to trace the entire breadth of that ecosystem here, but I will highlight a few organizations that span the gamut of professional expertise, candidate recruitment and campaign staffing, and communications to illustrate the point. Law for Black Lives is a professional organization that provides legal and research support to movement organizations in areas related to abolition, specifically for ending money bail, advocating for reparations, and creating legal frameworks and precedents for the invest/divest plank of the Vision for Black Lives platform. Similar advocacy groups that seek to organize other kinds of professionals in service of movement organizations and/or goals also exist, including Scholars for Black Lives and White Coats for Black Lives (comprising those in medical/pharmacy fields). On the campaign side there are a constellation of organizations that groom and support potential candidates and campaign staff. Organizations like Higher Heights for America work specifically with Black women to cultivate them as candidates. Collective PAC, which raised $6.5 million to support Black candidates in the 2018 election cycle, also runs an annual "boot camp" for aspiring candidates and staffers called Black Campaign School (McKinney 2018; Khalid 2018). Additionally, Shanelle Matthews leads two different communications shops that serve the movement: Channel Black and the Radical Communicators Network. Channel Black describes itself as "a storytelling and media training program that develops the strategy, intervention, and spokesperson skills of social movement leaders and impacted communities [whose] goal is to equip marginalized people with the tools and supports to develop and tell their own stories and have a say in how power and resources in the United States are distributed." And RadComms is a network of communications professionals that facilitate "cross-movement collaboration for people working in communications for social change" (Matthews, n.d.).

This political infrastructure is making measurable and positive strides. For example, on August 5, 2020, Cori Bush, an activist politicized by and supported through the movement, won the democratic primary in Missouri's 1st Congressional District. Bush, a nurse and single mother, became interested in politics after her experiences as a protestor during the Ferguson uprising in 2014. Her win was a stunning upset, unseating a fifty-year political dynasty to usher in a new era of visionary leadership that is not only representative of, but, more importantly, accountable to, the people of St. Louis. Bush mounted her campaign with little money, no connections to the traditional infrastructure of the local Democratic Party, and the reputation that she had earned as a fierce activist in the streets. In an interview that took place after her victory she commented, "They counted us out. They called me—I'm just the protestor, I'm just the activist with no name, no title and no real money. That's all they said that I was. But St. Louis showed up today" (Ballentine 2020).

At the same time that Bush won a resounding victory as a candidate, voters also overwhelmingly improved Medicare expansion in the state of Missouri. It is not only the candidates and their status as firsts that undergird the crucial nature of these electoral shifts, but also, and even more importantly, the policies that they usher in with them and the ideas that undergird them. This is one of the ways that protest can chart a course to power in politics. Bush is one of several activists that the Movement for Black Lives has encouraged to raise their voices and use their skills to represent communities that have too long been overpoliced, underserved, and unrepresented.

Freedom Summer 2020

The organizing work of M4BL took on new significance with the COVID-19 pandemic. The failure of elected leaders to respond adequately to the public health crisis intensified concerns about how we care for ourselves and for one another. Movement-resourced mutual aid networks grew in their capacity to provide the resources and solidarity needed in the absence of government support. These initiatives have called into question why food, housing, and healthcare are commodities rather than entitlements. They also made visible the disproportionate impact of the disease on Black and brown people and the poor.

From February 2020, in the face of soaring unemployment and rates of infection, there was a proliferation in campaigns to cancel rent, provide public healthcare, and release people from jails, prisons, and detention centers. #FreeThemAll campaigns have articulated the dangers of human caging amid COVID-19 and brought attention to the health crisis created by prisons and jails even before the pandemic. The police response to protests, including brutality, armored vehicles, curfew, tear gas, pepper spray, and rubber and wooden bullets, brought attention to glaring contradictions in funding and priorities— contradictions between countless police officers equipped with high-tech gear compared to insufficient numbers of health-care workers, shortages of essential personal protective equipment, and ex-orbitant healthcare costs that force millions into crippling debt; and between the government's immediate deployment of police to respond to protests and its failure to respond to the pandemic with mass testing and distribution of funds (Akbar 2020).

But these massive changes are complicated. By September 2020, white support for M4BL had contracted. In some polls, their support had sunk below the level of approval attained before the massive uprisings in June of that year. A Pew Research Center poll released September 16 noted:

> The recent decline in support for the Black Lives Matter movement is par-ticularly notable among White and Hispanic adults. In June, a majority of White adults (60%) said they supported the movement at least some-what; now, fewer than half (45%) express at least some support. The share of Hispanic adults who support the movement has decreased 11 percentage points, from 77% in June to 66% today. By comparison, support for the Black Lives Matter movement has remained virtually unchanged among Black and Asian adults. (Thomas and Horowitz 2020)

These findings point to the longue durée of the process initiated by the Movement for Black Lives. While there are inflection points where the move-ment makes dramatic, immediate impacts, the real work of movement is long-term. The goals of this radical movement include policy changes, but the goals are undergirded, in a deep way, by the belief that the structuring ide-ological systems of the twentieth century and the institutions and practices that formed to make the consequences of those ideologies real in people's lives need to be dismantled and built anew. This is a colossal proposition and, if it is successful, will be the work of several generations. However, we can see from the evidence amassed here that the Black liberation movement born in this, the twenty-first, century has laid the foundation for a politics that can shape the next era, one that centers human thriving from margin to center and builds from the bottom up.

Conclusion

On Futurity

> When I envision the future, I think of the world I crave for my daughters and my sons. It is thinking for the survival of the species— thinking for life.
>
> —Audre Lorde, "Man Child" in *Sister Outsider*

Futurity is a word with multivalent meanings; it indicates the future time, a future event, or renewed or continuing existence. Futurity is the conviction that the part of the story one is living in is not and cannot be the whole of it. This moment in time gives us a rare political opportunity to begin something new. We are living in a critical juncture where we can set the ideological terms on which the twenty-first century is lived. This movement provides a template of principles and ideas to overturn the twentieth-century paradigms of what constitutes proper and reasonable ways to arrange our political, social, and economic lives. I do not argue that the current iteration of the movement in defense of Black lives always lives up to their ideals, but neither has any paradigm that shapes common sense. Rather, I argue that radical Black feminist pragmatism is a good place to start.

Since the initial appearance of the Movement for Black Lives (M4BL) in 2013, the public opinion environment on the issues of race, racism, and policing have been transformed. But more than changing public opinion in the domain of race and criminal justice, the movement has influenced common sense perceptions of how political problems ought to be diagnosed, evaluated, and solved. This is because, in addition to causing people to reconsider the efficacy of the current criminal punishment system, the movement has managed to make structural analysis mainstream, reshaping the terrain of the politics of social justice.

Using the case of race and policing, the network of organizations that became M4BL has helped Americans understand structural relations in general, including the idea that an individual's life is conditioned by not only personal motivation and interpersonal encounters, which is the usual explanation in the ultra-individualist framework I have called neoliberal common sense, but also by edifices built for governance and systems of practice that operate impersonally based on ingrained assumptions about the comparative worth of some people's lives over others. For example, the popular conversation that #BlackLivesMatter facilitated rejecting the terminology of #AllLivesMatter not only built support for the movement, but also helped to spread the core argument of radical Black feminist pragmatism, which is that in order to address the problems we all face, we have to reason from margin to center and bottom to top, not by appeals to a universalism that neglects those suffering most acutely from the oppression and domination from which we all seek to escape.

In addition, despite the handwringing of a chorus of public intellectuals declaiming the dangers of identity politics, M4BL has been connecting the dots between racial, gender, and economic justice, making very plain that there are no dichotomous hierarchies but only a series of intersections. This is because RBFP and its most unique element, the politics of care, demands that we attend to the conditions preventing flourishing in people's lived experience. While the politics of the movement cannot be described as a class politics in the vein of the socialisms of the twentieth century, it is nevertheless a politics that understands class as a crucial *relation* among other social forces which structures the cumulation of advantage and disadvantage affecting persons, groups, and geographies. In addition, movement strives to center the poor, the disenfranchised, the ostracized, and the incarcerated. This centering of the marginalized is not done to meet the tenets of an abstract, immutable ordering of the world, but instead because they believe it is the birthright of every human being to live their best and fullest lives and it is only by starting with those who have been systematically left out that this becomes possible.

The notion of the world to come, of its fragility, has always animated Black political thought and culture. This is because to be Black in America puts one in a strange position with regard to time. As Ytasha Womack writes,

There's something about African American culture in particular that dictates that all cultural hallmarks and personal evolutions are recast in a historical lineage. Whether it's the concept of prophecy and speaking into the future or tropes of the past shadowing the present, whether by need or narrative, many speak as if the future, past, and present are one. The threads that bind can be as divergent as a tersely worded tweet, musical chord, fiery speech, ancient Kemetic symbol, Bible quote, starry night, or string theory, but there's an idea that the power of thought, word and imagination can somehow transcend time. Just as the right words and actions can speak the future into existence, the same can recast the past, too. (Womack 2013, 153)

And so, the movement speaks itself into time—anchored by the fulcrum of the world as it is while ready to pivot to face the past or conjure the future. This way of understanding futurity has a prefigurative element, but it is undergirded by a purposive pragmatism. The reason for acting in the present is not merely to pantomime a utopia, but instead to build a bridge from current conditions to ones that offer us all more safety, more freedom, more pleasure, and more capacity to develop ourselves and determine the world we share. This bridge-building is not merely mystical; it is, as Donna Kate Rushin wrote in her Bridge Poem, "the bridge to [our] own power," one that is built from relationships of reciprocity and political friendship that enable us to take concrete steps that mediate suffering while maintaining the ability to push at and expand the boarders of the possible. As Jessica Byrd writes, "We are radically reimagining the world so it will belong to all of us . . . our fight is a celebration of us and the new world we are creating" (Byrd 2020).

But this future is contingent. The fight against the structuring of the world under what bell hooks calls "white supremacist capitalist patriarchy" has been ongoing for at least four centuries. It seems to be what Audre Lorde calls the "shoreline" of modernity, the marker of its limit and the place from which we might embark. In her dissertation on the practice of Black feminist mothering, Alexis Pauline Gumbs writes, "we are the purveyors of the horizon," [of] approaches to sensibility that continue to recede, . . . who live on the shifting edge of the world . . . who know the truth of erosion and bet against it (Gumbs 2020, 1–2). In other words, we cannot sail over the sweep of history. We have been here—or nearly here—before. Even rendering an account of the massive protests in the summer of 2020 causes one to tell a story that contains within it a loop, a devastating refrain, an infuriating history in the round.

But let us begin on May 25, 2020. That day, four Minneapolis police officers participated in the callous murder of a Black man named George

Floyd, and the murder was captured on camera. The viral video of Floyd's killing was shared by a seventeen-year-old Black girl named Darnella Frazier, who happened to be walking by with her baby cousin. The recording of this police murder tore through the virtual world, opening up a reservoir of political rage and pain that had been simmering just beneath the surface of public sentiment and discourse. Beginning the next day, May 26, thousands of people started pouring into the streets. Protests began first in Minneapolis and then rapidly occurred in every major metropolitan area in the United States, followed quickly by suburban towns and rural counties, and finally spilled over American borders, with protests taking place in at least sixty other countries and on every continent except Antarctica.

George Floyd's murder caused a conflagration of protest activity in the summer of 2020 not only due to the casual depravity and sadism on display as Derrick Chauvin, appearing calm and composed with hands resting in his pockets, shoved his knee into Floyd's neck, choking him to death over the course of 8 minutes and 46 seconds. But also, because George Floyd pleaded, "I can't breathe" again and again, as he was slowly suffocated.

This phrase, "I can't breathe," has been repeated throughout the life of the Movement for Black Lives. The trauma that accompanies this phrase is a political portal, a return to the scene of Eric Garner's murder by police as he also pleaded for breath in the summer of 2014. The grim spectacle of a public lynching narrated by this phrase reminded people of not only these two incidents, but of all that had occurred in between—the cumulative weight of dehumanization, the deep devaluing of Black lives that has continued even amid organized resistance. Just as the killing of Mike Brown triggered a recursive anger about the failure to defend the importance of Trayvon Martin's Black life, and the killing of Breonna Taylor reminded people of their baffled fury at Sandra Bland's demise, Floyd's pained gasping breathed new life into large street protests in defense of Black lives.

These immense demonstrations were able to reemerge, and at a much greater scale, because protest is not merely the massing of a heartbroken mob, nor only a political tactic—it is also, crucially, a learning experience for both those involved and those observing. What they learn is more about the principles at stake, where they stand, and what they are willing to do to create the change they seek. That means that protest *creates* political possibilities that did not exist before it and could not exist without it. In this way, social movements radicalize politics as they educate the polity. It is for this reason that we have to understand social movement as cumulative. Currently, we are in a moment of political swailing; it has unique potentials, but it is also a part of a commonplace democratic pattern. Social movements recall democracy to itself. They highlight the institutions, habits, and systems that must be undone to move forward. Remember too that in society, we do not build from scratch, but instead reuse parts of the given combined with new ideas and designs that transform our shared public meanings and sociopolitical ideas, habits, and institutions.

This is not to say that the 2020 uprising was a replay of any other. It did not repeat 1968 or 2014. Each iteration of struggle in the streets teaches the organizers galvanizing people's consciousness, the activists showing up at actions, and the observers trying to figure out what is going on. Those who might have encountered with disturbed confusion the violence inflicted on Garner, Bland, and countless others had learned how to read what happened to George Floyd. By the summer of 2020, they knew, due to the organizing and public education efforts of the movement, that they were witnessing not just a horrific overuse of force by a few rogue police, but instead a graphic illustration of the structural contempt for Black life that manifests in every domain of American life. And so people who had been wounded and politically awakened by the phrase "I can't breathe" in 2014 were moved, in 2020, to act and act boldly because they had also learned that polite requests for half-measures do not yield anything like justice, because the racial terror of police murder and harassment has continued. Elizabeth Alexander conveys the litany of incidents in bleak verse:

> This one was shot in his grandmother's yard. This one was carrying a bag of Skittles. This one was playing with a toy gun in front of a gazebo. Black girl in bright bikini. Black boy holding cell phone. This one danced like a marionette as he was shot down in a Chicago intersection. The words, the names: Trayvon, Laquan, bikini, gazebo, loosies, Skittles, two seconds, I can't breathe, traffic stop, dashboard cam, sixteen times. His dead body lay in the street in the August heat for four hours. (Alexander 2020)

And the deaths are not the only situations that have led to this culmination. Recall that on the same day Floyd was murdered by police, our social media feeds had already swelled with the viral video of a Black bird-watcher in New York's Central Park, Christian Cooper, being threatened by Amy Cooper (no relation), a white woman who used manufactured tears to call in the police as a potentially deadly weapon against him in a dispute about leashing her dog. This was a very illustrative incident—an object lesson in everything that the movement has been telling America about white supremacy since 2013. This woman could use her whiteness, her femaleness, her tears, to mobilize agents of the state in a way that everyone understood would threaten Christian Cooper's life.

And remember, even this incident was a culmination of a previous litany of high-profile incidents of white people using their whiteness to terrorize Black people just going about their daily lives. With each iteration, the previous events seem to unfold again in the present tense. In April 2018, a barista at a Philadelphia Starbucks called the police because two Black men had come in and sat down. They were having a business meeting, but she claimed to feel afraid, so they were violently ejected by police. Over the rest of the summer a slew of incidents involving white women calling police on Black families and children lit up our news feeds. The perpetrators were given nicknames: "BBQ Becky" called the police on a Black family having a gathering in a public park. "Permit Patty" called the police on a Black eight-year-old selling lemonade on the sidewalk on the grounds that he had not obtained a permit. "Peppermint Patty" called the police on a Black woman who mistakenly used the wrong lane to exit a supermarket parking lot. When the Black woman pointed out that calling the police was a racist overreaction, the white woman chided her to "put away the nigger card," and then claimed on the phone with 911 dispatch that she was being "attacked." A group of Black friends who rented an Airbnb in California were met with multiple police cars and a helicopter because a white resident in the neighborhood found it disturbing that they did not smile and wave. A Black graduate student at Yale who fell asleep in a common study area while writing a paper was woken up for police interrogation because a white student had called them and questioned her right to be on campus.

The impact of this litany came not only because these everyday incidents were being publicized, nor even because they seemed to follow one another in quick succession and added to the pile of evidence of weaponized whiteness, but because each encounter entered public discourse on terms set by the Movement for Black Lives and provided an opportunity to further discuss what structural racism is, how it works, and why it affects the everyday lives of Black people and other people of color.

This public discourse allowed people to ponder the question Patrisse Khan-Cullors and asha bandele keep asking in *When They Call You a Terrorist*: "In what world does this make sense?" It is a startling question—one more at home in speculative fiction than in social science, but it is nevertheless the heart of the issue. In what world does this systematic anti-Black violence make sense? How can we build a world in which it doesn't?

This has been the mission of M4BL, to reveal the nonsense at the core of dominant ideologies and radically and pragmatically imagine a world in which anti-Black racism and violence; expropriation of every human activity for profit; dehumanization due to gender, gender expression, and sexuality; and a state apparatus that serves only to punish people rather than make them safe no longer make sense to us. This is why the movement has spent the last eight years helping people to connect the dots between the symptoms of anti-Black racism and their overarching and interconnected structural causes.

It is also important that in May 2020, the world had been grappling with its first pandemic in one hundred years, and much of America had been under stay-at-home orders to try to slow the spread of the novel coronavirus, COVID-19, for three months. The conditions created by the virus had cast 29 million Americans from work and tens of millions more were working from home. This forced reordering of time gave people a space for both attention and action that is normally unavailable amid the demands of the regular political economy, which dictates that most of our attention is focused on waged work. Under the hiatus imposed by the pandemic, people had the time to make the oft-heard protest chant "no justice, no peace" a reality. In so doing, the mass uprisings reshaped the political terrain of the United States and the world, and it is a perfect illustration of the argument at the heart of this book: social movements are not only an expressive function of those who have been too-long abused, but are also a specifically political tactic meant to call unresponsive decision-makers to surrender power—or find the courage to serve their constituents. Protest is one way a democratic people asserts its legitimate authority, and it is also a reminder that a people can refuse to be governed—by revoking their consent.

In this volume, I have argued that political scientists have generally given social movements too little credit for their role in democracy. What ought to have become clear in the protest cycle that has characterized this century, from Occupy Wall Street forward, is that social movements can change the way people understand reality. Protests that are connected to clear and reso-nant messages are not one-off events. As I showed in my book *The Politics of Common Sense*, resonant messages from political challengers furnish people with an alternate explanation of how things are and ought to be. If resonant messages persist over time, they begin to shape the way we encounter the world, even for people who do not (yet) agree. The movement has done the work necessary to earn what I have written about as *political acceptance* (Woodly 2015a). Political acceptance is not synonymous with agreement and does not mean a problem has been resolved. It does not prevent backlash or guarantee success. Instead, political acceptance is a threshold condition that marks a set of issues as urgent and necessary to address. Political acceptance means that political challengers no longer have to argue about whether their cause is a political problem; everyone *accepts* that it is, and they can focus instead on arguing about how to solve it.

Because of the passionate protest the world witnessed in Ferguson and other cities around the country in 2014, the clear and often contentious communication about why those protests were happening, and the organizations that were born to combat structural racism in the wake of that moment, no one can now deny the reality of systemic, racist police violence. So much about how people understand the task before us has changed. In 2015, Black Lives Matter was a contentious slogan. Less than a decade ago, the pull of "colorblindness" and "tolerance" as dominant ideologies made the slogan centering the suffering of Black people seem gauche, even offensive. After all, it was only six years ago that San Francisco 49ers quarterback Colin Kaepernick was pushed off his team and out of the NFL for insisting that America recognize the ongoing violent oppression of Black people.

While activists do well to call out the often vague and hollow statements of corporations and other entities that spent the summer tweeting messages of support or gesturing toward fighting injustice, we must also recognize that these gestures represent a transformation of the political context. Through the relentless campaign by the Movement for Black Lives to give Black people the language to talk about the structural depth and breadth of anti-Blackness and to educate all people about its reality, the movement has changed common sense.

In the six weeks after George Floyd's public execution, a Black Lives Matter protest had been held in all fifty states and in 40 percent of the counties in the United States. The scale of the 2020 protests is hard to fathom. By comparison, at the largest protests in the 1960s (the March on Washington in 1963, the antiwar March on the Pentagon in 1967), the decade that shaped American ideas about what protest is and means, hundreds of thousands of people showed up for Black civil rights and anti-imperialism. In 2017, the Women's March, a mobilization in response to the election of Donald

Trump, mobilized between 3 and 5 million participants for a single-day mobilization. The Movement for Black Lives brought tens of millions of people into the streets, where they remained for two months. In fact, between 8 percent and 10 percent of Americans claim that they have participated in a Black Lives Matter protest, which means between 25 and 30 million people have massed in public for the defense of Black lives. Moreover, this effort has been coordinated by a decentralized, highly networked cadre of Black leaders who explicitly name the dismantling of white supremacy, patriarchy, and rampant capitalism as its goal. No political scholar or professional would have predicted that such a thing was possible. Indeed, in 2013, when the movement began, these things *were not yet possible*. This is a future that had to be radically imagined and then practically enacted. Luckily, that is what the Movement for Black Lives is built to do. They do so by forcefully and disruptively challenging common political understandings of the way things are and presenting an executable vision of the way they might be. And they have been remarkably successful.

M4BL could not have foreseen the incredible impact that mass uprisings in late May and June of 2020 would have on the political environment of the nation and the world, but they were prepared to seize the political opportunity. In July, M4BL introduced the BREATHE Act, a suite of policy proposals authored by the movement's policy table in July 2020 and presented by congressional partners Ayanna Pressley and Rashida Tlaib. The proposed federal legislation includes guidelines for how to defund police agencies and reinvest those resources in programs and institutions that support the health, housing, and educational well-being of Black, brown, and poor communities. The movement did not know, could not have known, that they would help to reshape the political environment during the long COVID summer, creating a space in which their radically imagined policy proposals would become possible, but they were ready. Standing, as Lorde counseled, at the shoreline "looking inward and outward, at once before and after, seeking a now that can breed futures." They were ready because the movement had already spent years laying the philosophical and practical groundwork for transformative political change led from below by Black organizers. They were ready, because all along, the movement had been arguing in the future perfect tense.

So it made sense when movement strategist Jessica Byrd introduced the BREATHE Act legislation with an op-ed imagining what the moment we are living now would look like from a future in which more people are able to live and thrive:

> Imagine it's 2070. History classes all over the U.S. teach the 2020 Black Lives Matter Uprisings and the national campaign to defund police. Students are shocked to learn about police officers who once killed Black people. For these young people, public safety means community and skilled professionals coming together to resolve problems peacefully and everyone has access to the resources they need to heal and flourish.
>
> I'll be an elder, sitting on my porch telling stories over lemonade. With pride, I will share with anyone who will listen to how our mass multiracial, intergenerational and global movement led by Black people accelerated this march of history. (Byrd 2020)

This is the heart of the radical yet pragmatic imagination of the movement; it asks, "What will we have to have done in order to live in the future we envision?" And then it answers its own query in concrete terms as the new horizon of the possible emerges.

These observations taken together mean that the third decade of the twenty-first century might be a moment for reconstruction. If the public becomes repoliticized around the notion of care it would be a formidable, era defining force, and that is one outcome that has been made possible by the movement. But there will also be a drive toward retrenchment, just as there was in the 1880s after the Civil War and in the 1970s and 1980s after the civil rights movement.

We perceive time as though it progresses, but while it moves, the trajectory is not certain. This does not mean we are not at a new place. It simply means that we, like generations preceding us and those to come, cannot pretend that there is a universal momentum that favors justice. Instead, we have work to do where we are. It is our duty to invest in a "poetics of the possible" and to push forward conceptions of "what is and is not imaginable in [our] lifetimes" (Gumbs 2020, x). Radical Black feminist pragmatism gives us conceptual tools and practical strategies to both imagine and make the way. It will not be a straight road; iterations are to be expected because freedom is a process, we will always be getting free. However, this moment is a critical juncture in which we can make the way easier, to set the terms such that future generations are able to fight different battles.

Let me be clear, this movement is not built upon a plea. The speech act declaring #BlackLivesMatter is an encouragement and a demand. For worse and for better, we belong to each other. Those of us at the margins are not and have never been subdued into silence. It has never been a question of voice, but always one of the hearing. In this moment, because of this movement, the arena is changed. The acoustics have been reset. And because of this political shift, we are receiving an invitation. The ideas present in this movement are offering the substance, the matter, that can help us to craft a new era, to sail from the shoreline of modernity into a contemporary epoch that has not yet been named, to construct a polity in which human thriving makes sense. The task before us is how to answer.

So what shall we do?

APPENDIX A

Examples of Bailouts and Regular Bail-Out Actions

Bailout	Location	Primary Organizations Involved	Year	Number of People Bailed Out	Spending Info
#EndCashBail 2019[1]	Louisville, KY	Presbyterian Church/The Bail Project	2019	Over 50 people	$140K was spent on the bailout, with $10K coming from Presbyterian donations and $130k coming from the Bail Project
Anti-Nazi Protester bailout[2]	Newnan, GA	Atlanta Solidarity Fund	2018	12 counter-protestors arrested during a rally of fascist org	
Bail Fund for Boston #JewsAgainstICE[3]	Boston, MA	Boston Jews Against ICE	2019	12 activists arrested protesting ICE at Amazon's Cambridge HQ	Over $19K
Bay Area Dream Defenders' 2017 Mama's Day Bail Out[4]	Tampa Bay, FL	Bay Area Dream Defenders	2017	Over 4 people	Raised 25K—One woman's bail was $10k for driving with suspended license and missing court dates

[1] https://www.pcusa.org/news/2019/6/12/louisville-area-presbyterians-and-their-friends-ra/
[2] https://actionnetwork.org/fundraising/support-anti-nazi-protesters-in-newnan-ga
[3] https://www.gofundme.com/f/never-again-is-now-nobusinesswithice
[4] https://www.tampabay.com/news/humaninterest/dream-defenders-post-bail-for-four-mothers-to-raise-awareness-on-national/2323635/

Bailout	Location	Primary Organizations Involved	Year	Number of People Bailed Out	Spending Info
Black Father's Bail Out[5]	Philadelphia, PA	Philadelphia Community Bail Fund	2018	10 Black men	
Black Love Bail Out[6]	Bexar County, TX	National Bail Out Collective in collaboration with other advocacy orgs	2018	20 People	
Black Mama Bail Out[7]	Birmingham, AL	BLM Birmingham and The Ordinary People Society	2017	4 women[8]	$25K provided by Ordinary People and $13K raised by BLM
Black Mama's Bail Out[9]	Philadelphia, PA	Philadelphia Community Bail Fund	2017	13 Black women	$60K[10]
Coronavirus Bailout[11]	New Orleans, LA	Robert F. Kennedy Human Rights and the Safety and Freedom Fund at Operation Restoration	2020	22 people	
COVID Bail Out NYC[12]	New York, NY	Founded in April 2020 as a special fund by BAJI and Emergency Release Fund	2020	242 people	

5 https://www.usatoday.com/story/life/allthemoms/2018/06/15/national-bail-out-pays-bail-so-dads-can-home-fathers-day/706387002/
6 https://medium.com/in-justice-today/the-black-love-bail-out-aims-to-free-poor-defendants-and-teach-others-to-do-the-same-a33d93bfea00
7 https://www.al.com/news/2017/05/alabama_advocates_bail_women_o.html
8 https://southernersonnewground.org/a-labor-of-love/
9 https://decarceratepa.info/content/mamas-bail-out-day
10 https://www.inquirer.com/philly/opinion/commentary/black-women-incarceration-mothers-day-bailout-cash-bail-20180507.html
11 https://rfkhumanrights.org/news/new-orleans-covid-19-bail-out
12 https://indyweek.com/guides/archives/serena-sebring-organizer-southerners-new-ground-fights-entrenched-white-supremacy/

Campaign	Location	Organization	Year	Details	Amount
Durham Black August Bailout[13]	Durham, NC	Southerners On New Ground, Durham Chapter	2017	9 black mothers	Raised $492K
Free the People Day[14]	Nationwide	National Bail Fund Network	2018	The Bond Fund distributed money raised to the 60 community bail and bond funds that are part of its network	Raised over $47K[16]
"Freedom Should Be Free—No Cash Bail" Rally[15]	St. Louis, MO	Presbyterian Church, St. Louis Action Council, and Bail Project	2018	The money raised was given to local orgs to begin bailing out people	Raised over $190K
Freedom Summer Fund[17]	Nationwide	Community Justice Exchange	2019	Approximately 19 people[18]	
Funds for Freedom Campaign[19]	Nationwide	Robert F. Kennedy Human Rights Foundation and the Know Your Rights Camp	2020		$1 Million Distributed to over 30 local bail funds in 22 states
Juneteenth/Father's Day Bail Out[20]	Denver, CO	Colorado Freedom Fund	2018	21 people	Raised over $26K
Mama's Day Bail Out[21]	Denver, CO	Colorado Freedom Fund	2018	14 Black women in 5 Denver area jails	raised over $20k

13 https://indyweek.com/guides/archives/serena-sebring-organizer-southerners-new-ground-fights-entrenched-white-supremacy/
14 https://secure.actblue.com/donate/2019freethepeopleday
15 https://www.pcusa.org/news/2018/6/19/hundreds-presbyterians-join-march-st-louis-justice/
16 https://fox2now.com/news/presbyterian-convention-goers-march-on-st-louis-justice-center-to-bail-out-non-violent-offenders/amp/
17 https://secure.actblue.com/donate/freedomday
18 https://twitter.com/LGBTQ_Freedom/status/1149748353334501377
19 https://rfkhumanrights.org/2020-bail-out
20 https://fundly.com/coloradofreedom
21 https://fundly.com/coloradofreedom

Bailout	Location	Primary Organizations Involved	Year	Number of People Bailed Out	Spending Info
Mass Bail Out Action at NYC Jails[22]	New York, NY	Collaboration between Robert F. Kennedy Human Rights and various NYC grassroots orgs	2018	Over 100 people[23]	$2 Million[24]
Memphis Black Mama's Bail Out[25]	Memphis, TN	BLM Memphis	2019	6 Black Women	$30K
New Birth Easter Bail Out[26]	Lithonia, GA	Lithonia's New Birth Missionary Baptist Church alongside Scrapp DeLeon and Rapper T.I.	2019	23 people	Over $100k
Philadelphia Eagles Bail Out[27]	Philadelphia, PA	Philadelphia Eagles Social Justice Fund and the Philadelphia Community Bail Fund	2018	9 people	$50K
Shut Down GEO Bail Fund[28]	Baco Raton, FL	Broward Dream Defenders	2019	6 activists who interrupted operations at GEO Group HQ to highlight how the company, which operates private prisons	Raised over $6K

22 https://rfkhumanrights.org/news/rfk-bail-action
23 https://www.vice.com/en_us/article/zmdmy5/over-100-inmates-were-bailed-out-in-the-largest-mass-bail-in-history
24 https://thecrimereport.org/2019/01/31/can-the-mass-bailout-movement-prod-reform/
25 https://mlk50.com/2020/05/09/black-mamas-bail-out-and-grace-of-god-credited-with-release-after-4-years/
26 https://www.huffpost.com/entry/new-birth-missionary-baptist-church-bail-out_n_5cc0cbde4b01b6b3efc29c0
27 https://thehill.com/blogs/blog-briefing-room/news/418640-philadelphia-eagles-pay-bail-for-9-using-social-justice-funds
28 https://www.everribbon.com/ribbon/view/74891

SONG's 2017 Black Mamas Mother's Day Bail Out Campaign[29]	Southern States	Southerners on New Ground, Dream Defenders, Sister Song, and various Black Lives Matter chapters.	2017	64 Black women. Part of the first National Bail Out Collective-led bailout event during which around a 100 people were bailed out	Raised over $200K
Super Bowl 2020 Sex Worker Bail Out[30]	Nationwide	SWOP Behind Bars & LGBT Freedom Fund & Woodhull Freedom Foundation	2020	Approximately 12 sex workers	
Texas Immigrant Bailout[31]	Nationwide	Refugee and Immigrant Center for Education and Legal Services	2019	200 people from 40 facilities in 20 states; 56 people were in Texas	$21K
Workhouse Bailout[32]	St. Louis, MO	Action STL, The Bail Project, Arch City Defense.	2018–2020	3,500 people as of August 2020	

29 https://truthout.org/articles/southerners-on-new-ground-s-bail-out-continues-the-radical-tradition-of-black-august/
30 https://twitter.com/swopbehindbars/status/1223303688543973376
31 https://www.expressnews.com/news/local/article/Raices-leading-2-1-million-push-to-bail-out-200-14849821.php
32 https://www.theguardian.com/us-news/2020/aug/03/st-louis-workhouse-jail-legislation-close

Ongoing Bail Funds

State	Name of Bail Fund[1]	Area of Operation	Bail Types Funded	Organizational Focus[2]
Alabama	Shut Down Etowah's Etowah Freedom Fund	Gadsden	Immigration	
Arizona	Pima Monthly Meeting Immigration Bond Fund	Statewide	Immigration	
	Tucson Second Chance Community Bail Fund	Tucson	Criminal	
California	Al Otro Lado Vida Libre Bond Fund	Statewide	Immigration	
	Bay Area Anti-Repression Committee Bail Fund	San Francisco	Criminal	Activists
	Bay Area Immigration Bond Fund	San Francisco area	Immigration	
	Dede McClure Community Bail Fund	San Diego	Criminal	Activists
	Immigrant Families Defense Fund	East Bay area	Immigration	Families in California schools facing deportation
	Los Angeles People's City Council Freedom Fund	Los Angeles	Criminal	Activists

[1] This includes bail funds that are their own independent organization as well as bail funds that are an ongoing program of an organization or a coalition of organizations.

[2] Unlisted in this category are the criteria that are used by many bail funds in determining priority of cases: inability to pay; health concerns; number/needs of dependents; risk of discrimination due to identity; proximity to structural harm; risk of loss of employment, housing, or education; deportation risk.

State	Name of Bail Fund[1]	Area of Operation	Bail Types Funded	Organizational Focus[2]
	NorCal Resist Sacramento Region Bond Fund	Northern California	Immigration/ Criminal	Activists
	Orange County Justice Fund	Orange County	Immigration	
	San Diego Immigrant Rights Consortium Borderlands Get Free Fund	San Diego/ Imperial Counties	Immigration	
Colorado	Colorado Freedom Fund	Denver, Arapahoe, Jefferson, Adams, Douglas, El Paso, and Boulder Counties	Criminal	
	Immigrant Freedom Fund of Colorado	Aurora	Immigration	
Conneticut	Connecticut Bail Fund	Statewide	Immigration/ Criminal	COVID-19
Delaware				
Florida	FNB Bail Fund	Wilmington	Criminal	Activists
	Community Bail Fund	Statewide	Criminal	
	Fempower Community Bond Fund	Miami-Dade County	Criminal	
	Florida Justice Center Florida Bailout	Statewide	Criminal	Activists
	LGBTQ Freedom Fund	South Florida (Multi-State for Immigration)	Immigration/ Criminal	LGBTQ individuals/ Individuals with HIV/AIDS
Georgia	Atlanta Solidarity Fund	Atlanta area	Criminal	Activists
	Forsyth County Community Bail Fund	Forsyth County	Criminal	COVID-19/Activists
	Georgia Latino Alliance for Human Rights Georgia Immigration Bond Fund	Statewide	Immigration	

State	Organization	Location	Type	Population served
Hawaii	Hawaii Community Bail Fund	Statewide	Criminal	
Illinois	Believers Bail Out	Chicago	Immigration/Criminal	Muslims
	Champaign County Bailout Coalition	Champaign County	Criminal	
	Chicago Community Bond Fund	Cook County	Criminal	
	Winnebago Bond Project	Winnebago	Criminal	
Indiana	BLM Bloomington Bail Out Fund	Bloomington area	Criminal	Activists
Iowa	Prairielands Freedom Fund	Statewide	Immigration/Criminal	Activists
Kentucky	Louisville Community Bail Fund	Louisville area	Criminal	
Louisiana	New Orleans Safety & Freedom Fund	Orleans Parish	Criminal	
	YWCA Greater Baton Rouge Community Bail Fund	East Baton Rouge Parish	Criminal	Women
Maryland	Baltimore Action Legal Team Community Bail Fund	Baltimore area	Criminal	Covid-19/Home Detention
Massachusetts	Beyond Bail & Legal Defense Fund	Statewide	Immigration	
	Massachusetts Bail Fund	Statewide	Criminal	
Michigan	Kent County Immigration Bond for Our Neighbor's Defense Fund	Kent County	Immigration	
	The Woodward Foundation Detroit's Bail Fund	Detroit	Criminal	

State	Name of Bail Fund[1]	Area of Operation	Bail Types Funded	Organizational Focus[2]
Minnesota				
	Minnesota Freedom Fund	Statewide	Immigration/Criminal	BIPOC/Homeless individuals/ Activists
Mississippi				
	Mississippi Bail Fund Collective	Statewide	Criminal	
Missouri				
	Kansas City Community Bail Fund	Kansas City-area	Criminal	
	Race Matters Friends Community Bail Fund	Boone County	Criminal	
	Reale Justice Community Bail Fund	Kansas City-area	Criminal/Immigration	
	STL Jail & Legal Support Fund	St. Louis-area	Criminal	Activists
Nevada				
	Arriba Las Vegas Workers Center Las Vegas Family Unity Bond Fund	Statewide	Immigration	
	Progressive Leadership Alliance of Nevada	Reno/Las Vegas area	Criminal	
	Vegas Freedom Fund	Clark County	Criminal	Activists
New Hampshire				
	NH Conference UCC Immigrant and Refugee Support Group Immigrant Bond & Support Fund	Statewide	Immigration	
New York				
	Emergency Release Fund	NYC	Criminal	LGBTQ+/ Medically Vulnerable (COVID-19)
	Brooklyn Community Bail Fund	NYC	Criminal	
	COVID Bail Out	NYC	Criminal	COVID-19

State	Organization	Location	Type	Description
	Dollar Bail Brigade	NYC	Criminal	Pays bail on behalf of people incarcerated for $1
	New York Immigrant Freedom Fund	NYC	Immigration	
	No New Jails NYC	NYC	Criminal	
	OAR of Tompkins County Bail Fund	Tompkins County	Criminal	
	Revolutionary Abolitionist Liberation Fund	NYC	Criminal	People 25 years and under and people who have been incarcerated the longest
	Stop the Raids	NYC	Criminal	
	Swipe It Forward	NYC	Criminal	Individual arrested for fare-evasion
	The Liberty Fund	NYC	Criminal	Those charged with misdemeanor crimes
	Washington Square Legal Services Bail Fund	NYC	Criminal	Those charged with misdemeanor crimes
North Carolina	Alamance County Community Bail Fund	Alamance County	Criminal	
	Blue Ridge Anarchist Black Cross's Asheville Bail Fund	Asheville area	Criminal	Activists
	North Carolina Community Bail Fund of Durham	Durham area	Criminal	
Ohio	Beloved Community Church Cincinnati Bail Fund	Cincinnati	Criminal	Activists
	Central Ohio Freedom Fund	Columbus area	Criminal	
Oregon	Portland Freedom Fund	Multnomah, Clackamas, and Washington Counties	Criminal	BIPOC

State	Name of Bail Fund[1]	Area of Operation	Bail Types Funded	Organizational Focus[2]
Pennsylvania				
	Bukit Bail Fund of Pittsburgh	Allegheny County	Criminal	
	Dauphin County Bail Fund	Dauphin County	Criminal	
	New Sanctuary Movement of Philadelphia Community Fund for Bond and Legal Support	Philadelphia area	Immigration	
	Philadelphia Bail Fund	Philadelphia area	Criminal	
	Philadelphia Community Bail Fund	Philadelphia area	Criminal	
	Up Against the Law Legal Collective	Philadelphia area	Criminal	Activists
Tennessee				
	Hamilton County Community Bail Fund	Hamilton County	Immigration/Criminal	
	Just City Memphis Community Bail Fund	Shelby County	Criminal	
	Nashville Community Bail Fund	Nashville area	Criminal	
Texas				
	Hutto Community Deportation Defense & Bond Fund	Austin, TX area	Immigration	
	RAICES Texas Bond Fund	Statewide	Immigration	
	Restoring Justice Bail Fund	Harris County	Criminal	
	Tarrant County Bail Fund	Tarrant County	Criminal	COVID-19
Utah				
	Decarcerate Utah Salt Lake Community Bail Fund	Salt Lake County	Criminal	
Vermont				
	Vermont Freedom Bail Fund	Statewide	Immigration	

State	Organization	Location	Type	Population served
Virginia	Cville Immigrant Freedom Fund	Statewide	Immigration	
	Richmond Community Bail Fund	Central Virginia	Criminal	
	Roanoke Community Bail Fund	Roanoke area	Criminal	BIPOC Protesters
Washington	BLM Seattle Freedom Fund	Seattle	Criminal	
	Fair Fight Immigrant Bond Fund	Statewide	Immigration	
	Northwest Community Bail Fund	King, Snohomish, and Pierce Counties	Criminal	
Wisconsin	Free the 350 Bail Fund	Dane County	Criminal	Black people incarcerated in Dane County Jail System
Multi-state	3R Fund for Immigrants	Northern Kentucky/Cincinnati, Ohio	Immigration	
	Black Mama's Bail Out Action	Nationwide	Criminal	Black mothers
	FANG Bail Fund	Rhode Island/Massachusetts	Criminal	Activists
	First Friends of NJ & NY Bond Fund	New Jersey/New York	Immigration	
	Freedom for Immigrants National Detention Bond Fund	Nationwide	Immigration	
	Fronterizo Fianza Fund	West Texas/New Mexico	Immigration	
	New Sanctuary Coalition LIFE Bond Fund	Based in NYC, operates nationwide	Immigration	
	SWOP Behind Bars	Nationwide	Criminal	Sex workers
	The Bail Project	Nationwide	Criminal	
	Trans/Queer Migrant Freedom Bond Fund	Nationwide	Immigration	LGBTQ, prioritizing trans women and individuals with HIV+

Police Oversight Boards in the United States

State	Board	Location	Year Founded
Arkansas			
	Citizens' Review Board	Little Rock	2019
Arizona			
	Citizens' Panel for Review of Police Complaints and Use of Force	Chandler	2000
	Independent Police Auditor	Tucson	1997
California			
	Citizen Complaint Police Review Board	Tulare	1995
	Citizen Police Oversight Commission	Inglewood	2002
	Citizens' Law Enforcement Review Board	San Diego County	1990
	Civilian Oversight Commission	Los Angeles County	2016
	Commission on Police Practices	San Diego	2020
	Community & Police Relations Commission	National City	2003
	Community Police Review Commission	Richmond	1984
	Community Police Review Commission	Sacramento	2015
	Department of Police Accountability	San Francisco	2016
	Independent Police Auditor	Palo Alto	2006
	Independent Police Auditor	Santa Cruz	2003
	Office of Independent Review	Fresno	2009
	Office of the Independent Police Auditor	San Francisco Bay Area Rapid Transit (BART)	Revised in 2018
	Office of the Independent Police Auditor	San Jose	1993
	Police Advisory and Review Board	Novato	1992

State	Board	Location	Year Founded
	Police Commission	Oakland	2017
	Police Review Board	Anaheim	2007
	Police Review Commission	Berkeley	1973
	Police Station Citizens Advisory Committee	Claremont	2018
	The Citizen Police Complaint Commission	Long Beach	1990
	The Community Police Review Commission	Riverside	1998
	The Office of Independent Review	Orange County	2008, reorganized in 2015
	University of California, Davis Police Accountability Board	Davis	2014
Colorado			
	Citizen Oversight Board	Denver	2005
	Citizen Review Board	Fort Collins	1998, last amended in 2016
	Independent Review Board	Aurora	2014
Connecticut			
	Civilian Police Review Board	Hartford	1992
	Civilian Review Board	New Haven	2019
Florida			
	Citizens Police Review Board	Fort Myers	2009
	Citizens Police Review Board	Ft. Lauderdale	1994
	Citizen's Police Review Board	Naples	2001
	Citizens Review Board	Key West	2002
	Citizens' Police Review Board	Orlando	1992
	Civilian Investigative Panel	Miami	2002
	Civilian Police Review Committee	St. Petersburg	1991
	Independent Review Panel Working Group	Miami-Dade County	2016
	Orange County Citizens Review Board	Orange County	Disbanded in 2009 after losing subpoena power
	Police Advisory Council	Gainesville	2010
	Police Advisory Panels	Sarasota	2011
Georgia			
	The Atlanta Citizen Review Board	Atlanta	2007, granted subpoena power in 2010
Hawaii			
	Police Commission	Hawaii County	1979
	Police Commission	Honolulu	1932
	Police Commission	Kauai	1943

State	Board	Location	Year Founded
Idaho			
	Office of Police Oversight	Boise	1999
Illinois			
	Civilian Police Review Board	Urbana	2011
Indiana			
	Civilian Office of Police Accountability	Chicago	2016
Iowa			
	Community Police Review Board	Iowa City	1997
Kansas			
	Citizens Police Advisory Council	Olathe	1995
Kentucky			
	Citizens Commission on Police Accountability	Louisville	2003
Louisiana			
	The Office of the Independent Police Monitor	New Orleans	2010
Maine			
	Police Citizen Review Subcommittee	Portland	2001
Maryland			
	Citizen Complaint Oversight Panel	Prince George's County	1990
	Civilian Review Board	Baltimore	1999
Massachusetts			
	Community Ombudsman Oversight Panel	Boston	2007
	Community Police Hearing Board	Springfield	2010
	Police Review & Advisory Board	Cambridge	1984, adopted new rules and regulations in 2011
Michigan			
	Board of Police Commissioners	Detroit	1974
	Citizen's Police Review Board	Muskegon	1999
	Citizens Public Safety Review and Appeal Board	Kalamazoo	Relaunched in 2015 after a hiatus
	Police Civilian Appeal Board	Grand Rapids	1996; amended in 2003
	Police Oversight Commission	Ann Arbor	2018
Minnesota			
	Office of Police Conduct Review	Minneapolis	2012

State	Board	Location	Year Founded
	Police Civilian Internal Affairs Review Commission	St. Paul	Formed in 1993, significantly amended in 2016
	St. Cloud Police Citizens' Review Board	St. Cloud	1996
Missouri			
	Citizens Police Review Board	Columbia	2009
	Civilian Oversight Board	St. Louis	2014
	Office of Community Complaints	Kansas City	1943
	Police Civilian Review Board	Springfield	1999, reinstated in 2012
Montana			
	Police Commission	Missoula	1979
Nebraska			
	Citizen Complaint Review Board	Omaha	2014
Nevada			
	Citizen Review Board	Las Vegas	1997
New Hampshire			
	Police Commission	Portsmouth	1991
New Jersey			
	Police Oversight Board	Newark	2016
New Mexico			
	Civilian Police Oversight Agency	Albuquerque	2014 to replace prior entity
New York			
	Citizen Review Board	Syracuse	2011
	Civilian Complaint Review Board (CCRB)	New York	1953, restructured and given subpoena power in 1993
	Civilian Police Complaint Review Board	Village of Ossining	2000
	Civilian Police Review Board	Schenectady	2002
	Civilian Review Board	Rochester	2014
	Commission on Citizens' Rights and Community Relations	Buffalo	2000
	Community Police Board	Ithaca	1996
	Community Police Review Board	Albany	2000
	Police-Community Relations and Review Board	Newburgh	2014
North Carolina			
	Citizen Review Board	Charlotte-Mecklenburg	1997
	Citizens/Police Advisory Committee	Asheville	1989

State	Board	Location	Year Founded
	Citizens' Police Review Board	Winston-Salem	1993
	Civilian Police Review Board	Durham	2003, revised in 2014 and again in 2019
	Criminal Justice Advisory Commission	Greensboro	2018
Ohio			
	Citizen Complaint Authority	Cincinnati	2003
	Community Police Council	Dayton	2016
	Office of Professional Standards' Civilian Police Review Board	Cleveland	2016
Oklahoma			
	Citizen Advisory Board	Oklahoma City	2005
Oregon			
	Civilian Review Board	Eugene	2006
	Community Police Review Advisory Board	Corvallis	2007
	Independent Police Review	Portland	2001
Pennsylvania			
	Citizen Police Review Board	Pittsburgh	1997
	Police Advisory Commission	Philadelphia	1993, re-established in 2017
Rhode Island			
	Providence External Review Authority	Providence	Created in 2002, restarted in 2019 after staying dormant for a decade
South Carolina			
	Charleston Citizen Police Advisory Council	City of Charleston	2018
	Citizen Review Board	City of Columbia	2015
	Citizen Review Board	Richland County	2001
	Public Safety Citizen Review Board	City of Greenville	2005
Tennessee			
	Community Oversight Board	Nashville	2018
	Memphis Civilian Law Enforcement Review Board	Memphis	1994, restarted in 2016
	Police Advisory & Review Committee	Knoxville	2001
Texas			
	Chief's Advisory Action Board	San Antonio	2016
	Civilian Review Board	Galveston	Created in 2008, suspended in 2019

State	Board	Location	Year Founded
	Community Police Oversight Board	Dallas	2019, replaced previous oversight entity
	Community Police Review Commission	Austin	2020, prior oversight entity suspended in 2018
	Independent Police Oversight Board	Houston	2011
	Office of the Police Oversight Monitor	Fort Worth	2020
Utah			
	Police Civilian Review Board	Salt Lake City	2020
	Professional Standards Review Board	West Valley City	2013
Vermont			
	Citizen Police Communications Committee	Brattleboro	Amended in 2014
	State Police Advisory Commission	Statewide	Amended in 1979
Virginia			
	Investigation Review Panel	Virginia Beach	Re-established in 2013
	Police Civilian Review Board	Charlottesville	2019
	Police Civilian Review Panel	Fairfax County	2016
Washington			
	Citizen's Advisory/Review Board	Spokane	2000, amended in 2015
	Community Police Commission	Seattle	2012, amended in 2017
	Office of Law Enforcement Oversight	King County	2006, amended in 2015
Wisconsin			
	Fire and Police Commission	Statewide regulation with local iterations	1885, bill to overhaul commission under consideration in 2021

Progressive and Reform Prosecutors

Name	State	District	Progressive/ Reform	Election Year
Aisha Braveboy	MD	Prince George's County State's Attorney	Reform[a]	2018
Alexis King	CO	Jefferson/Gilpin County District Attorney	Reform	2020
Alonzo Payne	CO	San Luis Valley District Attorney	Progressive[c]	2020
Amy Ashworth	VA	Prince William County Commonwealth Attorney	Reform	2019
Amy Weirich	TN	Shelby County District Attorney	Reform	2011 (appointed)
Andrea Harrington	MA	Berkshire County District Attorney	Reform	2018
Andrew H. Warren	FL	Hillsborough State Attorney	Reform	2016
Beth McCann	CO	Denver County District Attorney	Reform	2016
Brian M. Middleton	TX	Fort Bend County District Attorney	Reform	2018
Bryan Porter	VA	Alexandria City Commonwealth Attorney	Reform	2013
Buta Biberaj	VA	Loudoun County Commonwealth Attorney	Reform	2019
Carol A. Siemon	MI	Ingham County Prosecuting Attorney	Reform	2016
Chesa Boudin	CA	San Francisco County District Attorney	Progressive	2019
Christian Gossett	WI	Winnebago County District Attorney	Reform	2006
Colette McEachin	VA	Richmond City Commonwealth Attorney	Reform	2019
Cyrus R. Vance, Jr.	NY	New York County District Attorney	Reform	2009

Name	State	District	Progressive/ Reform	Election Year
Dan Satterberg	WA	King County Prosecuting Attorney	Reform	2007
Danny Carr	AL	Jefferson County District Attorney - Birmingham Division	Progressive	2018
Darcel Clark	NY	Bronx County District Attorney	Reform	2015
Darius Pattillo	GA	Henry County District Attorney	Reform	2016
Dave Aronberg	FL	Palm Beach State Attorney	Reform	2012
David Soares	NY	Albany County District Attorney	Reform	2004
David Sullivan	MA	Franklin & Hampshire County District Attorney	Reform	2010
Diana Becton	CA	Contra Costa County District Attorney	Reform	2017
Eli Savit	MI	Washtenaw County Prosecuting Attorney	Progressive	2020
Eric Gonzalez	NY	Kings County District Attorney	Progressive	2016
Fani Willis	GA	Fulton County Georgia	Reform	2020
Faris Dixon	NC	Pitt County District Attorney	Reform	2018
Gary Tyack	OH	Franklin County Prosecuting Attorney	Reform	2020
George Gascón	CA	Los Angeles County District Attorney	Progressive	2020
George Hartwig	GA	Houston County District Attorney	Reform	2010
Gordon McLaughlin	CO	Jackson/Larimer County District Attorney	Reform	2020
Hillar Moore III	LA	East Baton Rouge Parish District Attorney	Reform	2008
J. Hanley	IL	Winnebago County State's Attorney	Reform	2020
Jack Stollsteimer	PA	Delaware County District Attorney	Reform	2019
James Stewart Sr.	LA	Caddo Parish District Attorney	Implemented some reforms[b]	2015

Name	State	District	Progressive/ Reform	Election Year
Jason Anderson	CA	San Bernardino County District Attorney	Implemented some reforms	2018
Jason R. Williams	LA	Orleans Parish District Attorney	Progressive	2020
Jeff Reisig	CA	Yolo County District Attorney	Reform	2006
Jeff Rosen	CA	Santa Clara County District Attorney	Reform	2010
Jim Hingeley	VA	Albemarle County Commonwealth Attorney	Progressive	2019
Jody Owens	MS	Hinds County District Attorney	Reform	2019
Joe Gonzales	TX	Bexar County District Attorney	Reform	2018
John Chisholm	WI	Milwaukee County District Attorney	Reform	2006
John Choi	MN	Ramsey County Attorney	Reform	2010
John Creuzot	TX	Dallas County District Attorney	Reform	2018
John Hummel	OR	Deschutes County District Attorney	Reform	
Jose Garza	TX	Travis County District Attorney	Progressive	2020
Joseph Platania	VA	Charlottesville City Commonwealth Attorney	Reform	2017
Justin Kollar	HI	Kauai County Chief prosecutor	Reform	2012
Karen McDonald	MI	Oakland County Prosecuting Attorney	Reform	2020
Karl Racine	DC	District of Columbia Attorney General	Reform	2014
Katherine Fernandez Rundle	FL	Miami-Dade State Attorney	Implemented some reforms	1993
Kent Volkmer	AZ	Pinal County Attorney	Reform	2016
Kim Ogg	TX	Harris County District Attorney	Reform	2016
Kimberly Gardner	MO	City of St. Louis Circuit Attorney	Progressive	2016

Name	State	District	Progressive/ Reform	Election Year
Kimberly M. Foxx	IL	Cook County State's Attorney	Progressive	2015
Kristin M. Bronson	CO	Denver City Attorney	Reform	2016
Larry Krasner	PA	Philadelphia City District Attorney	Progressive	2017
Locke Thompson	MO	Cole County Prosecuting Attorney	Reform	2018
Lynneice O. Washington	AL	Jefferson County District Attorney - Bessemer Division	Reform	2016
Marian Ryan	MA	Middlesex County District Attorney	Reform	2013 (appointed)
Marilyn Mosby	MD	Baltimore City State's Attorney	Reform	2014
Mark A. Gonzalez (D)	TX	Nueces County District Attorney	Reform	2016
Mark Dupree, Sr.	KS	Wyandotte County District Attorney	Reform	2016
Mary Carmack-Altwies	NM	Santa Fe/Rio Arriba/Los Alamos County District Attorney	Reform	2020
Mary Pat Donnelly	NY	Rensselaer County District Attorney	Reform	2018
Melinda Katz	NY	Queens County District Attorney	Progressive	2019
Melissa Nelson	FL	Clay/Duval/Nassau County State Attorney	Reform	2016
Michael Dougherty	CO	Boulder County District Attorney	Reform	2018
Michael O'Malley	OH	Cuyahoga County Prosecuting Attorney	Reform	2016
Mike O'Connell	KY	Jefferson County Attorney	Reform	2008 (appointed)
Mike Schmidt	OR	Multnomah County District Attorney	Reform	2020
Mimi Rocah	NY	Westchester County District Attorney	Progressive	2020
Monique Worrell	FL	Orange/Osceola County State Attorney	Progressive	2020

Name	State	District	Progressive/ Reform	Election Year
Nancy O'Maley	CA	Alameda County District Attorney	Implemented some reforms	2009
Natasha Irving	ME	Knox/Lincoln/Sagadahoc/ Waldo County District Attorney	Reform	2018
Parisa Dehghani-Tafti	VA	Arlington County Commonwealth Attorney	Progressive	2019
Patricia G. Conway	NH	Rockingham County Attorney	Reform	2014
Paul D. Connick Jr.	LA	Jefferson Parish District Attorney	Reform	1996
Pete Holmes	WA	Seattle City Attorney	Reform	2010
Pete Orput	MN	Washington County Attorney	Reform	2010
Phillip Terrell	LA	Rapides Parish District Attorney	Implemented some reforms	2014
Rachel Rollins	MA	Suffolk County District Attorney	Progressive	2018
Rachel Romano	WV	Harrison County Prosecuting Attorney	Implemented some reforms	2015
Raul Torrez	NM	Bernalillo County District Attorney	Reform	2016
Ryan Mears	IN	Marion County Prosecutor	Reform	2019
Sarah George	VT	Chittendon County State's Attorney	Reform	2017 (appointed)
Satana Deberry	NC	Durham County District Attorney	Progressive	2018
Scott Colom	MS	Lowndes/Oktibbeha/Clay/ Noxubee County District Attorney	Reform	2015
Shameca Collins	MS	Adams/Amite/Franklin/ Wilkinson County District Attorney	Reform	2019
Sherry Boston	GA	DeKalb County District Attorney	Reform	2016
Sim S. Gill	UT	Salt Lake County District Attorney	Reform	2010
Stephanie N. Morales	VA	Portsmouth City Commonwealth Attorney	Reform	2015
Steve T. Descano	VA	Fairfax County Commonwealth Attorney	Progressive	2019

Name	State	District	Progressive/ Reform	Election Year
Timothy D. Sini	NY	Suffolk County District Attorney	Reform	2017
Todd Thompson	KS	Leavenworth County District Attorney	Reform	2008
Tori Verber Salazar	CA	San Joaquin County District Attorney	Reform	2014
Wesley Bell	MO	St. Louis County Prosecuting Attorney	Progressive	2018
Zachary Klein	OH	Columbus City Attorney	Reform	2017

[a] **Reform prosecutor:** This category represents those prosecutors who have taken steps to implement reforms but are not decarceral. This category also includes prosecutors who have claimed membership with the progressive movement but have failed to live up to their promises or who have implemented some progressive reforms but who have failed to pursue progressive policies in critical areas such as policing.

To be classified as a reformist requires that a prosecutor takes initiative to implement reforms beyond carrying on or slightly expanding reforms from prior administrations. It is also sensitive to the overall context and length of a career. A six-term prosecutor whose only reform was setting up a drug court twenty years ago would not be considered a reformist. The category is also cognizant of the rhetoric the prosecutor uses. While using reformist/progressive rhetoric is not sufficient in and of itself, how they frame their policies is important. There is a difference between prosecutors who say they are declining to prosecute certain misdemeanor offenses because they lack the resources versus one who declines to prosecute those crimes because they do not believe those offenses should result in prison time. It reflects different things about what one can expect from their career and who they are looking towards as their base of support. It also reflects the influence of the movement on the scope of what a prosecutor is capable of doing and their reasons for making changes.

[b] **Implemented some reforms:** this is a subcategory of the reform category. This category indicates that the prosecutor does not claim progressivism but that reforms they did pursue were meaningful in the context of the movement's work toward criminal justice reform. This could be because they were elected as a rejection of a deeply controversial/conservative prosecutor, or because they are long-standing prosecutors who shifted their rhetoric and policies in recent years as pressure for criminal justice reform mounted.

[c] **Progressive prosecutor:** This category indicates a commitment to comprehensive decarceral solutions and restricting the power of the criminal justice system. Below are some key institutional habits of the progressive prosecutor[1]:

- They have an outsider status, such as a former defense attorney, activists, or prosecutors in reformist offices who challenge the DA from the left.

[1] Some of the criteria provided here are based on the Community Justice Exchange's Abolitionist Principles & Campaign Strategies for Prosecutor Organizing, see https://www.communityjusticeexchange.org/abolitionist-principles.

- They directly call out law enforcement, police associations and regressive prosecutors in their rhetoric and have a corresponding antagonistic/challenge-based relationship with them.
  - They work to hold police to account and limit their role and contact with the community.
- This excludes policies that seek to use police to intervene in a community or encourage greater contact between police and the communities they historically victimize, even if it is in the name of diversion.
- They seek to shrink the size of the criminal justice system, particularly their own office, by cutting budgets, staff, and scope of duties of the prosecutor's office.
  - This includes removing prosecutors who are committed to traditional law and order prosecution.
- They do not support hi-tech solutions to crime such as tagging "high-risk" individuals for intervention.
- They promote pretrial freedoms by working to forego cash bail as well as electronic monitoring.
- They seek to reduce long-term harm caused by the prison industrial complex by expunging criminal records and avoiding/limiting probation, parole, and other forms of extended surveillance.
- They work to decrease the range of issues that are criminalized and create alternatives to incarceration.
  - They pursue non-enforcement for certain crimes, especially crimes of poverty or drug offenses.
  - They create barriers between the criminal justice system, including the prosecutor's office, and social services/social workers, including schools and housing. This requires exerting pressure on other system stakeholders.
- They work to empower communities through funding community-based resources for community problems, separating these resources to the criminal justice system.
  - They do not rely on coercive measures or surveillance in designing diversion programs or other alternatives to incarceration.
- They pursue transparency by releasing, in an accessible way, as much data as possible to allow constituents to review the impact they have had in office.
  - This includes providing open and early discovery for defense.
- They avoid prosecutorial mechanism meant to maximize punishment and coerce defendants, such as stacking charges, up-charging, and plea bargaining.
  - Their diversion programs are accessible to all people regardless of ability to pay, and they do not place onerous demands on participants.

While few if any prosecutors will meet all of these, they each indicate a commitment to more than just reform of the system, but also advocate for the reduction of its power and influence. Many reformist prosecutors end up expanding the scope and reach of the criminal justice system even in the process of reducing jail populations. It should be noted that some prosecutors labeled as "progressive" ran on promises to implement progressive policies but have not been in office long enough to measure their success.

Movement Syllabi

Anon. 2018. "Prison Abolition Syllabus 2.0." *Black Perspectives*. https://www.aaihs.org/prison-abolition-syllabus-2-0/.

Barber, Lauren, Mankaprr Conteh, Alex Dean, Eric Jordan, and Ann Nguyen. 2017. "A Seat at the Table Syllabus." *Issuu*, February 8. https://issuu.com/ajcwfu/docs/seatatthetablefinal.

Benbow, Candice. 2016. "Lemonade Syllabus." *Issuu*, May 6. https://issuu.com/candicebenbow/docs/lemonade_syllabus_2016.

Bonilla, Yarimar, Marisol LeBrón, Sarah Molinari, Isabel G. Tamargo, and Kimberly Roa. n.d. "#PRSYLLABUS." *Puerto Rico Syllabus*. https://puertoricosyllabus.com/?fbclid=IwAR0RvchrbwBFKGBe6IBvpey_5ZBOEGG-MmHKPtLDPtVgP6AHew8dxEcbYFE.

"Ferguson Syllabus." n.d. *Sociologists for Justice*. https://sociologistsforjustice.org/ferguson-syllabus/.

Halley, Catherine. 2017. "Charlottesville Syllabus: Readings on the History of Hate in America." *JSTOR Daily*, August 16. https://daily.jstor.org/charlottesville-syllabi-history-hate-america/.

Harris-Perry, Melissa. 2018. "Race, Class, and Social Justice." Syllabus, Wake Forest University, Winston-Salem, NC. https://static1.squarespace.com/static/5b69f86ff407b482714e9084/t/5c3fa68cc2241b31b771de11/1547675276454/RaceClassSocialJusticeFall2018.pdf.

Harris-Perry, Melissa. 2020. "Disaster, Race, and American Politics." Syllabus, Wake Forest University, Winston-Salem, NC. https://docs.google.com/document/d/14uKFyc-Ii0rT5Q7YHoGelGq86FLIfG3kPBrYgc3Gcck/edit.

Johnson, Jessica Marie, and Martha S. Jones. 2018. "Black Womanhood." Syllabus, John Hopkins University, Baltimore, MD. http://dh.jmjafrx.com/2018/01/27/black-womanhood-the-syllabus/.

Kendi, Ibram X. 2019. "A Reading List for Ralph Northam." *The Atlantic*. https://www.theatlantic.com/ideas/archive/2019/02/antiracist-syllabus-governor-ralph-northam/582580/?utm_medium=social&utm_term=2019-02-12T14%3A40%3A35&utm_content=edit-promo&utm_campaign=the-atlantic&utm_source=facebook.

Neal, Mark Anthony. 2016. "#ColinKaepernickSyllabus." *NewBlackMan (in Exile)*, September 6. https://www.newblackmaninexile.net/2016/09/colinkaepernicksyllabus.html.

NYC Stands with Standing Rock Collective. 2016. "#StandingRockSyllabus." *NYC Stands with Standing Rock Collective*. https://nycstandswithstandingrock.wordpress.com/standingrocksyllabus/?fbclid=IwAR2g4_umNJNj8mBrDXMp5YYxeT6z7sJXRRsm5epFrnjk5-xCLi88QMlq6Ts.

Petrella, Christopher, and Ameer Loggins. 2017. "Freedom Dreams: The Colin Kaepernick Reading List." *GQ*. https://www.gq.com/story/the-colin-kaepernick-reading-list.

Purnell, Derecka. 2016. "Radical Political Action." *Boston Review*, March 7. http://bostonreview.net/reading-radicalism.

Stewart, Jessica Lynn, and Melissa Harris-Perry. 2019. "Black Women's Political Activism." Syllabus, Wake Forest University, Winston-Salem, NC. https://static1.squarespace.com/static/5b69f86ff407b482714e9084/t/5c3fa5528a922de4d8af32ee/1547674962714/Black+Women%27s+Political+Activism++syllabus+spring+2019.pdf.

The Red Papers. 2017. "A Women's Strike Syllabus." *The New Inquiry*. https://thenewinquiry.com/a-womens-strike-syllabus/.

UVa Graduate Student Coalition for Liberation. 2017. "The Charlottesville Syllabus." *Medium*, August 20. https://medium.com/@UVAGSC/the-charlottesville-syllabus-9e01573419d0.

Viewpoint. 2013. "Issue 5: Social Reproduction." *Viewpoint Magazine*. https://www.viewpointmag.com/2015/11/02/issue-5-social-reproduction/.

Williams, Chad, Keisha N. Blain, Melissa Morrone, Ryan P. Randall, and Cecily Walker. 2021. "#Charlestonsyllabus." *African American Intellectual History*. https://www.aaihs.org/resources/charlestonsyllabus/.

"Welfare Reform Syllabus." 2016. *Black Perspectives*. AAIHS, August 24. https://www.aaihs.org/welfare-reform-syllabus/.

Bibliography

Ackerman, Spencer. 2015. "Homan Square Revealed: How Chicago Police 'Disappeared' 7,000 People." *Guardian*, October 15, 2015. https://www.theguardian.com/us-news/2015/oct/19/homan-square-chicago-police-disappeared-thousands.

Ahmed, Sara. 2007. "A Phenomenology of Whiteness." *Feminist Theory* 8 (2): 149–68.

Akbar, Amna. 2020. "Opinion: The Left Is Remaking the World." *New York Times*, July 11, 2020. https://www.nytimes.com/2020/07/11/opinion/sunday/defund-police-cancel-rent.html.

Akili, Yolo. 2011. "The Immediate Need for Emotional Justice." *Crunk Feminist Collective*, November 16, 2011. http://www.crunkfeministcollective.com/2011/11/16/the-immediate-need-for-emotional-justice/.

Albrecht, Leslie. 2020. "People Donated Millions of Dollars to the Wrong Black Lives Matter Foundation—Read This before You Give to Any Charity." *MarketWatch,* July 6, 2020. https://www.marketwatch.com/story/people-donated-millions-of-dollars-to-the-wrong-black-lives-matter-foundation-read-this-before-you-give-to-any-charity-2020-07-01.

Alcindor, Yamiche. 2016. "After High Profile Shootings, Blacks Seek Prosecutors Seats." *New York Times,* November 5, 2016. http://www.nytimes.com/2016/11/06/us/politics/black-prosecutors.html?_r=0.

Alexander, Elizabeth. 2020. "The Trayvon Generation." *The New Yorker*, June 15, 2020.

Alexander, Michelle. 2011. *The New Jim Crow: Mass Incarceration in the Age of Colorblindness*. New York: New Press.

Alinsky, Saul. (1971) 1989. *Rules for Radicals: A Practical Primer for Realistic Radicals*. New York: Vintage Books.

Althusser, Louis. 1971. "Ideology and the Ideological State Apparatuses (Notes towards an Investigation)." In *Lenin and Philosophy and Other Essays*, by Louis Althusser, 127–86. New York: Monthly Review Press.

Anderson, Benedict. (1983) 2006. *Imagined Communities: Reflections on the Origin and Spread of Nationalism*. New York: Verso.

Anderson, Elizabeth S. 1999. "What Is the Point of Equality?" *Ethics* 109 (2): 287–337.

Anderson, Elizabeth. 2017. *Private Government: How Employers Rule Our Lives (And Why We Don't Talk About It)*. Princeton, NJ: Princeton University Press.

Anderson, Monica. 2016. "Social Media Causes Some Users to Rethink Their Views on an Issue." Pew Research Center, *FactTank: News in the Numbers*, November 7, 2016. https://www.pewresearch.org/fact-tank/2016/11/07/social-media-causes-some-users-to-rethink-their-views-on-an-issue/.

Annenburg Public Policy Center, University of Pennsylvania. 2016. "American's Knowledge of the Branches of Government Is Declining." *Cision PR Newswire*, News release, September 13, 2016. http://www.prnewswire.com/news-releases/americans-knowledge-of-the-branches-of-government-is-declining-300325968.html.

Arendt, Hannah. (1958) 1998. *The Human Condition*. 2nd ed. Introduction by Margaret Canovan. Chicago: University of Chicago Press.

Arendt, Hannah. 1994. *Essays in Understanding: 1930–1954*. New York: Schocken Books.

Arenge, Andrew, Stephanie Perry, and Dartunorro Clark. 2018. "Poll: 64 Percent of Americans Say Racism Remains a Major Problem." NBC News, May 28, 2017. https://www.nbcnews.com/politics/politics-news/poll-64-percent-americans-say-racism-remains-major-problem-n877536.

Armacost, Barbara E. 2020. "Police Shootings: Is Accountability the Enemy of Prevention?" *Ohio State Law Journal* 80 (5): 90786.

Atkinson, Anthony. 2015. *Inequality: What Can Be Done?* Cambridge, MA: Harvard University Press.

Averill, James R. 1982. *Anger and Aggression: An Essay on Emotion*. New York: Springer Verlag.

Bailey, Julius, and David J. Leonard. 2015. "Black Lives Matter: Post-Nihilistic Freedom Dreams." *Journal of Contemporary Rhetoric* 5 (3/4): 67–77.

Ballentine, Summer. 2020. "Protest Leader Bush Ousts 20-Year US Rep. Clay in Missouri." Associated Press, August 5, 2020. https://apnews.com/article/shootings-michael-brown-politics-racial-injustice-alexandria-ocasio-cortez-36ae43993c0fe43e67bcdd9539675997.

Balko, Radley. 2014a. "How Municipalities in St. Louis Co., MO, Profit from Poverty." *Washington Post*, September 3, 2014. https://www.washingtonpost.com/news/the-watch/wp/2014/09/03/how-st-louis-county-missouri-profits-from-poverty/?utm_term=.0e3d15af3e3a.

Balko, Radley. 2014b. *Rise of the Warrior Cop: The Militarization of America's Police Forces*. New York: PublicAffairs/Perseus Books.

Banks, Antoine J. 2014a. *Anger and Racial Politics: The Emotional Foundation of Racial Attitudes in America*. New York: Cambridge University Press.

Banks, Antoine. 2014b. "The Public's Anger: White Racial Attitudes and Opinions toward Healthcare Reform." *Political Behavior* 36 (September): 493–514.

Banks, Chloe. 2018. "Disciplining Black Activism: Post-racial Rhetoric, Public Memory and Decorum in News Media Framing of the Black Lives Matter Movement." *Continuum: Journal of Media and Cultural Studies* 32 (6) 709–20.

Bartels, Larry. 1988. *Presidential Primaries and the Dynamics of Public Choice*. Princeton, NJ: Princeton University Press.

Bartels, Larry. 2008. *Unequal Democracy: The Political Economy of the New Gilded Age*. Princeton, NJ: Princeton University Press.

Bazelon, Emily. 2019. *Charged: The New Movement to Transform American Prosecution and End Mass Incarceration*. New York: Random House.

Beal, Frances M. 1969. "Double Jeopardy: To Be Black and Female." Pamphlet. Later revised and published in *The Black Woman*, edited by Toni Cade Bambara (1970), and in *Sisterhood Is Powerful: An Anthology of Writings from the Women's Liberation Movement*, edited by Robin Morgan (1970).

Beckett, Katherine. 1997. *Making Crime Pay: Law and Order in Contemporary American Politics*. Studies in Crime and Public Policy. New York: Oxford University Press.

Bernard, Tanya Lucia. 2015. "The Movement for Black Lives Convening: An Offering of Love." *The Root*, August 7, 2015. http://www.theroot.com/the-movement-for-black-lives-convening-an-offering-of-1790860722.

Berstein, Mary. 2008. "Afterword: The Analytic Dimension of Identity: A Political Identity Framework." In *Identity Work Processes in Social Movements*, edited by Jo

Reger, Daniel J. Myers, and Rachel L. Einwohner, 277–97. Minneapolis: University of Minnesota Press.

Bingham, Amy. 2012. "Republicans, Democrats Can't Even Agree on Coffee." ABC News, June 18, 2012. http://abcnews.go.com/Politics/OTUS/republicans-democrats-agree-coffee/story?id=16581674#.T98-7c_NaEu.

Black Lives Matter. 2017. *Healing in Action: A Toolkit for Black Lives Matter Healing Justice and Direct Action.* Prepared for Black Lives Matter Global Network Foundation. https://blacklivesmatter.com/resources/.

Black Lives Matter Global Network Foundation. 2020. "Black Lives Matter Global Network Foundation Announces $6.5 Million Fund to Support Organizing Work." Black Lives Matter.com, June 11, 2020. https://blacklivesmatter.com/black-lives-matter-global-network-foundation-announces-6-5-million-fund-to-support-organizing-work/.

Bonilla-Silva, Edouardo. 2013. *Racism without Racists: Colorblind Racism and the Persistence of Racial Inequality in America.* New York: Rowman & Littlefield.

Bowman, Karlyn, Jennifer Marsico, and Heather Sims. 2014. *Is the American Dream Alive? Examining Americans Attitudes.* American Enterprise Institute Report, December 15, 2014.

Brave Heart, Maria Yellow Horse. 1999. "*Oyate Ptayela*: Rebuilding the Lakota Nation through Addressing Historical Trauma among Lakota Parents." *Journal of Human Behavior in the Social Environment* 2 (1–2): 109–26.

Braveman, Paula, Katherine Heck, Susan Egerter, Tyan Parker Dominguez, Christine Rinki, Kristen S. Marchi, and Michael Curtis. 2017. "Worry about Racial Discrimination: A Missing Piece of the Puzzle of Black-White Disparities in Preterm Birth?" *PLoS One* 12 (10): e0186151. doi:10.1371/journal.pone.0186151. eCollection 2017.

Brock, André. 2012. "From the Blackhand Side: Twitter as a Cultural Conversation." *Journal of Broadcasting and Electronic Media* 56 (4): 529–49.

brown, adrienne maree. 2017. *Emergent Strategy: Shaping Change, Changing Worlds.* Reprint edition. Chico, CA: AK Press.

brown, adrienne maree, and Walidah Imarisha, eds. 2015. *Octavia's Brood: Science Fiction Stories from Social Justice Movements.* New York: AK Press.

Bump, Phillip. 2016. "The Facts about Stop-and-Frisk in New York City." *Washington Post*, September 26, 2016. https://www.washingtonpost.com/news/the-fix/wp/2016/09/21/it-looks-like-rudy-giuliani-convinced-donald-trump-that-stop-and-frisk-actually-works/?utm_term=.9f7083634d83.

Byrd, Jessica. 2020. "The Genius of Resilience: Toward a New, Black National Convention." *The Root*, July 14, 2020. https://www.theroot.com/the-genius-of-resilience-toward-a-new-black-national-1844367817.

Capella, Joseph N., and Kathleen Hall Jamieson. 1997. *Spiral of Cynicism: The Press and the Public Good.* New York: Oxford University Press.

Caroll, Susan J., and Richard Fox. 2013. *Gender and Elections.* 3rd ed. Cambridge, MA: Cambridge University Press.

Carruthers, Charlene. 2018. *Unapologetic: A Black, Queer, and Feminist Mandate for Radical Movements.* Boston: Beacon Press.

Carruthers, Charlene, and adrienne maree brown. 2019. "Energizing Change: Charlene Carruthers and Adrienne Marie Brown in conversation at the Chicago Humanities Festival." Spring 2019. https://www.youtube.com/watch?v=vOm3mlLGpok#action=share.

Carruthers, Charlene, and Daniel Denvir. 2017. "Charlene Carruthers: Fighting for Black Lives Under Trump." *The Dig* (podcast), March 7, 2017. https://www.thedigradio.com/podcast/charlene-carruthers-fighting-for-black-lives-under-trump/.

Caspar, Monica J. 2014. "Black Lives Matter/Black Life Matters: A Conversation with Patrisse Cullors and Darnell L. Moore." *The Feminist Wire*, December 1, 2014. http://www.thefeministwire.com/2014/12/Black-lives-matter-Black-life-matters-conversation-patrisse-cullors-darnell-l-moore/.

CBS News Staff. 2016. "Black Lives Matter Condemns Dallas, Pushes Ahead with Protests." CBS News, July 8, 2016. https://www.cbsnews.com/news/dallas-shooting-black-lives-matter-leaders-respond/.

CBS News Staff. 2020. "Black Lives Matter Network Creates $12 Million Grand Fund to Fight Racism." CBS News, June 17, 2020. https://www.cbsnews.com/news/black-lives-matter-network-establishes-12m-grant-fund/.

Chang, Cindy, and Abby Sewell. 2014. "L.A. County Sheriff's Dept. to Get Civilian Oversight." *Los Angeles Times*, December 14, 2014. http://www.latimes.com/local/california/la-me-sheriff-oversight-20141210-story.html.

Chenoweth, Erica, and Jeremy Pressman. 2020. "Black Lives Matter Protests Were Overwhelmingly Peaceful, Our Research Finds." *Spokesman-Review*, October 20, 2020. https://www.spokesman.com/stories/2020/oct/20/erica-chenoweth-and-jeremy-pressman-black-lives-ma/.

Christo, Gina, and Wilnelia Rivera. 2019. "Jessica Byrd on Building the Movement and Owning the Journey." *Deep Democracy* (podcast), episode 7, October 30, 2019. https://www.stitcher.com/podcast/deep-democracy/e/64957672?autoplay=true.

Coates, TaNehisi. 2015. *Between the World and Me*. New York: Random House.

Cohen, Cathy J. 1999. *The Boundaries of Blackness: AIDS and the Breakdown of Black Politics*. Chicago: University of Chicago Press.

Cohn Nate, and Kevin Quealy. 2020. "How Public Opinion Has Moved on Black Lives Matter." *New York Times*, June 10, 2020. https://www.nytimes.com/interactive/2020/06/10/upshot/black-lives-matter-attitudes.html.

Cole, David. 1999. *No Equal Justice: Race and Class in the American Criminal Justice System*. New York: New Press.

Coleman, Justine. 2020. "Millions Mistakenly Raised for Black Lives Matter Group Not Associated with Movement." *The Hill*, June 15, 2020. https://thehill.com/blogs/blog-briefing-room/news/502850-millions-mistakenly-raised-for-black-lives-matter-group-not.

Collins, Patricia Hill. 1990. *Black Feminist Thought: Knowledge, Consciousness, and the Politics of Empowerment*. New York: Routledge.

Combahee River Collective. 1977. "The Combahee River Collective Statement." April 1977. http://circuitous.org/scraps/combahee.html.

Combahee River Collective. 1986. *Combahee River Collective Statement: Black Feminist Organizing in the Seventies and Eighties*. Albany, NY: Kitchen Table/Women of Color Press.

Cooper, Brittney. 2017. *Beyond Respectability: The Intellectual Thought of Race Women*. Urbana: University of Illinois Press.

Cooper, Brittney. 2018. *Eloquent Rage: A Black Feminist Discovers Her Superpower*. New York: St. Martin's Press.

Cordery, William. 2016. "Resourcing the Movement for Black Lives." Funders for Justice, March 17, 2016. https://fundersforjustice.org/resourcing-movement-black-lives/.

Crenshaw, Kimberlé. 1989. "Demarginalizing the Intersection of Race and Sex: A Black Feminist Critique of Antidiscrimination Doctrine, Feminist Theory and Antiracist Politics." *University of Chicago Legal Forum* 1: 139–67.

Crenshaw, Kimberlé. 1991. "Mapping the Margins: Intersectionality, Identity Politics, and Violence against Women of Color." *Stanford Law Review* 43 (6): 1241–99.

Crenshaw, Kimberlé, Andrea J. Ritchie, Rachel Anspach, Rachel Gilmer, and Luke Harris. 2015. *Say Her Name: Resisting Police Brutality against Black Women.* New York: African American Policy Forum. https://ncvc.dspacedirect.org/handle/20.500.11990/1926.

d'Entreves, Maurizio Passerin. 2019. "Hannah Arendt." In *Stanford Encyclopedia of Philosophy Archive*, fall 2019 edition. https://plato.stanford.edu/archives/fall2019/entries/arendt/.

Dahl, Robert. 2006. *A Preface to Democratic Theory.* Expanded edition. Chicago: University of Chicago Press.

Daley, Jim. 2021. "Killings by Police Declined after Black Lives Matter Protests." *Scientific American*, March 1, 2021. https://www.scientificamerican.com/article/killings-by-police-declined-after-black-lives-matter-protests1/.

Davis, Angela. 1983. *Women, Race, and Class.* New York: Vintage Books.

Davis, Angela J. 2007. *Arbitrary Justice: The Power of the American Prosecutor.* New York: Oxford University Press.

Dawson, Michael. 1994. *Behind the Mule: Race and Class in African American Politics.* Princeton, NJ: Princeton University Press.

Dawson, Michael. 2003. *Black Visions: The Roots of Contemporary African-American Political Ideologies.* Chicago: University of Chicago Press

Day, Elizabeth. 2015. "#BlackLivesMatter: The Birth of a New Civil Rights Movement." *Guardian*, July 19, 2015. https://www.theguardian.com/world/2015/jul/19/blacklivesmatter-birth-civil-rights-movement.

Deleuze, Gilles, and Felix Guattari. (1980) 2004. *A Thousand Plateaus: Capitalism and Schizophrenia.* London: Continuum.

DeSilver, Drew. 2015. "The Many Ways to Measure Economic Inequality." Pew Research Center, *FactTank: News in the Numbers,* September 22, 2015. http://www.pewresearch.org/fact-tank/2015/09/22/the-many-ways-to-measure-economic-inequality/.

Desilver, Drew. 2018. "For Most U.S. Workers, Wages Have Barely Budged for Decades." Pew Research Center, *FactTank: News in the Numbers,* August 7, 2018. https://www.pewresearch.org/fact-tank/2018/08/07/for-most-us-workers-real-wages-have-barely-budged-for-decades/.

Dewey, John. (1916) 2012. *Democracy and Education.* New York: Simon & Brown.

Dewey, John. (1927) 2016. *The Public and Its Problems.* Athens, OH: Swallow Press.

Dewey, John. (1934) 2005. *Art as Experience.* New York: Perigee Books.

Dewey, John. (1935) 1991. *Liberalism and Social Action.* Great Books in Philosophy edition. New York: Prometheus Books.

Dewey, John. (1938) 1997. *Experience and Education.* Touchstone Edition. New York: Simon & Schuster.

Dewey, John. (1946) 2007. *The Problems of Men.* New York: Philosophical Library.

Dittmar, Kelly E. 2015. "Women and the Vote: From Enfranchisement to Influence." In *Minority Voting in the United States,* edited by Kyle L. Kreider and Thomas J. Baldino, 99–126. New York: Praeger.

Donaghue, Erin. 2020. "'Horrific Spike' in Fatal Violence against Transgender Community." CBS News, July 14, 2020. https://www.cbsnews.com/news/transgender-community-fatal-violence-spike/.

Du Bois, W. E. B. (1903) 1994. *The Souls of Black Folks*. New York: Dover.

Durkheim, Emile. 1995. *Elementary Forms of Religious Life*. Translated by Karen E. Fields. New York: Free Press.

Dussel, Enrique. 1996. *The Underside of Modernity: Apel, Ricoeur, Rorty, Taylor and the Philosophy of Liberation*. Translated and edited by Eduardo Mendieta. New York: Humanities Press.

Dworkin, Ronald. 2000. *Sovereign Virtue: The Theory and Practice of Equality*. Cambridge, MA: Harvard University Press.

E-Poll Market Research. 2016. "Which TV Shows Do Democrats, Republicans Rate the Highest?" *Cision PR Newswire*, News release, July 20, 2016. http://www.prnewswire.com/news-releases/which-tv-shows-do-republicans-and-democrats-rate-the-highest-300301143.html.

Economic Mobility Project. 2009. "Opinion Poll on Economic Mobility and the American Dream." Pew Charitable Trusts, March 12, 2009. http://www.pewtrusts.org/en/research-and-analysis/analysis/2009/03/12/opinion-poll-on-economic-mobility-and-the-american-dream.

Edwards, Erica R. 2012. *Charisma and the Fictions of Black Leadership*. Minneapolis: University of Minnesota Press.

Edwards-Levy, Ariel. 2018. "Here's What America Thinks about the Me Too Movement Now." *Huffington Post*, August 22, 2018. http://www.pewresearch.org/fact-tank/2016/07/08/how-americans-view-the-black-lives-matter-movement/.

Ellison, Ralph. 2003. "Twentieth-Century Fiction and the Black Mask of Humanity." In *The Collected Essays of Ralph Ellison*, edited by John Callahan, 81–99. New York: Modern Library.

Elmasry, Mohamad Hamas, and Mohammed el-Nawawy. 2017. "Do Black Lives Matter? A content analysis of *New York Times* and *St. Louis Post-Dispatch* coverage of Michael Brown Protests." *Journalism Practice* 11 (7): 857–75.

Eshun, Kodwo. 2003. " Further Considerations on Afrofuturism." *CR: The New Centennial Review* 3 (2): 287–302.

Evans, Erin E. 2019. "#FreeBlackMamas Works to Bail Black Mothers out of Jail in Time for Mother's Day." NBC News, May 11, 2019. https://www.nbcnews.com/news/nbcblk/freeblackmamas-works-bail-black-mothers-out-jail-time-mother-s-n1004511.

Favreau, Jon. "Basket of Neanderthals." Interview with Svante Myrick. *Pod Save America* (podcast), March 4, 2021. https://crooked.com/podcast/basket-of-neanderthals/

Federal Election Commission. 2017. Federal Elections 2016: Election Results for the U.S. President, the U.S. Senate and the U.S. House of Representatives. Washington, DC: Federal Election Commission, December 2017. https://www.fec.gov/resources/cms-content/documents/federalelections2016.pdf.

Fingerhut, Hannah. 2016. "In Both Parties, Men and Women Differ over Whether Women Still Face Obstacles to Progress." Pew Research Center, *FactTank: News in the Numbers*, August 16, 2016. http://www.pewresearch.org/fact-tank/2016/08/16/in-both-parties-men-and-women-differ-over-whether-women-still-face-obstacles-to-progress/.

Fischer, Greg (mayor, Louisville, KY). 2017. "Mayor Fischer's Letter to Citizens Regarding Charlottesville." City News, August 13, 2017. https://louisvilleky.gov/news/mayor-fischers-letter-citizens-regarding-charlottesville.

Fisher, Berenice, and Joan Tronto. 1990. "Toward a Feminist Theory of Caring." In *Circles of Care: Work and Identity in Women's Lives*, edited by Emily Abel and Margaret Nelson, 4–34. Albany: State University of New York Press.

Flavin, Patrick. 2012. "Income Inequality and Policy Representation in the American States." *American Politics Research* 40 (1): 29–59.

Florini, S. 2014. "Tweets, Tweeps, and Signifyin': Communication and Cultural Performance on 'Black Twitter.'" *Television and News Media* 15 (3): 223–37.

Folayan, Sabaah, and Damon Davis, dirs. 2017. *Whose Streets?* Magnolia Pictures.

Follman, Mark. 2014. "Michael Brown's Mom Laid Flowers Where He Was Shot and Police Crushed Them." *Mother Jones*, August 27, 2014. https://www.motherjones.com/politics/2014/08/ferguson-st-louis-police-tactics-dogs-michael-brown/.

Ford, Dana. 2013. "Juror: 'No Doubt' Zimmerman Feared for His Life." CNN, July 16, 2013. http://www.cnn.com/2013/07/15/justice/zimmerman-juror-book/index.html.

Fraser, Nancy. 1990. "Rethinking the Public Sphere: A Contribution to the Critique of Actually Existing Democracy." *Social Texts* 25/26: 56–80.

Fry, Richard, and Rakesh Kochhar. 2014. "Americas Wealth Gap between Middle-Income and Upper-Income Families Widest on Record." Pew Research Center, *FactTank: News in the Numbers,* December 17, 2014. http://www.pewresearch.org/fact-tank/2014/12/17/wealth-gap-upper-middle-income/.

Frymer, Paul. 2010. *Uneasy Alliances: Race and Party Competition in America.* Princeton, NJ: Princeton University Press.

Gaertner, Samuel L., and John F. Dovidio. 2005. "Understanding and Addressing Contemporary Racism: From Aversive Racism to the Common Ingroup Identity Model." *Journal of Social Issues* 61 (3): 615–39.

Gallagher, Ryan J., Andrew J. Reagan, Christopher M. Danforth, and Peter Sheridan Dodds. 2018. "Divergent Discourse between Protests and Counter-Protests: #BlackLivesMatter and #AllLivesMatter." *PLoS One*, April 18, 2018. doi:10.1371/journal.pone.0195644.

Gallup. 2016. "Americans' Confidence in Institutions Stays Low." *Gallup News: Politics*, June 13, 2016. http://www.gallup.com/poll/192581/americans-confidence-institutions-stays-low.aspx.

Garza, Alicia. 2016. "A Herstory of the #BlackLivesMatter Movement." In *Are All the Women Still White? Rethinking Race, Expanding Feminisms,* edited by Janell Hobson, 23–28. Albany: State University of New York Press.

Garza, Alicia, Patrisse Cullors, and Opal Tometi. 2016. "An Interview with the Founders of Black Lives Matter." TEDWomen, October 2016. https://www.ted.com/talks/alicia_garza_patrisse_cullors_and_opal_tometi_an_interview_with_the_founders_of_Black_lives_matter.

Gaventa, John. 1980. *Power and Powerlessness: Quiescence and Rebellion in the Appalachian Valley.* Urbana: University of Illinois Press.

Gecan, Michael. 2004. *Going Public: An Organizer's Guide to Citizen Action.* New York: Anchor Books.

Germain, Jacqui. 2018. "How Brunch Helped Defeat a 7-Term Incumbent." *The Nation*, August 24, 2018. https://www.thenation.com/article/archive/how-brunch-helped-defeat-a-7-term-incumbent/.

Gilens, Martin, and Benjamin Page. 2014. "Testing Theories of American Politics: Elites, Interest Groups, and Average Citizens." *Perspectives on Politics* 12 (3): 564–81.

Gilmore, Ruth Wilson, and James Kilgore. "The Case for Abolition." The Marshall Project, June 19, 2019. https://www.themarshallproject.org/2019/06/19/the-case-for-abolition?fbclid=IwAR1WulH1-iCbugLSfX6yfogOJ2l7bJeFIwdvKvLYhssvEs PoWwSfsT5j6b8.

Goldmacher, Shane. 2020. "Racial Justice Groups Flooded with Millions in Donations in Wake of Floyd Death." New York Times, June 14, 2020, updated June 16, 2020. https://www.nytimes.com/2020/06/14/us/politics/black-lives-matter-racism-donations.html.

Gordon, Lewis. 1995. Bad Faith and Antiblack Racism. New York: Humanity Books.

Gould, Deborah. 2009. Moving Politics: Emotions and ACT UP's Fight against AIDS. Chicago: University of Chicago Press.

Gould, Deborah. 2012. "Political Despair." In Politics and the Emotions: The Affective Turn in Contemporary Political Studies, edited by Simon Thompson and Paul Hoggett, 95–114. New York: Bloomsbury.

Grattan, Laura. 2016. Populism's Power: Radical Grassroots Democracy in America. New York: Oxford University Press.

Green, Donald P., and Alan S. Gerber. 2019. Get Out the Vote: How to Increase Voter Turnout. 4th ed. Washington, DC: Brookings Institution Press.

Green, Donald P., and Michael Schwam-Baird. 2016. "Mobilization, Participation, and American Democracy: A Retrospective and Postscript." Party Politics 22 (2): 158–64.

Green, Kai M., Je Naé Taylor, Pascale Ifé Williams, and Christopher Roberts. 2019. "#BlackHealingMatters in a time of #BlackLivesMatter." Biography 41 (4): 909–41.

Griffith, Mark Winston. 2015. "Black Love Matters." The Nation, July 28, 2015. https://www.thenation.com/article/black-love-matters/.

Grimm, Andy. 2016. "Anita Alvarez Lost Every Predominantly Black Ward in Chicago." Chicago Sun Times, March 16, 2016. https://chicago.suntimes.com/2016/3/16/18399271/anita-alvarez-lost-every-predominantly-black-ward-in-chicago.

Gumbs, Alexis Pauline. 2020. Dub: Finding Ceremony. Durham, NC: Duke University Press.

Hall, Stuart. 1993. "Cultural Identity and Diaspora." In Identity: Community, Culture, Difference, edited by Jonathan Rutherford, 222–37. London: Lawrence and Wishart.

Haney López, Ian. 2015. Dog Whistle Politics: How Coded Racial Appeals Have Reinvented Racism and Wrecked the Middle Class. New York: Oxford University Press.

Haparimwi, Charlene. 2016. "On Being Unapologetically Black." Hooligan Mag (blog), April 6, 2016. http://www.hooliganmagazine.com/blog/2016/4/6/on-being-unapologetically-black

Harris, Christopher Paul. 2019. "Political Acts, Generational Minds: Race, Culture, and the Politics of the Wake." PhD diss., The New School, New York.

Harris, Fredrick. 2012. The Price of the Ticket: Barack Obama and the Rise and Decline of Black Politics. New York: Oxford.

Harris-Perry, Melissa. 2017. "How #SquadCare Saved My Life." Elle, July 24, 2017. https://www.elle.com/culture/career-politics/news/a46797/squad-care-melissa-harris-perry/.

Hattam, Victoria, and Joseph Lowndes. 2007. "The Ground beneath Our Feet: Language, Culture, and Political Change." In Formative Acts: American Politics in the Making, edited by Stephen Skowronck and Matthew Glassman, 199–222. Philadelphia: University of Pennsylvania Press.

Hauck, Grace. 2021. "Denver Successfully Sent Mental Health Professionals, Not Police, to Hundreds of Calls." USA Today, February 8, 2021. https://www.usatoday.com/story/

news/nation/2021/02/06/denver-sent-mental-health-help-not-police-hundreds-calls/4421364001/.

Hayes, Chris. 2017. *A Colony in a Nation*. New York: W. W. Norton.

Hearns, Elle, and Treva B. Lindsey. 2017. "Sister to Sister: Black Women Solidarity." *Huffington Post*, February 12, 2016, updated December 6, 2017. https://www.huffpost.com/entry/sister-to-sister-black-women-solidarity_b_9213772.

Helm, Chanelle. 2017. "White People, Here Are 10 Requests from a Black Lives Matter Leader." *Leo Weekly*, August 16, 2017.

Hemphill, Prentis. 2017. "Healing Justice Is How We Can Sustain Black Lives." *Huffington Post*, February 7, 2017. https://www.huffpost.com/entry/healing-justice_b_5899e8ade4b0c1284f282ffe?guccounter=1&guce_referrer=aHR0cHM6Ly93d3cuZ29vZ2xlLmNvbvbS8&guce_referrer_sig=AQAAADw7aDWVs2CcQ2gqzn8HPbCDDTNJyanJIadLuixzsR3is63_3DiAP8PuIne6q30N4uXjb-BQ6MrqATAhwYjt426hJ64RY04ZtPMW.

Hendricks, Obery M., Jr. 2007. *The Politics of Jesus: Rediscovering the True Revolutionary Nature of Jesus' Teachings and How They Have Been Corrupted*. New York: Three Leaves Press.

Herndon, Astead W., and Dionne Searcey. 2020. "How Trump and the Black Lives Matter Movement Changed Voters' Minds." *New York Times*, June 27, 2020, updated July 3, 2020. https://www.nytimes.com/2020/06/27/us/politics/trump-biden-protests-polling.html

Hess, Ursula. 2014. "Anger Is a Positive Emotion." In *The Positive Side of Negative Emotions*, edited by Gerrod Parrott, 55–75. New York: Guilford Press.

Hetheington, Marc J., and Thomas J. Rudolph. 2015. *Why Washington Won't Work: Polarization, Political Trust, and the Governing Crisis*. Chicago: University of Chicago Press.

Higginbotham, Evelyn Brooks. 1994. *Righteous Discontent: The Women's Movement in the Black Baptist Church, 1880–1920*. Cambridge, MA: Harvard University Press.

Hill, Sean, II. 2017. "Precarity in the Era of #BlackLivesMatter." *Women's Studies Quarterly* 45 (3/4): 94–109.

Hirsch, Marianne. 2012. *The Generation of Postmemory: Writing and Visual Culture after the Holocaust*. New York: Columbia University Press.

Hochschild, Jennifer. 1996. *Facing Up to the American Dream*. Princeton, NJ: Princeton University Press.

Holt, Lanier Frush. 2018. "Using The Elaboration Likelihood Model To Explain To Whom '#Black Lives Matter' . . . And To Whom It Does Not." *Journalism Practice* 12 (2): 146–61.

hooks, bell. (1984) 2015. *Feminist Theory: From Margin to Center*. 3rd ed. New York: Routledge.

Hooks, Mary. 2016. "The Mandate: A Call and Response from Black Lives Matter Atlanta." Transcript, July 14, 2016. Atlanta: Southerners on New Ground. https://southernersonnewground.org/themandate/.

Hopkins, Daniel J., and Samantha Washington. 2019. "The Rise of Trump, the Fall of Prejudice? Tracking White Americans' Racial Attitudes from 2008–2018 via a Panel Study." SSRN Paper, posted May 26, 2019, revised October 2, 2019. https://papers.ssrn.com/sol3/papers.cfm?abstract_id=3378076.

Horowitz, Juliana Menasce, Anna Brown, and Kiana Cox. 2019. "Race in America 2019." Pew Research Center, April 9, 2019. https://www.pewsocialtrends.org/2019/04/09/race-in-america-2019/.

Horowitz, Juliana Menasce, Ruth Igielnik, and Rakesh Kochhar. 2020. "Most Americans Say There Is Too Much Economic Inequality in the U.S., but Fewer Than Half Call It a Top Priority." Pew Research Center, January 9, 2020. https://www.pewresearch. org/social-trends/2020/01/09/most-americans-say-there-is-too-much-economic-inequality-in-the-u-s-but-fewer-than-half-call-it-a-top-priority/.

Horowitz, Juliana Menasce, and Gretchen Livingston. 2016. "How Americans View the Black Lives Matter Movement." Pew Research Center, *FactTank: News in the Numbers*, July 8, 2016. http://www.pewresearch.org/fact-tank/2016/07/08/how-americans-view-the-black-lives-matter-movement/.

Horton, Myles, Judith Kohl, and Herbert R. Kohl. 1998. *The Long Haul: An Autobiography*. New York: Teachers College Press.

Human Rights Network. 2020. "Fatal Violence against the Transgender and Gender Non-conforming Community in 2020." https://www.hrc.org/resources/violence-against-the-trans-and-gender-non-conforming-community-in-2020

Ince, Jelani, Fabio Rojas, and Clayton A. Davis. 2017. "The Social Media Response to Black Lives Matter: How Twitter Users Interact with Black Lives Matter through Hashtag Use." *Ethnic and Racial Studies* 40 (11): 1814–30.

Inouye, Mie. 2019. "Organizer as Radical Pedagogue: Myles Horton's Theory of Democratic Education." Paper presented at 2019 APSA Annual Meeting and Exhibition: Populism and Privilege, August 29–September, 2019, Washington, DC.

Jackson, Imani. 2018. "Black Lives Matter Cincinnati Changes Its Name, Issues Scathing Critique of National BLM Network." Black Youth Project, March 30, 2018. http://blackyouthproject.com/black-lives-matter-cincinnati-changes-its-name-issues-scathing-critique-of-national-blm/?utm_campaign=crowdfire&utm_content=crowdfire&utm_medium=social&utm_source=facebook_page#122353849684-fp#1522628546627.

James, William. 1880. "Great Men, Great Thoughts, and the Environment." Lecture delivered before the Harvard Natural History Society, published in the *Atlantic Monthly*, October 1880. https://www.uky.edu/~eushe2/Pajares/jgreatmen.html.

Johnson, Heather Beth. 2006. *The American Dream and the Power of Wealth: Choosing Schools and Inheriting Inequality in the Land of Opportunity*. New York: Routledge.

Johnston, Hank. 2011. *States and Social Movements*. New York: Polity.

Jones, Bryan D. 1994. *Reconceiving Decision-Making in Democratic Politics: Attention, Choice and Public Policy*. Chicago: University of Chicago.

Jones, Bryan D., and Frank R. Baumgartner. 2005. *The Politics of Attention: How Government Prioritizes Problems*. Chicago: University of Chicago Press.

Jones, Michael L. 2018. "Black Lives Matter Starts Housing Program to Ensure Low Income Families Can Stay in West End." *Louisville Future*, November 26, 2018. https://louisvillefuture.com/archived-news/Black-lives-matters-starts-housing-programs-to-ensure-low-income-families-can-stay-in-the-west-end/.

Jones-Eversley, Sharon, A. Christson Adedoyin, Michael A. Robinson, and Sharon E. Moore. 2017. "Protesting Black Inequality: A Commentary on the Civil Rights Movement and Black Lives Matter." *Journal of Community Practice* 25 (3/4): 309–24.

Justice Roundtable. 2020. "Endorse the Movement for Black Lives." https://justiceroundtable.org/endorse-the-movement-for-black-lives/.

Kaba, Mariame. 2021. *We Do This 'Til We Free Us: Abolitionist Organizing and Transforming Justice*. Chicago: Haymarket Books.

Kaba, Mariame, and John Duda. 2017. "Towards the Horizon of Abolition: A Conversation with Mariame Kaba." The Next System Project, November 9, 2017. https://thenextsystem. org/learn/stories/towards-horizon-abolition-conversation-mariame-kaba.

Katznelson, Ira. 1981. *City Trenches: Urban Politics and the Patterning of Class in the United States*. New York: Pantheon Books.

Kaur, Manjeet. 2021. "Seattle Cut Its Police Budget. Now the Public Will Decide How to Spend the Money." *The Appeal*, January 28, 2021. https://theappeal.org/politicalreport/ seattle-participatory-budgeting-defund-police/.

Kelly, Nathan J. 2009. *The Politics of Income Inequality in the United States*. Cambridge: Cambridge University Press.

Keshner, Andrew. 2019. "Child-Care Costs in America Have Soared to Nearly $10K per Year. *MarketWatch*, March 8, 2019. https://www.marketwatch.com/story/child-care-costs-just-hit-a-new-high-2018-10-22.

Khan-Cullors, Patrisse. 2016. "We Didn't Start a Movement, We Started a Network." *Medium.com*, February 22, 2016. https://medium.com/@patrissemariecullorsbrignac/ we-didn-t-start-a-movement-we-started-a-network-90f9b5717668.

Khan-Cullors, Patrisse. 2019. "Abolition and Reparations: Histories of Resistance, Transformative Justice, and Accountability." *Harvard Law Review* 132 (6): 1684–94. https://harvardlawreview.org/2019/04/abolition-and-reparations-histories-of-resistance-transformative-justice-and-accountability/.

Khan-Cullors, Patrisse, and asha bandele. 2018. *When They Call You a Terrorist: A Black Lives Matter Memoir*. New York: St. Martin's Press.

Khalid, Asma. 2018. "Black Campaign School Seeks to Build Black Political Power." NPR, August 6, 2018. https://www.npr.org/2018/08/06/634670780/black-campaign-school-seeks-to-build-black-political-power.

Kinder, Donald, and Lynn Sanders. 1996. *Divided by Color: Racial Politics and Democratic Ideals*. Chicago: University of Chicago Press.

King, Jamilah. 2015. "#BlackLivesMatter: How Three Friends Turned A Spontaneous Facebook Post into a Global Phenomenon" *California Sunday Magazine*, March 1, 2015. http://www.barenose.com/be_stumble/2015/03/05/how-three-friends-turned-a-spontaneous-facebook-post-into-a-global-phenomenon/.

Kochhar, Rakesh, and Anthony Cilluffo. 2017. "How Wealth Inequality Has Changed in the U.S. since the Great Recession, by Race, Ethnicity, and Income." Pew Research Center, *FactTank: News in the Numbers*, November 1, 2017. https://www.pewresearch. org/fact-tank/2017/11/01/how-wealth-inequality-has-changed-in-the-u-s-since-the-great-recession-by-race-ethnicity-and-income/.

Kochhar, Rakesh, and Richard Fry. 2014. "Wealth Inequality has Widened along Racial, Ethnic Lines since End of Great Recession." Pew Research Center, *FactTank: News in the Numbers,* December 12, 2014. http://www.pewresearch.org/fact-tank/2014/12/12/ racial-wealth-gaps-great-recession/.

Kushner, Rachel. 2019. "Is Prison Necessary? Ruth Wilson Gilmore Might Change Your Mind." *New York Times*, April 17, 2019. https://www.nytimes.com/2019/04/17/maga-zine/prison-abolition-ruth-wilson-gilmore.html.

Lartey, Jamiles, and Ryan Felton. 2016. "Black Lives Matter Activists Face Familiar Anxiety in Aftermath of Dallas Shooting." *Guardian*, July 9, 2016. https://www.theguardian. com/us-news/2016/jul/09/black-lives-matter-dallas-protest-shooting.

Lartey, Jamiles, and Simone Weichselbaum. 2020. "Before George Floyd's Death, Minneapolis Police Failed to Adopt Reforms, Remove Bad Officers." The Marshall Project, May 28, 2020. https://www.themarshallproject.org/2020/05/28/before-george-floyd-s-death-minneapolis-police-failed-to-adopt-reforms-remove-bad-officers.

Leopold, Joy, and Myrtle P. Bell. 2017. "News Media and the Racialization of Protest: An Analysis of Black Lives Matter Articles." Equality, Diversity and Inclusion: An International Journal 36 (3): 720–35.

Lerman, Amy E., and Vesla M. Weaver. 2014. Arresting Citizenship: The Democratic Consequences of American Crime Control. Chicago: University of Chicago Press.

Lien, Pei-Te. 2001. Making of Asian America: Through Political Participation. Philadelphia: Temple University Press.

Loewen, James W. 2006. Sundown Towns: A Hidden Dimension of American Racism. New York: Touchstone.

Lomax, Tamura, Stephanie Troutman, and Heather Laine Talley. 2015. "Lessons from Ferguson." The Feminist Wire, September 5, 2015. http://www.thefeministwire.com/2014/09/things-learned-ferguson.

López, Ian F. Haney. 2004. Racism on Trial: The Chicano Fight for Justice. Cambridge, MA: Belknap Press of Harvard University Press.

Lorde, Audre. 1981. "The Uses of Anger: Women Responding to Racism." Keynote Presentation at National Women's Studies Association Conference, Storrs, Connecticut, June 1981. https://www.blackpast.org/african-american-history/1981-audre-lorde-uses-anger-women-responding-racism/.

Lorde, Audre. 2007. Sister Outsider: Speeches and Essays. Berkeley, CA: Crossing Press.

Lowery, Wesley. 2016. They Can't Kill Us All: Ferguson, Baltimore, and a New Era in America's Racial Justice Movement. New York: Little, Brown.

Lowery, Wesley. 2017. "Black Lives Matter: The Birth of a Movement." Guardian, January 17, 2017. https://www.theguardian.com/us-news/2017/jan/17/black-lives-matter-birth-of-a-movement.

Lowery, Wesley. 2021. "The Most Ambitious Effort Yet to Reform Policing May Be Happening in Ithaca, NY." GQ Magazine, February 21, 2021. https://www.gq.com/story/ithaca-mayor-svante-myrick-police-reform.

Lukes, Steven. 2005. Power: A Radical View. 2nd ed. New York: Palgrave Macmillan.

Lupia, Arthur. 2015. Uninformed: Why People Seem to Know So Little about Politics and What We Can Do about It. New York: Oxford University Press.

Lurie, Julia. 2014. "10 Hours in Ferguson: A Visual Timeline of Michael Brown's Death and Its Aftermath," Mother Jones, August 27, 2014. https://www.motherjones.com/politics/2014/08/timeline-michael-brown-shooting-ferguson/.

Luxemburg, Rosa. 1972. Selected Political Writings (Writings of the Left). Edited by Robert Looker. London: Jonathan Cape.

M4BL.org. 2020. Vision for Black Lives: 2020 Policy Platform. https://m4bl.org/policy-platforms/.

Makalani, Minkah. 2017. "Black Lives Matter and the Limits of Formal Black Politics." South Atlantic Quarterly 116 (3): 529–52.

Marasco, Robyn. 2017. The Highway of Despair: Critical Theory after Hegel. New York: Columbia University Press.

Marin, Mara. 2017. Connected by Commitment: Oppression and Our Responsibility to Undermine It. New York: Oxford University Press.

Martin, Courtney E. 2019. "Closing the Racial Wealth Gap." *New York Times*, April 23, 2019. https://www.nytimes.com/2019/04/23/opinion/closing-the-racial-wealth-gap.html.

Matthews, Shanelle, and Miski Noor. 2017. *Celebrating Four Years of Organizing to Protect Black Lives*. Prepared for Black Lives Matter Global Network Foundation. https://richmondpledge.org/wp-content/uploads/Module-5-Pre-Session-BLM-Anniversary-Report.pdf.

Mauer, Marc. 2006. *Race to Incarcerate*. New York: New Press.

Mauer, Marc, and Ryan S. King. 2007. *The 25-Year Quagmire: The War on Drugs and Its Impact on American Society*. Washington, DC: The Sentencing Project.

Mazumder, Shom. 2019. "Black Lives Matter Protests Reduced Whites' Racial Prejudice and Boosted Democratic Party Vote Share." *Data for Progress* (blog), May 5, 2019. https://www.dataforprogress.org/blog/2019/5/5/black-lives-matter-protests-reduced-whites-racial-prejudice-and-boosted-democratic-party-vote-shares.

McAdam, Doug. 1982. *Political Process and the Development of Black Insurgency 1930–1970*. Chicago: University of Chicago Press.

McAlevey, Jane F. 2016. *No Shortcuts: Organizing for Power in the New Gilded Age*. New York: Oxford University Press.

McFadden, Syreeta. 2014. "Ferguson, Goddamn: No Indictment for Darren Wilson Is No Surprise. This Is Why We Protest." *Guardian*, November 24, 2014. https://www.theguardian.com/commentisfree/2014/nov/24/ferguson-no-indictment-darren-wilson-protest.

McIntosh, Kriston, Emily Moss, Ryan Nunn, and Jay Shambaugh. 2020. "Examining the Black-White Wealth Gap." Brookings Institute, Up Front (blog), February 27, 2020. https://www.brookings.edu/blog/up-front/2020/02/27/examining-the-black-white-wealth-gap/.

McIvor, David W. 2016. *Mourning in America: Race and the Politics of Loss*. Ithaca, NY: Cornell University Press.

McKinney, Jeffrey. "This PAC Is Raising $12 million to Get Black Politicians Elected in 2020." *Black Enterprise*, December 28, 2018. https://www.blackenterprise.com/12-million-to-get-black-politicians-elected/.

McNulty, James K., and V. Michelle Russell. 2010. "When "Negative" Behaviors Are Positive: A Contextual Analysis of the Long-Term Effects of Problem-Solving Behaviors on Changes in Relationship Satisfaction." *Journal of Personality and Social Psychology* 98 (4): 587–604.

Mettler, Suzanne. 2011. *The Submerged State: How Invisible Government Policies Undermine American Democracy*. Chicago: University of Chicago Press.

Mills, Charles W. 1997. *The Racial Contract*. Ithaca, NY: Cornell University Press.

Mitchell, Nikita. 2017. "Why We Organize: A Letter From Our Organizing Director." In *Celebrating Four Years of Organizing to Protect Black Lives*, by Shanelle Matthews and Miski Noor. Prepared for Black Lives Matter Global Network Foundation. https://richmondpledge.org/wp-content/uploads/Module-5-Pre-Session-BLM-Anniversary-Report.pdf.

Monmouth University. 2020. "Partisanship Drives Latest Shift in Race Relations Attitudes: Majority Hopeful That Movement Will Have a Positive Impact." Monmouth University Polling Institute, July 8, 2020. https://www.monmouth.edu/polling-institute/reports/monmouthpoll_us_070820/.

Moore, Darnell L., and Patrisse Cullors. 2014. "Five Ways to Never Forget Ferguson and Deliver Real Justice for Michael Brown," *Guardian*, September 4, 2014. https://www.theguardian.com/commentisfree/2014/sep/04/never-forget-ferguson-justice-for-michael-brown.

Morales, Mark, and Laura Ly. 2019. "Released NYPD Emails Show Extensive Surveillance of Black Lives Matter Protestors." CNN, January 18, 2019. https://www.cnn.com/2019/01/18/us/nypd-black-lives-matter-surveillance/index.html.

Morris, Aldon D. 1984. *The Origins of the Civil Rights Movement: Black Communities Organizing for Change.* New York: Free Press.

Morris, Susana M. 2012. "Black Girls Are from the Future: Afrofuturist Feminism in Octavia E. Butler's *Fledgling.*" *Women's Studies Quarterly* 40 (3/4): 146–66.

Morrison, Aaron. 2016. "Black Lives Matter Is Evolving and Some Early Supporters Aren't Too Thrilled." *Mic*, September 13, 2016. https://www.mic.com/articles/153799/black-lives-matter-is-evolving-and-some-early-supporters-aren-t-too-thrilled.

Moses, Robert P., Mieko Kamii, Susan McAllister Swap, and Jeffrey Howard. 1989. "The Algebra Project: Organizing in the Spirit of Ella." *Harvard Educational Review* 59 (4): 423–43.

Moses, Wilson Jeremiah. 1996. *Classic Black Nationalism: From the American Revolution to Marcus Garvey.* New York: New York University Press.

Movement for Black Lives. 2018. "Electoral Justice." Project Launch Video. https://www.youtube.com/watch?v=8z8einKu6Z4.

Movement for Black Lives. 2020. "Vision for Black Lives: 2020 Platform." https://m4bl.org/policy-platforms/.

Mundt, Marcia, Karen Ross, and Charla M. Burnett. 2018. "Scaling Social Movements through Social Media: The Case of Black Lives Matter." *Social Media and Society* 4 (4): 1–14.

Museum of the City of New York. 2017. "The Movement for Black Lives Now." Panel discussion, September 19, 2017. https://www.youtube.com/watch?v=-j1Eh6fG1QQ&feature=youtu.be.

Nash, Jennifer C. 2019. *Black Feminism Reimagined: After Intersectionality.* Durham, NC: Duke University Press.

NAREB (National Association of Real Estate Brokers). 2013. *The State of Housing in Black America: Official Report, 2013.* Lanham, MD: NAREB. https://issuu.com/jenningslj/docs/shiba_report_for_posting.

Neal, Samantha. 2017."Views of Racism as a Major Problem Increase Sharply, Especially among Democrats." Pew Research Center, *FactTank: Numbers in the Numbers*, August 29, 2017. https://www.pewresearch.org/fact-tank/2017/08/29/views-of-racism-as-a-major-problem-increase-sharply-especially-among-democrats/.

Nelson, Alondra. 2002. "Introduction: Future Texts." *Social Text* 20 (2): 1–16.

Nelson, Matt. 2015. "Introduction." In *Ferguson Is America: Roots of Rebellion*, by Jamala Rogers, xv–xxii. St. Louis: Mira Digital Publishing.

NOBLE (National Organization of Black Law Enforcement Executives). 2017. "NOBLE Expresses Concern of the Black Identity Extremists FBI Assessment, Proposes Changes and Recommendations." Press Release, November 27, 2017. http://noblenational.org/wp-content/uploads/2018/01/FBI-Black-Identity-Extremists-NOBLE-Press-Statement.pdf.

North Star Fund. n.d. "Our Vision." https://northstarfund.org/about/.

Nozick, Robert. 1974. *Anarchy, State, and Utopia.* New York: Basic Books.

Nussbaum, Martha C. 2004. "Beyond the Social Contract: Toward Global Justice." *Tanner Lectures on Human Values* 24 (2004): 415–507.

Nyhan, Brendan, and Jason Reifler. 2010. "When Corrections Fail: The Persistence of Political Misperceptions." *Political Behavior* 32: 303–30.

Ober, Josiah. 1991. *Mass and Elite in Democratic Athens: Rhetoric, Ideology, and the Power of the People*. Princeton, NJ: Princeton University Press.

O'Brian, Hettie. 2019. "How Mindfulness Privatized a Social Problem." *New Statesman*, July 17, 2019. https://www.newstatesman.com/politics/health/2019/07/how-mindfulness-privatised-social-problem?fbclid=IwAR2atV4IMDYVIBphSY5X6eqieUw0W_LDnSw1ol9DJXw-cqsKJst8u5A7qw4.

O'Connor, Meg. 2021a. "Austin May Use Money Cut from Police Budget to Establish Permanent Supportive Housing." *The Appeal*, January 26, 2021. https://theappeal.org/austin-police-budget-homeless-housing/.

O'Connor, Meg. 2021b. "State Lawmakers Are Pushing New Bills to Reduce Reliance on Police." *The Appeal*, February 2, 2021. https://theappeal.org/politicalreport/state-lawmakers-are-pushing-new-bills-to-reduce-reliance-on-police/.

Oliver, Mary. 2017. *Devotions: The Selected Poems of Mary Oliver*. New York: Penguin Press, 2017.

Olson, Mancur. 1971. *The Logic of Collective Action: Public Goods and the Theory of Groups*. Cambridge, MA: Harvard University Press.

Olteanu, Alexandra, Ingmar Weber, and Daniel Gatica-Perez. 2016. "Characterizing the Demographics behind the #BlackLivesMatter Movement." *AAAI Spring Symposium Series, 2016*, vol. 1, 310–13.

Organization for Black Struggle. n.d. "About Us." Accessed July 30, 2017, http://www.obs-stl.org/about-us/.

Page, Benjamin I., Larry M. Bartels, and Jason Seawright. 2013. "Democracy and the Policy Preferences of Wealthy Americans." *Perspectives on Politics* 11 (1): 51–73.

Page, Cara, and Kindred Healing Justice Collective. n.d. Black Emotional and Mental Health Collective website. Accessed April 4, 2020, https://www.beam.community/healing-justice.

Patterson, Brandon E. 2017. "Black Lives Matter Is Bailing Out Women for Mother's Day." *Mother Jones*, May 12, 2017. https://www.motherjones.com/politics/2017/05/black-lives-matter-mothers-day-bail-out/.

Patterson, Orlando. 1982. *Slavery and Social Death: A Comparative Study*. Cambridge, MA: Harvard University Press.

Patterson, Thomas E. 2005. " Of Polls, Mountains: U.S. Journalists and Their Use of Election Surveys." *Public Opinion Quarterly* 69 (5): 716–24.

Payne, Charles M. 2007. *I've Got the Light of Freedom: The Organizing Tradition and the Mississippi Freedom Struggle*. 2nd ed. Berkeley: University of California Press.

Perry, Imani. 2018. *Vexy Thing: On Gender and Liberation*. Durham, NC: Duke University Press.

Pettit, Phillip. 2001. *A Theory of Freedom*. New York: Polity Press.

Pew Research Center. 2013. "Big Racial Divide on Zimmerman Verdict: Whites Say Too Much Focus on Race, Blacks Disagree." Pew Research Center: U.S. Politics & Policy, July 22, 2013. http://www.people-press.org/2013/07/22/big-racial-divide-over-zimmerman-verdict/.

Pew Research Center. 2014. "Ideological 'Silos.'" Pew Research Center: U.S. Politics & Policy, June 10, 2014. http://www.people-press.org/2014/06/12/section-3-political-polarization-and-personal-life/pp-2014-06-12-polarization-3-02/.

Pew Research Center. 2015. "Beyond Distrust: How Americans View Their Government." Pew Research Center: U.S. Politics & Policy, November 23, 2015. http://www.people-press.org/2015/11/23/1-trust-in-government-1958-2015/.

Pew Research Center. 2016a. "On Views of Race and Inequality, Blacks and Whites Are Worlds Part." Pew Research Center: Social & Demographic Trends, June 27, 2016. http://www.pewsocialtrends.org/2016/06/27/1-demographic-trends-and-economic-well-being/.

Pew Research Center. 2016b. "The Parties on the Eve of the 2016 Election: Two Coalitions, Moving Further Apart—2. Party Affiliation among Voters: 1992–2016." Pew Research Center: U.S. Politics & Policy, September 13, 2016. https://www.people-press.org/2016/09/13/2-party-affiliation-among-voters-1992-2016/.

Pew Research Center. 2016c. "Partisanship and Political Animosity in 2016." Pew Research Center: U.S. Politics & Policy, June 22, 2016. https://www.pewresearch.org/politics/2016/06/22/partisanship-and-political-animosity-in-2016/.

Pew Research Center. 2017. "Majority Says Country Needs to Continue Making Changes for Racial Equality." Pew Research Center: U.S. Politics & Policy, October 4, 2017. https://www.people-press.org/2017/10/05/4-race-immigration-and-discrimination/4_1-10/.

Pew Research Center. 2019. "Public Trust in Government: 1959–2019." Pew Research Center: U.S. Politics & Policy, April 11, 2019. https://www.pewresearch.org/politics/2019/04/11/public-trust-in-government-1958-2019/.

Pfeffer, Fabian T., Sheldon Danziger, and Robert F. Schoeni. 2013. "Wealth Disparities before and after the Great Recession." *Annals of the American Academy of Political and Social Science* 650 (1): 98–123.

Phulwani, Vijay. 2016. "The Poor Man's Machiavelli: Saul Alinsky and the Morality of Power." *American Political Science Review* 110 (4): 863–75.

Pichardo, Nelson A. 1997. "New Social Movements: A Critical Review." *Annual Review of Sociology* 23 (August): 411–30.

Piepzna-Samarasinha, Leah Laksshmi. 2016. "A Not-So-Brief Personal History of the Healing Justice Movement, 2010–2016." *MICE Magazine*, Fall 2016. http://micemagazine.ca/issue-two/not-so-brief-personal-history-healing-justice-movement-2010%E2%80%932016.

Piepzna-Samarasinha, Leah Laksshmi. 2019. *Care Work: Dreaming Disability Justice*. Vancouver: Arsenal Pulp Press.

Piketty, Thomas. 2015. *The Economics of Inequality*. Translated by Arthur Goldhammer. Cambridge, MA: Belknap Press of Harvard University Press.

Pineda, Erin. 2019. "The Organized Crowd: Organizing, Mobilizing and Democratic Agency." Paper presented at 2019 APSA Annual Meeting and Exhibition: Populism and Privilege, August 29–September, 2019, Washington, DC.

Pinto, Nick. 2020. "Criminal Justice Reformers Are Rethinking the Crusade against Cash Bail." *New Republic*, April 6, 2020. https://newrepublic.com/article/156823/limits-money-bail-fund-criminal-justice-reform.

Pishko, Jessica. 2016a. "Is Angela Corey the Cruelest Prosecutor in America?" *The Nation*, August 16, 2016. https://www.thenation.com/article/archive/is-angela-corey-the-cruelest-prosecutor-in-america/.

Pishko, Jessica. 2016b. "Voters Have Ousted Notorious Florida Prosecutor Angela Corey." *The Nation*, August 31, 2016. https://www.thenation.com/article/archive/voters-have-ousted-notorious-florida-prosecutor-angela-corey/.

Pitkin, Hanna. 1981. "Justice: On Relating Public and Private." *Political Theory* 9 (3): 327–52.

Piven, Frances Fox. 1977. *Poor People's Movements: Why They Succeed, How They Fail*. New York: Pantheon Books.

Polletta, Francesca. 2006. *It Was Like A Fever: Storytelling in Protest and Politics*. Chicago: University of Chicago Press.

Polletta, Francesca, and James M. Jasper. 2001. "Collective Identity and Social Movements." *Annual Review of Sociology* 27 (August): 283–305.

Praelli, Lorella. 2019. "Organizing Is the Art of the Possible." Presentation by president of Community Change Action, August 13, 2019. https://www.youtube.com/watch?v=I_l35D9z2mw.

ProPublica. 2017–. Lost Mothers: Maternal Care and Preventable Death. Series. https://www.propublica.org/series/lost-mothers.

PRRI Staff. 2019. "Fractured Nation: Widening Partisan Polarization and Key Issues in 2020 Presidential Elections." Washington, DC: PRRI (Public Religion Research Institute), October 20, 2019. https://www.prri.org/research/fractured-nation-widening-partisan-polarization-and-key-issues-in-2020-presidential-elections/.

Ransby, Barbara. 2015. "Ella Taught Me: Shattering the Myth of the Leaderless Movement." *Colorlines*, June 12, 2015. https://www.colorlines.com/articles/ella-taught-me-shattering-myth-leaderless-movement?fbclid=IwAR3_2p8gO-rspz6-I83hiX9b1WUAj-5vjdg_qaMySFTpktQtgeZkEOKU5XA.

Ransby, Barbara. 2017. "Black Lives Matter Is Democracy in Action." *New York Times*, October 21, 2017. https://www.nytimes.com/2017/10/21/opinion/sunday/black-lives-matter-leadership.html.

Ransby, Barbara. 2018. *Making All Black Lives Matter: Reimagining Freedom in the 21st Century*. American Studies Now: Critical Histories of the Present 6. Oakland: University of California Press.

Rainie, Lee, Scott Keeter, and Andrew Perrin. 2019. "Trust and Distrust in America." Pew Research Center, July 22, 2019. https://www.pewresearch.org/politics/2019/07/22/trust-and-distrust-in-america/.

Rawls, John. 1971. *Theories of Justice*. Cambridge, MA: Harvard University Press.

Ray, Rashawn, Melissa Brown, Neil Fraistat, and Edward Summers. 2017. "Ferguson and the Death of Michael Brown on Twitter: #BlackLivesMatter, #TCOT, and the Evolution of Collective Identities." *Ethnic and Racial Studies* 40 (11): 1797–1813. https://doi.org/10.1080/01419870.2017.1335422.

Real Clear Politics. 2016. *Trump: Favorable/Unfavorable*. Data for October 17–21, 2016. http://www.realclearpolitics.com/epolls/other/trump_favorableunfavorable-5493.html.

Reid, Omar G., Sekou Mims, and Larry Higginbottom. 2004. *Post Traumatic Slavery Disorder*. New York: Xlibris.

Richardson, Allissa V. 2019. "Dismantling Respectability: The Rise of New Womanist Communication Models in the Era of Black Lives Matter." *Journal of Communication* 69 (2): 193–219.

Rising Majority. n.d. "About Us." https://therisingmajority.com/about-us/.

Roberts, Neil. 2015. *Freedom as Marronage*. Chicago: University of Chicago Press.

Robinson, Cedric J. (1983) 2000. *Black Marxism: The Making of the Black Radical Tradition*. Foreword by Robin D. C. Kelley, with a new preface by the author. Chapel Hill: University of North Carolina Press.

Robinson, Dean E. 2001. *Black Nationalism in American Politics and Thought*. Cambridge: Cambridge University Press.

Roediger, David. 2016. "Making Solidarity Uneasy: Cautions on a Keyword from Black Lives Matter to the Past." *American Quarterly* 68 (2): 223–48.

Rogers, Jamala. 2015. *Ferguson Is America: Roots of Rebellion*. St. Louis: Mira Digital Publishing.

Rogers, Melvin L. 2007. "Action and Inquiry in Dewey's Philosophy." *Transactions of the Charles S. Pierce Society: A Quarterly Journal in American Philosophy* 23 (1): 90–115.

Rogers, Melvin L. 2009. "Democracy, Elites and Power: John Dewey Reconsidered." *Contemporary Political Theory* 8 (1): 68–89. https://doi.org/10.1057/cpt.2008.25.

Rogers, Melvin L. 2010. "Dewey and His Vision for Democracy." *Contemporary Pragmatism* 7 (1): 69–91.

Rogers, Melvin L. 2012. *The Undiscovered Dewey: Religion Morality, and the Ethos of Democracy*. Paperback edition. New York: Columbia University Press.

Rosenstone, Steven J., and John Mark Hansen. 1993. *Mobilization, Participation, and Democracy in America*. New York: Macmillan.

Ross, Loretta. 2007. "What Is Reproductive Justice?" In *Reproductive Justice Briefing Book: A Primer on Reproductive Justice and Social Change*. Berkeley, CA: Berkeley School of Law. https://www.law.berkeley.edu/php-programs/courses/fileDL.php?fID=4051.

Rueckert, Phineas. 2018. "Real World Superheroes Are Registering Voters at *Black Panther* Screenings across the Country." *Global Citizen*, February 20, 2018. https://www.globalcitizen.org/en/content/electoral-justice-project-wakanda-black-panther/.

Sabl, Andrew. 2002. *Ruling Passions: Political Offices and Democratic Ethics*. Princeton, NJ: Princeton University Press.

Saez, Emmanuel. "The Evolution of Top Incomes in the United States" (updated version of "Striking It Richer: The Evolution of Top Incomes in the United States"). *Pathways Magazine* (Stanford Center for the Study of Poverty and Inequality), Winter 2008, 6–7. https://eml.berkeley.edu/~saez/saez-UStopincomes-2018.pdf.

Sandel, Michael J. 1982. *Liberalism and the Limits of Justice*. Cambridge: Cambridge University Press.

Sandler, Todd. 2015. "Collective Action: Fifty Years Later." *Public Choice* 164 (3–4): 195–216.

Sawyer, Jeremy, and Anup Gampa. 2018. "Implicit and Explicit Racial Attitudes Changed during Black Lives Matter." *Personality and Social Psychology Bulletin* 44 (7): 1039–59.

Schaeffer, Katherine. 2020. "6 Facts about Economic Inequality in the U.S." Pew Research Center, *FactTank: News in the Numbers*, February 7, 2020. https://www.pewresearch.org/fact-tank/2020/02/07/6-facts-about-economic-inequality-in-the-u-s/.

Schattschneider, E. E. 1960. *The Semisovereign People: A Realist's View of Democracy in America*. New York: Holt, Rinehart & Winston.

Schlozman, Kay Lehman, Henry Brady, and Sidney Verba. 2012. *The Unheavenly Chorus: Unequal Political Voice and the Broken Promise of American Democracy*. Princeton, NJ: Princeton University Press.

Schroeder, Juliana, Michael Kardas, and Nicholas Epley. 2017. "The Humanizing Voice: Speech Reveals, and Text Conceals, a More Thoughtful Mind in the Midst of Disagreement." *Psychological Science* 28 (12): 1745–62.

Schuschke, Joshua, and Brendesha M. Tynes. 2016. "Online Community Empowerment, Emotional Connection, and Armed Love in the Black Lives Matter Movement." In *Emotions, Technology, and Social Media*, edited by Sharon Tettegah, 25–47. New York: Academic Press.

Scott, Eugene. 2020. "Majority of Americans Say Race Discrimination Is a Big Problem in the U.S." *Washington Post*, July 10, 2020. https://www.washingtonpost.com/politics/2020/07/10/majority-americans-say-race-discrimination-is-big-problem-us/.

Sears, David, James Sidanius, and Lawrence Bobo, eds. 2000. *Racialized Politics: The Debate about Racism in America*. Chicago: University of Chicago Press.

Sen, Amartya. 1992. *Inequality Reexamined*. Cambridge, MA: Harvard University Press.

Sen, Rinku. 2003. *Stir It Up: Lessons in Community Organizing and Advocacy*. San Francisco: Jossey-Bass.

Shapiro, Ian, and Casiano Hacker-Cordon, eds. 1999. *Democracy's Value*. Cambridge: Cambridge University Press.

Sharma, Sanjay. 2013. "Black Twitter? Racial Hashtags, Networks and Contagion." *New Formations* 78 (19): 46–64.

Sharpe, Christina. 2016. *In the Wake: On Blackness and Being*. Durham, NC: Duke University Press.

Shear, Michael, and Liam Stack. 2016. "Obama Says Movements Like Black Lives Matter 'Can't Just Keep On Yelling.'" *New York Times*, April 23, 2016. http://www.nytimes.com/2016/04/24/us/obama-says-movements-like-black-lives-matter-cant-just-keep-on-yelling.html.

Sides, John, Michael Tesler, and Lynn Vavreck. 2018. *Identity Crisis: The 2016 Presidential Campaign and the Battle for the Meaning of America*. Princeton, NJ: Princeton University Press.

Silva, Tylah. 2017. "Welcome to the New Black Renaissance." *Study Breaks*, March 27, 2017. https://studybreaks.com/culture/black-renaissance/.

Sinclair, R. K. 1988. *Democracy and Participation in Athens*. Cambridge: Cambridge University Press.

Sinyanwe, Samuel. 2021. *2020 Police Violence Report*. Mapping Police Violence. https://policeviolencereport.org/.

Sister Song. n.d. "Sister Song" and "Reproductive Justice." https://www.sistersong.net/mission and https://www.sistersong.net/reproductive-justice.

Skelton, Renee, and Vernice Miller. 2016. "The Environmental Justice Movement." New York: NRDC, March 17, 2016. https://www.nrdc.org/stories/environmental-justice-movement.

Smith, Barbara, Charlene Carruthers, and Reina Gossett. 2016. "Black Feminism and the Movement for Black Lives." Panel discussion, National Gay and Lesbian Task Force, Creating Change Conference, January 23, 2016. Recording accessed March 20, 2017, https://www.youtube.com/watch?v=eV3nnFheQRo.

Smith, Christen A. 2016. "Facing the Dragon: Black Mothering, Sequelae, and Gendered Necropolitics in the Americas." *Transforming Anthropology* 24 (1): 31–48.

Smith, Jordan. 2016. "Overzealous Prosecutors Ousted across the Country, Showing There Is Still Hope for Reform." *The Intercept*, November 10, 2016. https://theintercept.com/2016/11/10/overzealous-prosecutors-ousted-across-the-country-showing-there-is-still-hope-for-reform/.

Smith, Tom W., and Jaesok Son. 2013. *Trends in Public Attitudes about Confidence in Institutions: General Social Survey 2012, Final Report*. Presented at NORC at the University of Chicago, May 2013. http://www.norc.org/PDFs/GSS%20Reports/Trends%20in%20Confidence%20Institutions_Final.pdf.

Snow, David A., and Doug McAdam. 2000. "Identity Work Processes in the Context of Social Movements: Clarifying the Identity/Movement Nexus." In *Self, Identity and Social Movements*, edited by Sheldon Stryker, Timothy J. Owens, and Robert White, 41–67. Minneapolis: University of Minnesota Press

Solomon, Akiba. 2015. "Get on the Bus: Inside Black Life Matters 'Freedom Ride' to Ferguson." *Colorlines*, September 5, 2015. http://www.colorlines.com/articles/get-bus-inside-black-life-matters-freedom-ride-ferguson.

Sotero, Michelle. 2006. "A Conceptual Model of Historical Trauma: Implications for Public Health Practice and Research." *Journal of Health Disparities Research and Practice* 1 (1): 93–108.

Southwick, Steven, George A. Bonanno, Ann S. Masten, Catherine Panter-Brick, and Rachel Yehuda. 2014. "Resilience Definitions, Theory, and Challenges: Interdisciplinary Perspectives." *European Journal of Psychotraumatology* 5 (1): article 25338. https://www.ncbi.nlm.nih.gov/pmc/articles/PMC4185134/.

Sparks, Grace. 2020. "Polls Show Widespread Support for Black Lives Matter Protests and Varied Views on How to Reform Police." CNN Politics, June 18, 2020. https://www.cnn.com/2020/06/18/politics/protests-polling-support-movement-policies-kaiser-quinnipiac/index.html.

Speer, Paul W., and Joseph Hughey. 1995. "Community Organizing: An Ecological Route to Power and Empowerment." *American Journal of Community Psychology* 23 (5): 729–48.

Speri, Alice. 2019. "Fear of a Black Homeland: The Strange Tale of the FBI's Fictional 'Black Identity Extremist' Movement." *The Intercept*, March 23, 2019. https://theintercept.com/2019/03/23/black-identity-extremist-fbi-domestic-terrorism/.

St. John's Church (The Beloved Community). n.d. "Mission." Accessed July 31, 2017, http://sjuccstl.org/our-mission/.

Stewart, Tracie L., Ioana M. Latu, Nyla B. Branscombe, and H. Ted Denney. 2010. "Yes We Can! Prejudice Reduction through Seeing (Inequality) and Believing (in Social Change)." *Psychological Science* 21 (11): 155–62.

Stout, Jeffrey. 2010. *Blessed Are the Organized: Grassroots Democracy in America.* Princeton, NJ: Princeton University Press.

Swarts, Heidi J. 2008. *Organizing Urban America: Secular and Faith-Based Progressive Movements.* Minneapolis: University of Minnesota Press.

Syedullah, Jasmine. forthcoming. "Becoming More Ourselves: Four Emergent Strategies of Black Feminist Congregational Abolition." *Palimpsest Special Issue: Black Feminist Practices of Care.*

Taber, Charles S., and Milton Lodge. 2006. "Motivated Skepticism in the Evaluation of Political Belief." *American Journal of Political Science* 50 (3): 755–69.

Tarrow, Sidney. 1998. *Power in Movement: Social Movements and Contentious Politics.* 2nd ed. Cambridge: Cambridge University Press.

Taylor, Je Naé, and Kai Green, interview with Kate Werning. 2018. "Interventional Healing and Accountability—BYP100 Healing & Safety Council." Transcript, Irresistible.org, *Healing Justice Podcast*, episode 27, May 15, 2018. https://irresistible.org/podcast/27.

Temin, Peter. 2018. "Finance and Economic Growth: Eating the Family Cow." Working Paper No. 86. New York: Institute for New Economic Thinking, December 17, 2018. https://www.ineteconomics.org/research/research-papers/finance-in-economic-growth-eating-the-family-cow.

Thomas, Deja, and Juliana Menasche Horowitz. 2020. "Support for Black Lives Matter Has Decreased since June but Remains Strong among Black Americans." Pew Research Center, *FactTank: News in the Numbers*, September 16, 2020. https://www.pewresearch.org/fact-tank/2020/09/16/support-for-black-lives-matter-has-decreased-since-june-but-remains-strong-among-black-americans/.

Thompson, Simon, and Paul Hoggett. 2012. *Politics and the Emotions: The Affective Turn in Contemporary Political Studies*. New York: Bloomsbury.

Threadcraft, Shatema. 2016. *Intimate Justice: The Black Female Body and the Body Politic*. New York: Oxford University Press.

Three Point Strategies. n.d. "M4BL: Electoral Justice Project." https://www.threepointstrategies.org/what-weve-done.

Thurston, Chloe N. 2018. "Black Lives Matter, American Political Development, and the Politics of Visibility." *Politics, Groups, and Identities* 6 (1): 162–70.

Toussaint, Kristin. 2020. "The Controversy over How the Minnesota Freedom Fund Is Spending Its Donations, Explained." *Fast Company*, June 18, 2020. https://www.fastcompany.com/90517597/the-controversy-over-how-the-minnesota-freedom-fund-is-spending-its-donations-explained.

Townes, Emilie M. 2006. *Womanist Ethics and the Cultural Production of Evil*. Black Religion, Womanist Thought, Social Justice. New York: Palgrave Macmillan

Tronto, Joan. 2013. *Caring Democracy: Markets, Equality, and Justice*. New York: New York University Press.

Twenge, Jean M., W. Keith Campbell, and Nathan T. Carter. 2014. "Declines in Trust in Others and Confidence in Institutions among American Adults and Late Adolescents, 1972–2012." *Psychological Science* 25 (10): 1914–23.

Uetricht, Micah. 2016. "The Criminal-Justice Crusade of Kim Foxx." *Chicago Reader*, March 9, 2016. http://www.chicagoreader.com/chicago/kim-foxx-bid-unseat-anita-alvarez-cook-county/Content?oid=21359641.

US Congress Joint Economic Committee. 2010. "Unemployment Disproportionately Impacts African Americans." *Weekly Economic Digest*, March 17, 2010. https://www.jec.senate.gov/public/_cache/files/7ff3e9c2-136b-4047-97ce-5aa85ac2ce77/wed-03-17-10.pdf.

US Department of Justice. 2015. *Investigation of the Ferguson Police Department*. Washington, DC: US Department of Justice, Civil Rights Division, March 4, 2015. Available online from the *Washington Post*, at https://apps.washingtonpost.com/g/documents/national/department-of-justice-report-on-the-ferguson-mo-police-department/1435/.

Vaughn, Kenya. 2014. "Rev. Starsky Wilson Parallels Christianity and Ferguson Protests." *St. Louis American*, September 11, 2014. http://www.stlamerican.com/religion/local_religion/rev-starsky-wilson-parallels-christianity-and-ferguson-protests/article_fa222d4a-3933-11e4-bb37-7ff6f39a6ed1.html.

Verba, Sidney, Kay Lehman Schlozman, and Henry E. Brady. 1995. *Voice and Equality: Civic Voluntarism in American Politics*. Cambridge, MA: Harvard University Press.

Walther, Eva, and Claudie Trasselli. 2003. "I Like Her, Because I Like Myself: Self-Evaluation as a Source of Interpersonal Attitudes." *Experimental Psychology* 50 (4): 239–46. doi:10.1026//1618- 3169.50.4.239.

Walzer, Michael. 1983. *Spheres of Justice: A Defense of Pluralism and Equality*. New York: Basic Books.

Warfield, Zenobia Jefferies. 2019. "Black Lives Matter Is Making Single Moms Homeowners." *Yes!*, February 5, 2019. https://www.yesmagazine.org/social-justice/2019/02/05/Black-lives-matter-is-making-single-moms-homeowners/.

Weber, Max. (1922) 2013. *Economy and Society*. 2 vols. Edited by Guenther Roth and Claus Wittich. Berkeley: University of California Press.

Weber, Max. 2004. *The Vocation Lectures*. Edited and with an introduction by David Owen and Tracy B. Strong. Translation by Rodney Livingstone. New York: Hackett Classics.

Weill-Greenberg, Elizabeth. 2020. "San Francisco Voters Abolish Mandatory Staffing Levels for Police." *The Appeal*, November 4, 2020. https://theappeal.org/san-francisco-abolish-mandatory-police-staffing-levels/.

West, Cornell. 1989. *The American Evasion of Pragmatism: A Genealogy of Pragmatism*. Madison: University of Wisconsin Press.

Wikipedia. 2020. "Disability Justice." https://en.wikipedia.org/wiki/Disability_justice.

Williams, D. R., H. W. Neighbors, and J. S. Jackson. 2008. "Racial/Ethnic Discrimination and Health: Findings from Community Studies." *American Journal of Public Health* 93 (2): 200–208.

Williams, Pascale Ife, and Chris Roberts. 2018. "Preventative Healing & Accountability." Transcript. Irresistible.org, *Healing Justice Podcast*, episode 26, May 8, 2018. https://irresistible.org/podcast/26.

Wines, Michael. 2014. "Are Police Bigoted? Race and Police Shootings: Are Blacks Targeted More?" *New York Times*, August 30, 2014. https://www.nytimes.com/2014/08/31/sunday-review/race-and-police-shootings-are-blacks-targeted-more.html.

Winter, Jana, Marquise Francis, and Sean Naylor. 2020. "New Terrorism Guide Shows FBI Still Classifying Black 'Extremists' as Domestic Terrorism Threat." Yahoo News, December 30, 2020. https://sports.yahoo.com/new-terrorism-guide-shows-fbi-still-classifying-black-extremists-as-domestic-terrorism-threat-190650561.html.

Wolin, Sheldon S. 1994. "Fugitive Democracy." *Constellations* 1 (1): 11–25.

Womack, Ytasha. 2013. *Afrofuturism: The World of Black Sci-Fi and Fantasy Culture*. Chicago: Lawrence Hill Books.

Woodly, Deva R. 2008. "New Competencies in Democratic Communication? Blogs, Agenda-Setting, and Political Participation." *Public Choice* 134 (1/2): 109–23.

Woodly, Deva R. 2015a. *The Politics of Common Sense: How Social Movements Use Public Discourse to Change Politics and Win Acceptance*. New York: Oxford University Press.

Woodly, Deva R. 2015b. "Seeing Collectivity: Structural Relation through the Lens of Youngian Seriality." *Contemporary Political Theory* 14 (3): 213–33.

Wright, Michelle M. 2015. *The Physics of Blackness: Beyond the Middle Passage Epistemology*. Minneapolis: University of Minnesota Press.

Yang, Guobin. 2016. "Narrative Agency in Hashtag Activism: The Case of #BlackLives Matter." *Media and Communication* 4 (4): 13–27.

Yehuda, Rachel, Nikolaos P. Daskalakis, Linda M. Bierer, Heather N. Bader, Torsten Klengel, Florian Holsboer, and Elisabeth B. Binder. 2016. "Holocaust Exposure Induced Intergenerational Effects on FKBP5 Methylation." *Biological Psychiatry* 80 (5): 372–80.

Yehuda, Rachel, Stephanie Mulherin Engel, Sarah R. Brand, Jonathan Seckl, Sue M. Marcus, and Gertrud S. Berkowitz. 2005. "Transgenerational Effects of Post-Traumatic Stress Disorder in Babies of Mothers Exposed to World Trade Center Attacks During Pregnancy." *Journal of Clinical Endocrinology & Metabolism* 90 (7): 4115–4118.

Young, Damon. 2016. "How to Be Unapologetically Black." *The Root*, February 26, 2016.http://verysmartbrothas.com/how-to-be-unapologetically-Black/.

Young, Iris Marion. (1990) 2011. *Justice and the Politics of Difference*. Princeton, NJ: Princeton University Press.

Websites

Action St. Louis. n.d. "About Action St. Louis." https://actionstl.org/mission-vision.
Law for Black Lives. n.d. "About the Squad." http://www.law4blacklives.org/new-page.
Matthews, Shanelle. n.d. "Hello, Shanelle: Projects." https://helloshanelle.com/projects.
People's Advocacy Institute. n.d. "What We Do." https://www.peoplesadvocacyinstitute.com/what-we-do.

Quoted Author Interviews and Personal Communications

Byrd, Jessica. Interview with author, March 12, 2018.
Cadet. Jewel. Interview with author, December 27, 2017.
Carruthers, Charlene. Interview with author, July 12, 2017.
Cooper, Brittney (activist, assoc. professor Africana Studies, Rutgers University). Interview with author, March 21, 2017.
Hatcher, Paris. Comments in reading discussion, September 16, 2018.
Hooks, Mary. Interview with author, October 19, 2018.
Khan-Cullors, Patrisse. Interview with author, July 17, 2017.
Matthews, Shanelle (communications director, Black Lives Matter Global Network Foundation). Interview with author, March 8, 2017.
Mitchell, Maurice (cofounder of BlackBird). Interview with author, June 30, 2017.
Police officer, Cobb County, Georgia. Interview with author, November 13, 2017.

Index